Human Architecture: Journal of the Sociology of Self-Knowledge

Monograph Series: Tayyebeh Series in East-West Research and Translation

About OKCIR

Omar Khayyam Center for Integrative Research in
Utopia, Mysticism, and Science (Utopystics)

www.okcir.com

OKCIR (est. 2002) is an independent research, pedagogical, and publishing initiative dedicated to exploring, in a simultaneously world-historical and self-reflective framework, the human search for a just global society.

Since the world's utopian, mystical, and scientific movements have been the primary sources of inspiration, knowledge, and/or practice in this field, OKCIR aims to critically reexamine the shortcomings and contributions of these world-historical traditions—seeking to clearly understand why they have failed to bring about the good society, and what each can integratively contribute toward realizing that end.

The center aims to develop new conceptual (methodological, theoretical, historical), practical, pedagogical, inspirational and disseminative structures of knowledge whereby the individual can radically understand and determine how world-history and her/his selves constitute one another.

OKCIR promotes creative exercises in liberating sociology and alternative pluriversities of knowledge production and publication in the global cyberspace. As a virtual research center, its publications are available in part freely online in its open-stacks digital library, in part via subscription to its own or other academic database member-stacks, and others for purchase online via the Okcir Store and other online distributors. Selected publications are also available in print for online purchase by libraries, institutions, and interested print readers.

OKCIR pursues innovative editorial, digital, and print publishing practices reflecting its substantive goals, and is the publisher of *Human Architecture: Journal of the Sociology of Self-Knowledge* (ISSN: 1540-5699, est. 2002) which explores issues pertaining to the center's interests. *Human Architecture* is a hybrid scholarly journal whose edited and monographed issues are simultaneously published also as individual books in hardcover, softcover, and pdf and/or epub ebook formats (with separately assigned ISBNs).

Tayyebeh Series in East-West Research and Translation (2014-) and Ahead Publishing House (imprint: Okcir Press) (1991-) respectively honor Tayyebeh Tamjidi (1928-2020) and Mohammed (Ahad) Tamjidi (1930-2007) whose parental love and support made the life and works of Mohammad H. (Behrooz) Tamdgidi, the founder of OKCIR, possible.

The Series on Which the Present Book is Based

Omar Khayyam's Secret: Hermeneutics of the Robaiyat in Quantum Sociological Imagination:
Book 1*: New Khayyami Studies: Quantumizing the Newtonian Structures of C. Wright Mills's Sociological Imagination for A New Hermeneutic Method* (Okcir Press, 2021)

Omar Khayyam's Secret: Hermeneutics of the Robaiyat in Quantum Sociological Imagination:
Book 2*: Khayyami Millennium: Reporting the Discovery and the Reconfirmation of the True Dates of Birth and Passing of Omar Khayyam (AD 1021-1123)* (Okcir Press, 2021)

Omar Khayyam's Secret: Hermeneutics of the Robaiyat in Quantum Sociological Imagination:
Book 3*: Khayyami Astronomy: How Omar Khayyam's Newly Discovered True Birth Date Horoscope Reveals the Origins of His Pen Name and Independently Confirms His Authorship of the Robaiyat* (Okcir Press, 2021)

Omar Khayyam's Secret: Hermeneutics of the Robaiyat in Quantum Sociological Imagination:
Book 4*: Khayyami Philosophy: The Ontological Structures of the Robaiyat in Omar Khayyam's Last Written Keepsake Treatise on the Science of the Universals of Existence* (Okcir Press, 2021)

Omar Khayyam's Secret: Hermeneutics of the Robaiyat in Quantum Sociological Imagination:
Book 5*: Khayyami Theology: The Epistemological Structures of the Robaiyat in All the Philosophical Writings of Omar Khayyam Leading to His Last Keepsake Treatise* (Okcir Press, 2022)

Omar Khayyam's Secret: Hermeneutics of the Robaiyat in Quantum Sociological Imagination:
Book 6*: Khayyami Science: The Methodological Structures of the Robaiyat in All the Scientific Works of Omar Khayyam* (Okcir Press, 2023)

Omar Khayyam's Secret: Hermeneutics of the Robaiyat in Quantum Sociological Imagination:
Book 7*: Khayyami Art: The Art of Poetic Secrecy for a Lasting Existence: Tracing the Robaiyat in Nowrooznameh, Isfahan's North Dome, and Other Poems of Omar Khayyam, and Solving the Riddle of His Robaiyat Attributability* (Okcir Press, 2024)

Omar Khayyam's Secret: Hermeneutics of the Robaiyat in Quantum Sociological Imagination:
Book 8*: Khayyami Robaiyat: Part 1 of 3: Quatrains 1-338: Songs of Doubt Addressing the Question "Does Happiness Exist?": Explained with New English Verse Translations and Organized Logically Following Omar Khayyam's Own Three-Phased Method of Inquiry* (Okcir Press, 2024)

Omar Khayyam's Secret: Hermeneutics of the Robaiyat in Quantum Sociological Imagination:
Book 9*: Khayyami Robaiyat: Part 2 of 3: Quatrains 339-685: Songs of Hope Addressing the Question "What Is Happiness?": Explained with New English Verse Translations and Organized Logically Following Omar Khayyam's Own Three-Phased Method of Inquiry* (Okcir Press, 2024)

Omar Khayyam's Secret: Hermeneutics of the Robaiyat in Quantum Sociological Imagination:
Book 10*: Khayyami Robaiyat: Part 3 of 3: Quatrains 686-1000: Songs of Joy Addressing the Question "Why Can Happiness Exist?": Explained with New English Verse Translations and Organized Logically Following Omar Khayyam's Own Three-Phased Method of Inquiry* (Okcir Press, 2024)

Omar Khayyam's Secret: Hermeneutics of the Robaiyat in Quantum Sociological Imagination:
Book 11*: Khayyami Robaiyat: Re-Sewing the Tentmaker's Tent: 1000 Bittersweet Wine Sips from Omar Khayyam's Tavern of Happiness* (Okcir Press, 2024)

Omar Khayyam's Secret: Hermeneutics of the Robaiyat in Quantum Sociological Imagination:
Book 12*: Khayyami Legacy: The Collected Works of Omar Khayyam (AD 1021-1123) Culminating in His Secretive 1000 Robaiyat Autobiography. With Forewords by Winston E. Langley and Jafar Aghayani Chavoshi.* (Okcir Press, 2025)

Khayyam's Tent

A Secretive Autobiography

1000 Bittersweet Robaiyat Sips
from His Tavern of Happiness

About this Book

This book offers the original Robaiyat of Omar Khayyam (AD 1021-1123) as a tent of 1000 logically sewn quatrains serving the poetic Wine of his secretive autobiography. It is an epic, at once a personal, world-historical, and cosmic search for true human happiness. He composed it to be highly readable so that it can be read by all, continually, and today, before it is too late, like a prayer book or a rosary of pearls or ruby stones, since it was meant to be not only reflective but also generative of search for happiness. If you begin reading it, you must do so at least once to its end, so that in later readings any of its parts can be recalled amid the unitary architecture of its philosophical, spiritual, and scientific wisdom rendered as an astounding and most beautiful work of art. Khayyam was right; there is nothing on Earth like his Wine.

His poetic "book of life" was intended to be released posthumously, so its existence was not known to his contemporaries. Following his death, it was released but became scattered and its logical unity was shattered by natural and social disasters and scribal poetry alphabetizing styles, some quatrains wandering into other poets' works and others becoming misattributed to him. The Robaiyat as shared in this book were logically re-sewn and newly translated in verse by the sociologist Mohammad H. Tamdgidi during his integrative study of all of Khayyam's works as reported in his unprecedented 12-book series *Omar Khayyam's Secret: Hermeneutics of the Robaiyat in Quantum Sociological Imagination* (2021-2025).

Following a summary of his series' findings, Tamdgidi presents in this book nothing else but Khayyam's Robaiyat, including the Persian originals and his verse translations (his study of them having been shared in his series, especially its Books 8-11). The poems, comprising songs of doubt, hope, and joy, are logically organized to address three questions, based on the 3-phased method of inquiry Khayyam himself introduced in his other writings.

Quatrains 1-338 of Part 1, Songs of Doubt, open by explaining his epic's secretiveness and address the question "Does Happiness Exist?" Their order follows a logically inductive reasoning through which Khayyam delves from surface portraits of unhappiness to their deeper chain of causes. Quatrains 339-685 of Part 2, Songs of Hope, address the second question "What Is Happiness?" Their order follows a logically deductive reasoning through which he moves from methodological to explanatory and practical quatrains. Quatrains 686-1000 of Part 3, Songs of Joy, address the third question "Why Can Happiness Exist?" Still deductively ordered, they show how happiness can be made possible through his poetry's Wine itself, realizing that one can never become truly happy by bringing sadness to others since human self and society are always twin-born and universal. Hurting another is always a hurting of that self in you that represents that other. For Khayyam, happiness can be possible by way of joyful, creative, and constructive humanizing efforts by own example, like his Robaiyat, which must also start from our inner and interpersonal todays and spread globally.

Khayyam's Robaiyat represented the tent of which he was a "tentmaker," his poetic pen name having been inspired by his *true birth date* horoscope chart as discovered by Tamdgidi and reported in his series for the first time. The metaphor also underlies the numerical geometry of its triangular unity, proportional to the dazzling Grand Tent (Triplicity) features of his birth chart, the same way he embedded his own triangular golden rule in the mysterious design of Isfahan's North Dome. A metaphor of the Robaiyat as Simorgh (or Phoenix) songs is also hidden in its deep structure. Khayyam's Robaiyat are his Simorgh's millennial rebirth songs served in his tented tavern as 1000 sips of his bittersweet poetic Wine of happiness.

Khayyam's Tent

A Secretive Autobiography

1000 Bittersweet Robaiyat Sips from His Tavern of Happiness

OMAR KHAYYAM

Logically Re-Sewn and Translated in Verse
by Mohammad H. Tamdgidi

خیمهٔ خیام: حسب حالی رازآمیز: هزار جرعه رباعیات تلخ و شیرین از میکدهٔ سعادت او
(عمر خیام - بازدوزی منطقی و ترجمهٔ منظوم از محمدحسین تمجیدی)

Human Architecture: Journal of the Sociology of Self-Knowledge • XXVI • 2025
Monograph Series: Tayyebeh Series in East-West Research and Translation

Khayyam's Tent
A Secretive Autobiography: 1000 Bittersweet Robaiyat Sips
from His Tavern of Happiness
OMAR KHAYYAM
Logically Re-Sewn and Translated in Verse by Mohammad H. Tamdgidi

خیمهٔ خیام: حسب حالی رازآمیز: هزار جرعه رباعیات تلخ و شیرین از میکدهٔ سعادت او
(عمر خیام - بازدوزی منطقی و ترجمهٔ منظوم از محمدحسین تمجیدی)

Copyright © 2025 by Mohammad-Hossein Tamdgidi

All English verse translations of the Robaiyat (quatrains) attributed to Omar Khayyam appearing in this book and of its parent series, Copyright © 2025 by Mohammad-Hossein Tamdgidi.

All rights reserved. No part of this publication may be transmitted or reproduced in any media or form, including electronic, mechanical, photocopy, recording, or informational storage and retrieval systems, without the express written permission of the author and publisher except for brief passages fairly used for the purpose of review or study while fully acknowledging its source.

First Edition: June 10, 2025
Okcir Press • P. O. Box 393, Belmont, MA 02478, USA • www.okcir.com
For ordering or other inquiries contact: info[at]okcir.com

Okcir Press is an imprint of Ahead Publishing House, which is a division of OKCIR:
Omar Khayyam Center for Integrative Research in Utopia, Mysticism, and Science (Utopystics)

Library of Congress Control Number: 2025908981

Publisher Cataloging in Publication Data

Khayyam's Tent: A Secretive Autobiography: 1000 Bittersweet Robaiyat Sips from Omar His Tavern of Happiness / Omar Khayyam, AD 1021-1123 / Logically Re-Sewn and Translated in Verse by Mohammad H. Tamdgidi, 1959- / First Edition: June 10, 2025

Human Architecture: Journal of the Sociology of Self-Knowledge • Volume XXVI • 2025
Monograph Series: Tayyebeh Series in East-West Research and Translation

212 pages • 6x9 inches • Includes illustration and index.
ISBN-13: 978-1-64098-058-7 • ISBN-10: 1-64098-058-X (hardcover : alk. paper)
ISBN-13: 978-1-64098-059-4 • ISBN-10: 1-64098-059-8 (softcover : alk. paper)
ISBN-13: 978-1-64098-060-0 • ISBN-10: 1-64098-060-1 (EPub ebook)
ISBN-13: 978-1-64098-061-7 • ISBN-10: 1-64098-061-X (PDF ebook)

1. Omar Khayyam—Robaiyat (Rubaiyat or Quatrains). 2. Omar Khayyam—Autobiography.
3. Omar Khayyam—Birth Millennium (2021). 4. Omar Khayyam—9th Death Centennial (2023).
I. Omar Khayyam (AD 1021-1123) II. Title

Front cover image: "North Dome, Jameʿ Mosque, Isfahan, Iran" (Dreamstime: 97224654) / Back Cover includes image of the Statue of Omar Khayyam, by Abolhasan Seddiqi, Laleh Park, Tehran, Iran / back cover image includes image "Tent Sewn" (Dreamstime: 322852906); Jacket flap image: "Phoenix Rising" (Dreamstime: 11454618)

Cover and Text Design: Ahead Publishing House, Belmont, MA, USA

The paper used in the print editions of this book is of archival quality and meets the minimum requirements of ANSI/NISO Z39.48-1992 (R1997) (Permanence of Paper). The production of this book on demand protects the environment by printing only the number of copies that are purchased.

for Omar Khayyam (AD 1021-1123)
who "Phoenix-like flew to the peak empyrean sphere"

In Celebration of the Millennium of Omar Khayyam's True Birth Date in AD 1021 and in Commemoration of the 9th Centennial of His True Date of Passing in AD 1123

»گفتمش چیست گفتۀ خیّام

گفت پیراست حسب حالی چند«

"I asked, 'What are Khayyam's sayings?'
He said, 'Prunings of his life tales, some.'"
— Omar Khayyam

and for my mother,
Tayyebeh Tamjidi
(March 20, 1928 - December 31, 2020)

About the Series Author and Translator

Other books beside this book and its originating series by Mohammad H. Tamdgidi

Liberating Sociology: From Newtonian Toward Quantum Imaginations: Volume I: Unriddling the Quantum Enigma (Okcir Press, 2020)

Gurdjieff and Hypnosis: A Hermeneutic Study (Palgrave Macmillan, 2009)

Advancing Utopistics: The Three Component Parts and Errors of Marxism (Routledge/Paradigm, 2007)

Mohammad-Hossein (a.k.a. 'Behrooz') Tamdgidi (pronounced "tamjidi") is the founder and editor respectively of OKCIR: Omar Khayyam Center for Integrative Research in Utopia, Mysticism, and Science (Utopystics) and its publication, *Human Architecture: Journal of the Sociology of Self-Knowledge* (ISSN: 1540-5699) which have served since 2002 to frame his independent research, pedagogical, and publishing initiatives. Formerly an associate professor of sociology specializing in social theory at the University of Massachusetts (UMass) Boston, he has also previously taught sociology as full-time lecturer at SUNY-Oneonta, and also as adjunct lecturer at SUNY-Binghamton. He has authored numerous books and edited more than thirty journal collections, in addition to other peer reviewed articles and chapters.

Tamdgidi's areas of scholarly and applied interest are the sociology of self-knowledge, human architecture, and utopystics—three fields of inquiry he invented in his doctoral studies and has since pursued as respectively intertwined theoretical, methodological and applied fields of inquiry altogether contributing to what he calls the quantum sociological imagination. His research, teaching, and publications have been framed by an interest in understanding how world-historical social structures and personal selves constitute one another. This line of inquiry has itself been a result of his longstanding interest in understanding the underlying causes of failures of the world's utopian, mystical, and scientific movements in bringing about a just global society.

It was during his undergraduate studies at U.C. Berkeley and in the course of his mentorship by the painter and design architect Jesse Reichek (1916-2005) that Tamdgidi's notion and project "human architecture" was born. During his graduate studies at SUNY-Binghamton, he was mentored in methods, theory, and world-systems studies by Terence K. Hopkins (1928-1997) and Immanuel Wallerstein (1930-2019), and further in dialectics by Dale Tomich (1946-2024) and on space and society by Anthony D. King (1931-2022), amid a uniquely autonomous and flexible transdisciplinary Graduate Program in Sociology founded by T. K. Hopkins.

Tamdgidi holds a Ph.D. and M.A. in sociology in conjunction with a graduate certificate in Middle Eastern studies from Binghamton University (SUNY). He received his B.A. in architecture from U. C. Berkeley, following enrollment as an undergraduate student of civil engineering in the Technical College of the University of Tehran, Iran. In Dec. 2013 he retired early from his tenured and promoted position at UMass Boston in order to pursue his independent scholarship in quantum sociological imagination and its application in Khayyami studies through the conduit of his research center, OKCIR.

"... a masterpiece in Omar Khayyam studies ..."

— **Jafar Aghayani Chavoshi** (Ph.D., University of Paris, 1997), Professor of Philosophy of Science at Sharif University of Technology, Tehran, Iran, specializing in Philosophy, Epistemology, and History of Mathematics and Science, and in Omar Khayyam Studies. From his Foreword to the last book of Tamdgidi's 12-Book *Omar Khayyam's Secret* series.

"Indeed, for this reader, who was exposed at an early age to Khayyam, through the work of Edward FitzGerald, encountering the *Omar Khayyam's Secret* series was like the astronauts who experienced seeing the Earth for the first time from outer space. It was nothing I could have imagined, from prior experience. ... In Khayyam's work, especially his poetry, one finds the pathos of the tragedian, with the author of *Gilgamesh*, Sophocles, Shakespeare, and Goethe calling; one comes face to face with anxiety, doubt, and the absurd, and tastes Dostoevsky, Kierkegaard, Camus, and Kobo Abe; one confronts subtleties of the most refined kind and meets Buddha, Pushkin, and the practical genius of Da Vinci and Bacon; and one, confronted with the heart and matters of faith and reason, love and happiness, finds voices from Aristotle, St. Augustine, and Aquinas, to Zara Jacob, Jefferson, and Bonhoeffer. Happiness, for example, is not only a state of well-being, but a process of continuing liberation. ... While Khayyam's life is a major story of fierce intellectual passion and a like devotion to ideals of philosophy, science, and poetry (and modes of living that combined those of the solitary and the celebrated, the private and the public), there is an area that is also part of his identity that cannot be overlooked without an injustice to scholarship, history, and human culture. It is the role of satire—that which humorously criticizes defects of reason, science, philosophy (including theology), politics, history, custom (however sacred), even in face of deep disappointments or lived catastrophes. Welcoming the comedy, as Aristophanes, Cervantes, Vico, Erasmus, Santayana, and Chekhov knew, is part of coming to know, of wisdom, of ensuring human flourishing. One may say that Khayyam could be regarded as the first true humanist. All that is human find unhidden expressions through him."

— **Winston E. Langley,** Professor Emeritus of Political Science & International Relations, Senior Fellow at the McCormack Graduate School for Policy & Global Studies, and a former Provost (2008-2017) of the University of Massachusetts Boston. From his Foreword to the last book of Tamdgidi's 12-Book *Omar Khayyam's Secret* series.

«... شاهکاری در مطالعات عمر خیام ...»

- دکتر جعفر آقایانی چاوشی (دکترای دانشگاه پاریس، ۱۹۹۷)، استاد فلسفه علم در دانشگاه صنعتی شریف در تهران، ایران، متخصص فلسفه، شناخت‌شناسی و تاریخ ریاضیات و علوم، و از پیشگامان ایران در مطالعات علمی عمر خیام. از دیباچۀ او برای آخرین کتاب مجموعۀ ۱۲ جلدی «راز عمر خیام».

«در واقع، برای اینجانب که در سنین جوانی با رباعیات خیام از منظر ادوارد فیتزجرالد آشنا شدم، مواجهه با مجموعۀ «راز عمر خیام» مانند تجربۀ فضانوردانی بود که برای اولین بار کرۀ زمین را از فضا مشاهده کردند. چنین تجربه‌ای برایم از قبل حتی متصوّر نبود. ... در آثار خیام، به ویژه در شعر او، دل‌مشغولی‌های غم‌نگارانی را می‌یابیم که پیشۀ نویسندۀ گیلگمش یا نویسندگانی نظیر سوفوکل، شکسپیر و گوته بوده است. با چنان اضطراب، تردید، و عبث‌نگری‌هایی روبرو می‌شویم که طعم داستایفسکی، کی‌یرکگور، کامو و کوبو آبه را به ما می چشانند. به تیزبینی‌های بس دقیقی بر می خوریم که حس می کنیم در محضر بودا، پوشکین و نبوغ عملی داوینچی و بیکن هستیم. و کسی که اهل دل و مسائل ایمان و عقل و عشق و سعادت است، با سخنانی از نظایر ارسطو، سنت آگوستین و آکویناس گرفته تا زارا ژاکوب، جفرسون و بونهوفر مواجه می‌شود. برای مثال، سعادت نه فقط حالتی از بهزیستی، بلکه فرآیندی از آزاده‌زیستی مداوم نیز هست. ... اگرچه زندگی خیام خود داستان شور و شوق جدّی روشنفکری است که به آرمان‌های فلسفه، علم و شعر (و شیوه هایی از زندگی که انزواگزینی و شهرت یا خصوصی و عمومی را با هم می‌آمیزند) عمیقاً وفادار می‌باشد، جایی را نیز به آنچه بخشی از هویت اوست اختصاص می‌دهد، بخشی که نمی توان آنرا ناعادلانه در پژوهش، تاریخ و فرهنگ بشری نادیده گرفت. و آن نقش طنز است — آنچه که با شوخ‌طبعی معایب عقل، علم، فلسفه (از جمله الهیات)، سیاست، تاریخ، عُرف (هرچند مقدس) را هنگام مواجهه با ناامیدی‌های عمیق یا فجایع زندگی نقد می‌کند. همانطور که آریستوفان، سروانتس، ویکو، اراسموس، سانتایانا و چخوف می‌دانستند، استقبال از کمدی بخشی از شناخت، خرد، و تضمین شکوفایی انسان است. شاید بتوان گفت خیام نخستین انسان گرای واقعی بوده است. هر آنچه انسانی است از طریق او به وضوح جلوه‌گر می‌شود.»

- دکتر وینستون ای. لنگلی، استاد بازنشستۀ علوم سیاسی و روابط بین الملل، عضو ارشد دانشکدۀ تحصیلات تکمیلی مک کورمک برای سیاست گذاری و مطالعات جهانی، و مدیر هیئت علمی (پرووست) سابق (۲۰۰۸-۲۰۱۷) دانشگاه ماساچوست در بوستون. از دیباچۀ او برای آخرین کتاب مجموعۀ ۱۲ جلدی «راز عمر خیام».

Contents

About OKCIR—i

The Series on Which the Present Book is Based—ii

About this Book—iv

About the Series Author and Translator—viii

Acknowledgments—xiii

Introduction: A Summary of the Findings of the 12-Book "Omar Khayyam's Secret" Series Resulting in the Present Book: How a Method Framed in the Quantum Sociological Imagination Helped Solve the Riddles of Omar Khayyam's Life and His Robaiyat amid All His Works—*1*

The Robaiyat of Omar Khayyam: Part 1 of 3: Songs of Doubt Addressing the Question "Does Happiness Exist?"

    I. Secret Book of Life (راز دفتر عمر)—p. *23*

    II. Alas! (افسوس)—p. *28*

    III. Times (زمانه)—p. *35*

    IV. Spheres (افلاک)—p. *39*

    V. Chance and Fate (قضا و قدر)—p. *47*

    VI. Puzzle (معمّا)—p. *50*

    VII. O God! (خدایا)—p. *55*

    VIII. Tavern Voice (ندا از میخانه)—p. *66*

    IX. O Wine-Tender (ای ساقی)—p. *72*

The Robaiyat of Omar Khayyam: Part 2 of 3: Songs of Hope Addressing the Question "What Is Happiness?"

    X. Drunken Way (راه مستی)—p. *79*

    XI. Willfulness (اراده)—p. *89*

    XII. Foes and Friends (دوست و دشمن)—p. *93*

    XIII. Wealth (ثروت)—p. *102*

    XIV. Today (امروز)—p. *110*

    XV. Pottery (کوزه گری)—p. *121*

    XVI. Cemetery (گورستان)—p. *124*

    XVII. Paradise and Hell (بهشت و جهنم)—p. *127*

The Robaiyat of Omar Khayyam: Part 3 of 3: Songs of Joy Addressing the Question "Why Can Happiness Exist?"

    XVIII. Garden (باغ)—p. *135*

    XIX. Wine (شراب)—p. *142*

    XX. Love (عشق)—p. *157*

    XXI. Night (شب)—p. *162*

    XXII. Death and Survival (مرگ و بقا)—p. *165*

    XXIII. Liberation (رهایی)—p. *170*

    XXIV. Return (بازگشت)—p. *182*

Robaiyat Index—185

Acknowledgments

Without the contributions of countless scholars, past and present, in Iran and abroad, who have explored the life and works of Omar Khayyam over the centuries, the conduct of this study would have been impossible. The list of these individuals is long, and I hope my engagements with some of their works throughout the *Omar Khayyam's Secret* series of which this book is a result may serve as expressions of my deep appreciation for their valuable contributions.

I thank my wife Anna D. Beckwith for her patience and encouragements during the many decades it took me to conduct this research on Khayyam. I also thank Ramón Grosfoguel for his kind early interest in my work, including that on Khayyam, and for inviting me to offer a seminar presentation on Khayyam in March 2011 at U.C. Berkeley. I also appreciate the interest Lewis R. Gordon has taken in my research in quantum sociological imagination. I wish them the best of health and work.

What ultimately made this study possible have been the love, support, and sacrifices of my parents, Tayyebeh Tamjidi (1928-2020) and Mohammed (Ahad) Tamjidi (1930-2007). My only wish and hope are that this engagement with the immortal spirit of Omar Khayyam will keep the names and memories of both my parents, and my endless love for them, alive forever. This series is especially dedicated, beside Omar Khayyam himself, to the memory of my mother and in celebration of the universe of love, search for justice, and spiritual curiosity she bequeathed to me.

Although according to Khayyam, after we live this life, there will be no returns in body, in spirit the enigma of death can be differently solved, and it happens that I received back my own Nowroozi gifts from my mother, and perhaps even from Khayyam himself, by way of two forewords from two distinguished scholars who have cared sincerely to write them for the series of which this book is a final result.

Dr. Aghayani Chavoshi is Professor of Philosophy of Science at Sharif University of Technology in Tehran, Iran, specializing in philosophy, epistemology, and history of mathematics and science, being also a pioneer in scientific Khayyam studies. He is a respected and recognized Iranian specialist in the history of science in Iran and Islam whose works I also cited in Book 6 of the series on *Khayyami Science* regarding some of the differently extant works of Khayyam in arithmetic and calendar reform. His foreword to the last book of the series, of which I have shared a quote as an epigraph for this book, spoke volumes to the requirements of scientific progress, that is, the need to appreciatively evaluate new studies in Khayyami studies.

Dr. Winston E. Langley's foreword to the last book of the series, of which I have also quoted an epigraph for this book, exemplifies what Dr. Chavoshi invited others to do, by way of an in-depth and thoughtful review of the entire series, and I am fortunate to have received a box full of his Nowroozi gifts, filled to the brim. I had imagined myself, every now and then, being in the presence of Omar Khayyam somewhere in the spheres above in an afterlife, hearing his few words of appreciation for my series'

xiii

work; but, of course, I was reminded each time while reading his Robaiyat that there will be no bodily afterlife coming. So, I have been most fortunate that here, in *this* world, before I too am gone, I have received Khayyam's thanks in spirit by way of Dr. Langley's foreword to the last book of the *Omar Khayyam's Secret* series, in his always eloquently expressed way.

Dr. Langley, Professor Emeritus of Political Science & International Relations, Senior Fellow at the McCormack Graduate School for Policy & Global Studies, and a former Provost (2008-2017) of the University of Massachusetts (UMass) Boston, has been familiar with and supportive of my studies in the context of my research, teaching, and service work at UMass Boston (2003-2013) as a tenure-track and then tenured associate professor of sociology. In my own university experience, going back to my undergraduate and graduate studies, I came to know several remarkable professors whose spirits rose above and beyond academic life, always reminding me that, despite their limitations, universities can also house utopystic spacetimes for advancing alternative perspectives. Dr. Langley represents a merging of all such dear individuals' spiritual gifts in one person, having been a universally respected university Provost as well, having deep empathy for others and being respectful of other cultural and spiritual voices in the sincerest of ways, as his foreword to the last book of my series demonstrated, passages of which are also epigraphing this book.

Khayyam, inspired by the allegorical spiritual works of all genuine spiritual traditions, had tapped into the insight that to bring about healing to human-caused suffering one has to reach the depths of human souls—their hearts, minds, and sensations—through poetry. So, I find his Robaiyat to be his poetic manifesto of a way of creating a better world in a different, othersystemic and utopystic, way, healing the human tree's roots starting from our intra/interpersonal todays, during what Langley aptly calls, as Khayyam had proposed, "meditation chambers" of reading his epic poem continually while reflecting on the meaning of our personal troubles in relation to the public issues of our times in a cosmic context. If a critical mass of us makes similar efforts, I do believe we can write happier chapters for our species.

Omar Khayyam's Robaiyat as shared in this book deserves to be read by all, at least once in one's lifetime, and continually. If you begin reading it, you *must* do so to its end. Once it has been read thoroughly with the presence of mind, heart, and sensibilities, any of its quatrains or parts thereof can then be understood properly in the context of the unitary logical architecture of its truly astounding spiritual beauty.

I sincerely believe that had this work of art by Omar Khayyam been known earlier to humanity in its logical integrity, and taken to heart for what it intends to do, we would have been living in a better world today. But, it is still not too late. All it takes, as Khayyam invites us to do continually in our todays, is to taste the Sips of its unitary spiritual Wine of happiness, bittersweet as it is, in a mindful way. And yes, as he also advised, the best moments to Drink the Sips are those magical early morning hours, when we have not yet become as fragmented as we will likely become later in the day.

— M. H. (Behrooz) Tamdgidi, May 2025

Introduction: A Summary of the Findings of the 12-Book "Omar Khayyam's Secret" Series Resulting in the Present Book: How a Method Framed in the Quantum Sociological Imagination Helped Solve the Riddles of Omar Khayyam's Life and His Robaiyat amid All His Works

Omar Khayyam's Secret: Hermeneutics of the Robaiyat in Quantum Sociological Imagination is a 12-book series on the life and works of Omar Khayyam whose publication began in 2021 and was completed in 2025. Each book of the series is independently readable, although it will be best understood as a part of the series. The last book of the series published in April 2025 served as a synopsis volume in which the collected works of Omar Khayyam and a summary of the series' findings studying them in a unitary way was included.

In the series, I shared the results of my research on Khayyam, the enigmatic 11th/12th centuries Persian Muslim sage, philosopher, astronomer, mathematician, physician, writer, and poet from Neyshabour, Iran, whose life and works had remained behind a veil of deep mystery. The purpose of my research was to find answers to the many puzzles surrounding Khayyam, especially regarding the existence, nature, and purpose of the Robaiyat in his life and works. To explore the questions posed in the series, I advanced a new hermeneutic method of textual analysis, informed by what I call the quantum sociological imagination, to gather and study all the attributed philosophical, religious, scientific, and literary writings of Khayyam.

In Book 1, I developed the quantum sociological imagination method framing my hermeneutic study in the series. In the preface I explained the origins of the series and how the study was itself a moment in the trajectory of a broader research project. In the introduction, I described how centuries of Khayyami studies,

1

especially during the last two, had reached an impasse in shedding light on his life and works, especially his Robaiyat.

The four chapters of Book 1 were then dedicated to developing the quantum sociological imagination as a new hermeneutic method framing the Khayyami studies in the series. The method built, in an applied way, on the results of my recent work in the sociology of scientific knowledge, *Liberating Sociology: From Newtonian Toward Quantum Imagination: Volume 1: Unriddling the Quantum Enigma* (2020), where I explored extensively, in greater depth, and in the context of understanding the so-called "quantum enigma," the Newtonian and quantum ways of imagining reality. In the first book of the series, I shared a summary of the findings of that research amid new applied insights developed in relation to Khayyami studies.

In the first chapter, I raised a set of eight questions about the structure of C. Wright Mills's sociological imagination as a potential framework for Khayyami studies. In the second chapter, I showed how those questions were symptomatic of Newtonian structures that still continue to frame Mills's sociological imagination. In the third chapter, I explored how the sociological imagination can be reinvented to be more in tune with the findings of quantum science, and in the last chapter the implications of the quantum sociological imagination for devising a hermeneutic method for new Khayyami studies were outlined.

The most important and pivotal implication of the application of the quantum sociological imagination for the study of Khayyam's Robaiyat is this. The basic insight of the quantum vision of reality is that each particle (and this is not limited just to light phenomena) is at once congealed and spread-out. In my unriddling the quantum enigma (2020) I showed that there is no duality separating microscopic from macroscopic worlds from one another as far as the applicability of such a quantum vision is concerned, since such a duality is itself a result of leftover Newtonian distortions in our own lenses as observers. Consequently, applying such a quantum vision to the sociological imagination and to Khayyami studies is also possible. I argued that Khayyam's quatrains must have also existed at once locally in the quatrains themselves and also spread-out in all of his writings. Therefore, even if the attributability of specific quatrains to him is doubted, his Robaiyat can be rediscovered and the riddle of specific quatrains' attributability to him solved by way of studying the Robaiyat as spread out in all of his extant writings.

The Newtonian way of imagining reality has been metaphorically compared to what I have argued (2020) to be itself an ideologically distorted "billiard balls game" way of imagining reality—ideologically distorted, since in fact even the billiard balls game can be imagined in a quantum way if our Newtonian lenses are rectified. The Newtonian way of imagining reality may be broadly characterized as having eight notional attributes—namely, its notions of (1) dualism, (2) atomism, (3) separability, (4) (subjectless) objectivity, (5) determinism (including its associated notion of predictability), (6) continuity, (7) disciplinarity, and (8) scientism.

To elaborate, the notional attributes of the Newtonian imagination are the following: 1. Dualism: It assumes that an object must be either A and non-A and cannot be both at the same time; 2. Atomism: Its micro unit of analysis of the object allows for separability of objects in an atomistic way; 3. Separability: Its macro unit of analysis allows for separability of objects as if they came into being on their own and apart from one another; 4. (Subjectless) Objectivity: It assumes that the object being observed can be understood apart from the role the observer plays in understanding and constituting it; 5. Determinism: It assumes that there are predeterministic causes and consequences governing objects that render their development always predictable; 6. Continuity: It assumes that objects are constituted by the influence of continuous chains of local-causations; 7. Disciplinarity: It assumes that reality can be understood by way of fragmented disciplinary lenses whose knowledge can be truly understood apart from the knowledge of reality as a whole; and 8. Scientism: It presumes the superiority of Western, Newtonian scientific way of thinking about reality, treating other cultural approaches to science as outdated and defective.

In Book 1, I suggested that the same eight-fold model to describe the attributes of the Newtonian way of thinking can be reframed to arrive at the quantum way of imagining reality, characterized as having eight sets of attributes: 1. Simultaneity (not "duality," nor "complementarity"): That reality is constituted of folds that can be best imaginable as superposed concentric part/whole circles where A can be at once non-A; 2. Superpositionality: That such a superposed reality constitutes the micro world, rendering it as not being atomistic but being comprised of superposed folds; 3. Inseparability: That such a superposed reality also constitutes the macro world as well, each part of which is constituted as an organic part of the whole reality; 4. Relativity (or, subject-included objectivity): That objectivity can only be achieved if the subject observing the object is always treated as being a part of the object, treating the knowledge and reality of the object as not being independent of, but also constituted by, the observer; 5. Probability: Given the superposed nature of reality, microscopically as well as macroscopically, its transformation can be at once determined and probabilistic; 6. Transcontinuity (which is a term I prefer to call what is commonly referred to in quantum science as "discontinuity"): That reality by its superposed nature allows for transcontinuous, creative leaps to take place that can defy prior established local causal chains; 7. Transdisciplinarity: That reality can be best understood in a transdisciplinary (not just disciplinary, nor interdisciplinary or multidisciplinary, since the latter two still presume the disciplines) way, by regarding the knowledge of each of its folds as a part of the reality as a whole; 8. Transculturalism: Embracing all culturally variant ways of going about understanding reality that defy the presumed superiority of one cultural tradition over another.

Following the above considerations, in Book 1, I proposed that quantumizing the Newtonian in favor of a quantum sociological imagination invites the following considerations regarding each of which I offered illustrations, and from each of which I drew inspiration for Khayyami studies: 1. From dualism to simultaneity (not "duality," nor "complementarity"): Personal troubles and public issues can be at once one another and dialectically constituting of one another; 2. From atomism to superpositionality: One can be constituted of a multitude of selves, some having personal troubles, others not, and some being at once troubled and troubling; 3. From separability to inseparability: Public issues are not constituted just locally, communally, or nationally, but also world-historically; 4. From subjectless objectivity to relativity (subject-included objectivity): Those who study the relation of personal troubles and public issues can also be themselves personally troubled and shaped by public issues of their times affecting their sociological imaginations, and even be themselves the source of personal troubles and public issues of their subjects; 5. Reimagining causal patterns creatively from determinism to probability: Personal troubles and public issues are not predeterminable and predictable always, but are subject to probabilities and chances, and the same insight applies to resolutions one can bring to such troubles and issues; 6. Reimagining causal chains also as causal leaps, from continuity to "transcontinuity" (also known as "discontinuity"): Lack of creativity can play a role in causing personal troubles and public issues, and their resolution can significantly depend on the application of creative cognitive and transformative methods; 7. Reimagining sociology from disciplinarity toward transdisciplinarity: The sociological imagination can be most successful in understanding the interplay of personal trouble and public issues when it is conducted in a transdisciplinary way; and 8. Reimagining science from eurocentrism to tansculturalism: The sociological imagination can be most successful in understanding the interplay of personal trouble and public issues when it is conducted in a transcultural way.

In Book 1, I showed how by reimagining the elements of the sociological imagination in terms of superposing circles we can arrive at a non-dualistic, both/and, conception of elements that previously could only be imagined in terms of a formal, either/or logic characterizing the Newtonian way of imagining reality.

The implications of the quantum sociological imagination for Khayyami studies can therefore be highly significant. We can find that Khayyam was personally troubled in life about the existential troubles of humanity as a whole, his own personal troubles offering deep insights into how he went about understanding human existence, the reverse being equally true—suggesting that even a brief piece of his writings can shed light on his entire life and works. We can find that atoms of his quatrains are not separate micro units of his poetry but integrally superposed parts of a larger narrative of his effort in understanding human life. We can find that the broader public issues influencing, and being influenced by, his personal troubles were, in his view, not just local, communal, or even world-historical, but, given his spiritual worldview, encompassing astronomical/astrological, theological, and philosophical dimensions, requiring the study of all his treatises, not in isolation from one another, but as superposed folds of his unitary research work.

We can find that his study of human personal troubles and public issues is not just contemplative and one-sidedly objective, but deeply self-reflective, self-critical, as well as conceptually constitutive and transformative of their realities—rendering his Robaiyat as not being contemplative of, but also healing and transformative for, the personal troubles and public issues facing humankind. We can find that he was aware not only of matters of deterministic fate, but also of probabilistic chance, not dualizing them artificially but containing quantum visions where one can be at once the other. We can find that he regarded predeterministic worldviews, scientific or religious, as being inadequate when dualized and separated from one another, being deficient on their own in understanding human troubles and issues, aiming instead for creative, poetic, pathways for appreciating and transcending their approaches.

We can find that his method was deeply and widely transdisciplinary and transcultural, not boxing his worldview in one or another rigid dogma, instead preferring a freethinking way of going about understanding human existence. We can find that such a method is itself required for understanding Khayyam's life and works in a transdisciplinary and transcultural way, beyond artificial ways of separating his science from his philosophy, theology, astronomy, astrology, art, and poetic work, ways that treat the fields as being separable billiard balls to be juggled against one another. We can instead treat them as being superposed, overlapping, folds of a unitary approach to understanding and transforming human life in favor of just outcomes. In short, we can find that to understand his views, and his Robaiyat, we need to read and understand *all* his treatises, and not just his quatrains, rather than treating them in isolation from one another, as if they are inherently separable.

Moreover, I argued that using the notion of "Khayyami" as a reference both to the person and to the tradition associated with him can offer a sociologically imaginative quantum device involving a language of simultaneity when referring to Khayyam's life, works, and legacy—especially when it comes to the study of the attributed Robaiyat. Therefore, the notion can have significant methodological, substantive, and practical value for framing and conducting our Khayyami studies.

Overall, applying such a quantum method to the study of the Robaiyat requires that we do not study the quatrains in isolation from one another and from the rest of the extant works of Khayyam, but undertake a careful study of *all* his works, as if his Robaiyat had a spread-out presence in them throughout. This explains why for the study of his Robaiyat I had to conduct the 12-book series research.

The second book of the series was subtitled *Khayyami Millennium: Reporting the Discovery and the Reconfirmation of the True Dates of Birth and Passing of Omar Khayyam (AD 1021-1123)*. In the book, I laid down an essential foundation for the series by revisiting the unresolved questions surrounding the dates of birth and passing of Omar Khayyam.

Critically reexamining the manner in which Omar Khayyam's birth horoscope as reported in Zahireddin Abolhassan Beyhaqi's *Tatemmat Sewan al-Hekmat (Supplement to the Chest of Wisdom)* was used by Swāmi Govinda Tīrtha in his book *The Nectar of Grace: Omar Khayyam's Life and Works* (1941) to determine Khayyam's birth date, I uncovered a number of serious internal inconsistencies and factual inaccuracies that prevented Tīrtha (and, since then, other scholars more or less taking his results for granted) from arriving at a reliable date for Khayyam's birth, hurling Khayyami studies into decades of confusion regarding Khayyam's life and works. I then shared in the book the detailed account of my own discovery of Khayyam's true date of birth for the first time on 412 LH, or June 10, AD 1021, in the Gregorian calendar.

I then turned my attention to the task of definitively establishing the true date of passing of Omar Khayyam. Conducting an in-depth, superposed analysis of Beyhaqi's *Tatemmat Sewan el-Hekmat (Supplement to the Chest of Wisdom)*, Abdorrahman Khazeni's *Mizan ol-Hekmat (Balance of Wisdom)*, Nezami Arouzi's *Chahar Maqaleh (Four Discourses)*, and Yar Ahmad Rashidi Tabrizi's *Tarabkhaneh (House of Joy)*, amid other relevant texts, I reconfirmed and further discovered, in a textually reliable way, the date and time in which the poet mathematician, astronomer, and calendar reformer died as a solar centenarian, completing his 102nd solar year age—517 LH, or AD 1123, in the Gregorian calendar.

Notably, these discoveries were made and reported in 2021 just in time as we approached the first solar millennium of Omar Khayyam's birth date on June 10, AD 1021 (Gregorian), at sunrise of Neyshabour, Iran, and the ninth solar centennial of his passing in AD 1123, likely also on June 10 (Gregorian), on the eve also of his birthday, closing the circle of his life's "coming and going."

The third book of the series, published together with the two preceding books of the series, was subtitled, *Khayyami Astronomy: How Omar Khayyam's Newly Discovered True Birth Date Horoscope Reveals the Origins of His Pen Name and Independently Confirms His Authorship of the Robaiyat.*

Omar Khayyam's true birth date horoscope, as newly discovered in the series (see Figure 1), is comprised of a dazzling number of Air Triplicities (called in Persian astrology Khargāh or "Grand Tent") sharing a vertex on a Sun-Mercury Samimi (Cazimi) point on the same Ascendant degree 18 of Gemini. Among other features, his Venus, Sextile with Moon, also plays a lifelong, secretively creative role to intentionally balance his chart. These features would not have escaped the attention of Omar Khayyam, a master astronomer and expert in astrological matters, no matter how much he embraced, doubted, or rejected astrological interpretations.

In Book 3, conducting a hermeneutic analysis of Khayyam's horoscope, I reported having discovered the inspirational origins of Khayyam's pen name ("tentmaker") in his horoscope. The long-held myth that "Khayyam" was a family name, even if true, in no way takes away from the new finding; it only adds to its intrigue.

My hermeneutic analysis of Khayyam's horoscope in intersection with extant Khayyami Robaiyat also led me to discover an entirely neglected signature quatrain that I proved could not be from anyone but Khayyam, one that provides a reliably independent confirmation of his authorship of the Robaiyat. I also showed how another neglected quatrain reporting its poet to have aged to a hundred is from Khayyam. This meant that all the extant Khayyami quatrains were now in need of hermeneutic reevaluation.

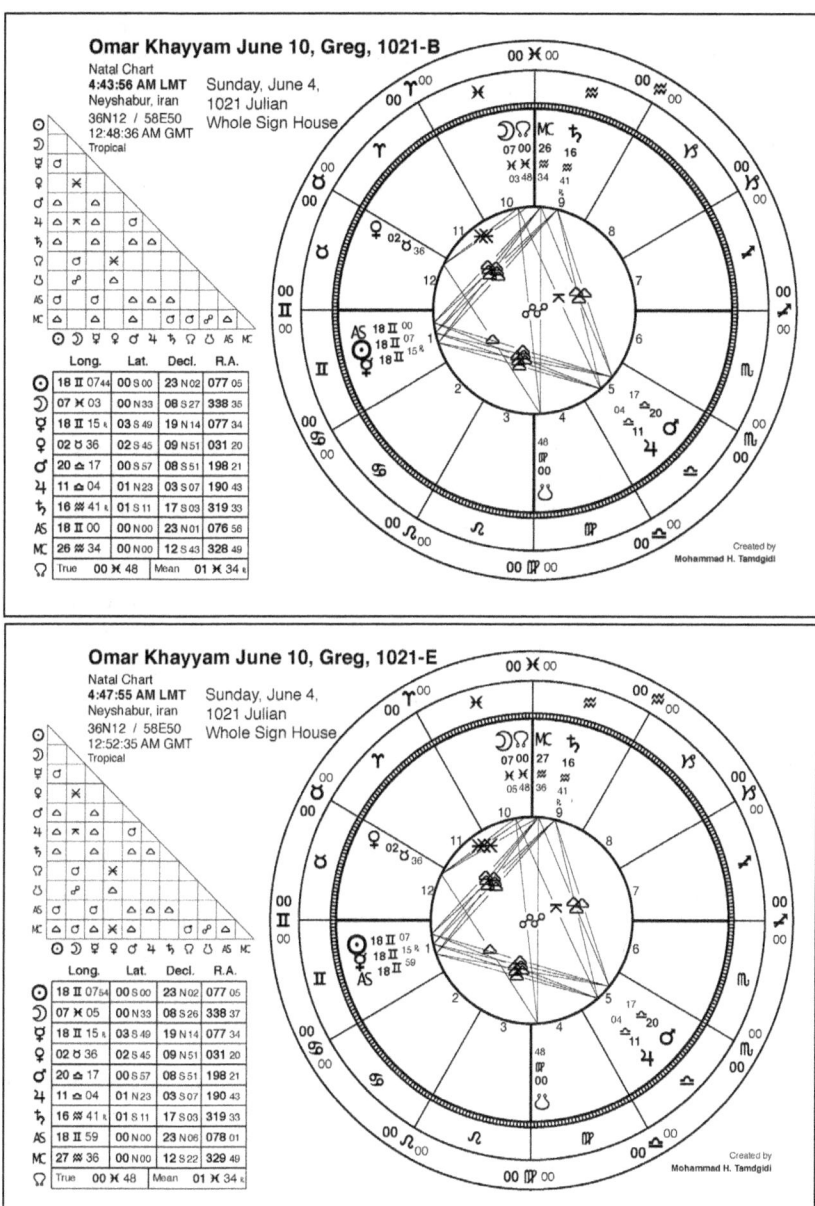

Figure 1: The 11th Century Known-Planets Natal Charts of the Beginning and the Ending Seconds of the Nearly Four Minutes During which Omar Khayyam's Birth Took Place in AD 1021

My further study of a sample of fifty Khayyami Robaiyat led me to conclude that their poet definitively intended the poems to remain in veil, that they were a collection of interrelated quatrains and not separate quatrains written marginally in pastime, that they were meant to offer a life's intellectual journey as in a "book of life," that the poems' critically nuanced engagement with astrology was not incidental but essential throughout the collection, and that, judging from the signature quatrain discovered, 1000 quatrains were intended to comprise the collection. It appears that, after all, "The Khayyam who stitched his tents of wisdom" was a trope that had its inspirational origins in Omar Khayyam's horoscope heavens.

The fourth book of the series was subtitled *Khayyami Philosophy: The Ontological Structures of the Robaiyat in Omar Khayyam's Last Written Keepsake Treatise on the Science of the Universals of Existence*.

Having confirmed in the prior three books of the series the true dates of birth and passing of Omar Khayyam, his pen name origins, and his authorship of a robaiyat collection, in Book 4 I explored the origins, nature, and purpose of such a collection by applying the series' quantum sociological imagination method to hermeneutically explore the ontological structures of the Robaiyat in Khayyam's last written treatise on the universals of existence.

Khayyam's treatise, found in the early 20th century and still largely ignored or misread, radically challenges the mythical narratives built over the centuries about him as one who thought existence is unknowable, having died not solving its riddles. Strangely, his treatise instead offers a logically coherent and brilliant worldview of someone who has found his answers as far as human existence is concerned. Khayyam even goes so far as confidently saying he hopes his peers would agree that his brief treatise is more useful than volumes.

Offering the Persian text and my new English translation of the treatise, I undertook in the fourth book a detailed clause-based hermeneutic study of the treatise. I also explored its broader intellectual and historical contexts by examining its relation to the book "Savior from Error" by Khayyam's junior (by more than three decades) contemporary foe, Muhammad Ghazali, while questioning the long-held belief that the treatise was requested by and addressed to Fakhr ol-Molk, a son of the famous vizier Nezam ol-Molk.

I found instead that the treatise was written in AD 1095-96, a few years earlier than thought, for another son of Nezam ol-Molk, Moayyed ol-Molk, who served at the time Soltan Muhammad, Malekshah's son. The treatise was intended as a philosophical foundation to move the post-Malekshah Iran in a more independent direction by way of influencing his son, Muhammad. In his book, likely written to please Ahmad Sanjar (Malekshah's younger son who disliked Khayyam) and his vizier at the time, Fakhr ol-Molk, Ghazali anonymously chastised Khayyam as a philosopher, duplicitously feeding the cynical metaphors that some theologians and Sufis hurled at Khayyam down the centuries.

Khayyam's treatise unveils his vision of existence as a participatory universe where the subject has objective status, shedding a new light on the ontological structures of the Robaiyat. His "succession order" thesis of existence is an alternative Islamic creationist-evolutionary worldview that offers a prescient quantum conceptualist vision of the universe as a unitary, relatively self-reliant, self-knowing, and self-creative, substance lovingly created by an absolutely good God in His own image. Existence is essentially good but, due to its good volitionally self-creative nature, can be potentially subject to incidental defects that are nevertheless knowable and curable to build *both* a spiritually fulfilling *and* a joyful life in *this* world. Other than God's Necessary Existence there is no "another world"; judgment days, heavens, and hells are definitely real *this-worldly*, not otherworldly, existents. In Khayyam's view, human existence can be what good we artfully make of it, starting here-and-now from our own personal selves in our *this-worldly* lifetimes. It is to creatively realize such an existence that the Robaiyat must have been intended.

The fifth book of the series was subtitled *Khayyami Theology: The Epistemological Structures of the Robaiyat in All the Philosophical Writings of Omar Khayyam Leading to His Last Keepsake Treatise.*

Book 5 was devoted to an in-depth examination of all of Omar Khayyam's philosophical treatises written before and leading to his last keepsake treatise on the science of the universals of existence which I had examined already in depth in Book 4 of the series. The purpose of the study of these texts, applying the quantum hermeneutic method developed for the series, was to arrive at an understanding of the structures of the theological epistemology informing any collection of quatrains or Robaiyat Khayyam may have written in his life.

In the book, to understand the theological epistemology (or, way of knowing God) framing Khayyam's Robaiyat as spread out in all his philosophical works, I offered the texts and my updated Persian and new English translations and analyses of six writings that preceded Khayyam's last treatise on the universals of existence.

The six primary texts included: 1: Khayyam's annotated Persian translation of Avicenna's sermon in Arabic on God and creation; 2: Khayyam's treatise in Arabic addressed to Nasawi (who I showed has been wrongly regarded as an Avicenna pupil) on the created world and worship duty; 3-5: Khayyam's three treatises in Arabic (which I showed were all addressed to Abu Taher, to whom Khayyam also dedicated his treatise in algebra) that are separate chapters of a three-part treatise on existence on topics such as the necessity of contradiction, determinism, survival, attributes of existents, and the light of intellect on 'existent' as the subject matter of universal science; and 6: Khayyam's treatise in Arabic addressed to Moshkavi (who I revealed was a supportive Shia intellectual) in response to three questions on soul's survival, on the necessity of accidents, and on the nature of time.

In the book, I showed that the most fruitful way of understanding Khayyam's six texts is by regarding them as efforts made at defending his "succession order" thesis implicitly revealed when commenting on Avicenna's sermon and finalized in his last keepsake treatise. The texts served to offer the theological epistemology behind Khayyam's thesis, revealing his creative conceptualist view of existence that informed his poetic way of going about knowing God, creation, and himself within a unitary Islamic creationist-evolutionary worldview.

It was learned that Khayyam's way of knowing God and existence is non-dualistic, non-atomistic, and unitary in worldview, allowing for subject-included objectivity, probabilistic determinism, transcontinuous (or 'discontinuous') creative causality, transdisciplinarity, and transculturalism; it thus fulfils in a prescient way all the eight attributes of the quantum vision (Tamdgidi 2020). Poetry is most conducive to unitary knowing, and subject-included objectivity must necessarily be self-reflective and thus engage intellective, emotional, and sensible modes of knowing. This explains why Khayyam transcended scholastic learning in favor of a poetic encounter with reality. What he meant by 'Drunkenness,' calling it the highest state of mind known to him, can thus be best understood as a unitary, quantum state of mind achieved by way of his poetry as a meditative art of self-purification (what he called "tazkiyeh-ye nafs"). The goal, metaphorically, is to move from a way of knowing things as divisible grapes to a pure and unitary way of knowing them as indivisible Wine—paralleling what we call today moving from chunky Newtonian toward unitary quantum visions of reality.

I posited that the key for entering Khayyam's secret tent is realizing that what he primarily meant by 'Wine' in his Robaiyat was self-referentially his Robaiyat *itself*, a key openly hidden therein thanks to his theological epistemology. For him, the Robaiyat was a lifelong work on himself, serving also human spiritual awakening to its place and duty in the succession order of God's creation. It also served his aspiration for a lasting soul. He knew the now-proven worth of his secret *magnum opus*, and that is why he so much praised his 'Wine.'

The sixth book of the series was subtitled *Khayyami Science: The Methodological Structures of the Robaiyat in All the Scientific Works of Omar Khayyam.*

In Book 6, I shared the Arabic texts, my new English translations (based on others' or my new Persian translations, also included in the volume), and hermeneutic analyses of five extant scientific writings of Khayyam: a treatise in music on tetrachords; two treatises on balance, one being on how to measure the weights of precious metals in a body composed of them; a treatise on dividing a circle quadrant to achieve a certain proportionality; a treatise on classifying and solving all cubic (and lower degree) algebraic equations using geometric methods; and a treatise on explaining three postulation problems in Euclid's book *Elements*. Khayyam wrote three other non-extant scientific treatises on nature, geography, and music, while a treatise in arithmetic is differently extant since it influenced the work of later Islamic and Western scientists. His work in astronomy on solar calendar reform is also differently extant in the calendar used in Iran today. A short tract on astrology attributed to him has been neglected.

I studied the scientific works in relation to Khayyam's own theological, philosophical, and astronomical views. The study revealed that Khayyam's science was informed by a unifying methodological attention to ratios and proportionality. So, given such a way of thinking, likewise, any quatrain he wrote cannot be adequately understood without considering its place in the relational whole of its parent collection. Khayyam's Robaiyat is found to be, as a critique of fatalistic astrology, his most important scientific work in astronomy rendered in poetic form.

Studying Khayyam's scientific works in relation to those of other scientists out of the context of his own philosophical, theological, and astronomical views, would be like comparing the roundness of two fruits while ignoring that they are apples and oranges. Khayyam was a relational, holistic, and self-including objective thinker, being systems and causal-chains discerning, creative, transdisciplinary, transcultural, and applied in method. He applied a poetic geometric imagination to solving algebraic problems and his logically methodical thinking did not spare even Euclid of criticism. His treatise on Euclid unified numerical and magnitudinal notions of ratio and proportionality by way of broadening the notion of number to include both rational and irrational numbers, transcending its Greek atomistic tradition.

I argued that Khayyam's classification of algebraic equations, being capped at cubic types, tells of his applied scientific intentions that can be interpreted, in the context of his own Islamic philosophy and theology, as an effort in building an algebraic and numerical theory of everything that is not only symbolic of body's three dimensions, but also of the three-foldness of intellect, soul, and body as essential types of a unitary substance created by God to evolve relatively on its own in a two-fold succession order of coming from and going to its Source. Although the succession order poses limits, as captured in the astrological imagination, existence is not fatalistic. Khayyam's conceptualist view of the human subject as an objective creative force in a participatory universe allows for the possibility of human self-determination and freedom depending on his or her self-awakening, a cause for which the Robaiyat was intended. Its collection would be a balanced unity of wisdom gems ascending from multiplicity toward unity using Wine and various astrological, geometrical, numerical, calendrical, and musical tropes in relationally classified quatrains that follow a logical succession order.

Book 7 of the series was subtitled *Khayyami Art: The Art of Poetic Secrecy for a Lasting Existence: Tracing the Robaiyat in Nowrooznameh, Isfahan's North Dome, and Other Poems of Omar Khayyam, and Solving the Riddle of His Robaiyat Attributability.*

In Book 7, I shared an updated edition of Omar Khayyam's Persian book *Nowrooznameh (The Book on Nowrooz)*, and for the first time my new English translation of it, followed by my analysis of its text. I then visited recent findings about the possible contribution of Khayyam to the design of Isfahan's North Dome. Next, I shared the texts, and my new English translations and analyses of Khayyam's other Arabic and Persian poems. And finally, I studied the debates surrounding the attributability of the Robaiyat to Omar Khayyam.

In the book, I verifiably showed that *Nowrooznameh* is a book written by Khayyam, arguing that its unreasonable and unjustifiable neglect has prevented

Khayyami studies from answering important questions about Khayyam's life, works, and his times. *Nowrooznameh* is primarily a work in literary art, rather than in science, tasked not with reporting on past truths but with creating new truths in the spirit of Khayyam's conceptualist view of reality. Iran in fact owes the continuity of its ancient calendar month names to the way Khayyam artfully recast their meanings in the book in order to prevent their being dismissed (given their Zoroastrian roots) during the Islamic solar calendar reform underway under his invited direction.

The book also sheds light on the mysterious function of Isfahan's North Dome, revealing it as having been to serve as a space, as part of an observatory complex, for the annual Nowrooz celebrations and leap-year declarations of the new calendar. The North Dome, to whose design Khayyam verifiably contributed and in fact bears symbols of his unitary view of a world created for happiness by God, marks where the world's most accurate solar calendar of the time was calculated. It deserves to be named after Omar Khayyam (*not* Taj ol-Molk) and declared as a cultural world heritage site. *Nowrooznameh* is also a pioneer in the prince-guidance books genre that anticipated the likes of Machiavelli's *The Prince* by centuries, the difference being that Khayyam's purpose was to inculcate his Iranian and Islamic love for justice and the pursuit of happiness in the young successors of Soltan Malekshah. Iran is famed for its ways of converting its invaders into its own culture, and *Nowrooznameh* offers a textbook example for how it was done by Khayyam.

Most significantly, however, *Nowrooznameh* offers by way of its intricately multilayered meanings the mediating link between Khayyam's philosophical, theological, and scientific works, and his Robaiyat, showing through metaphorical clues of his beautiful prose how his poetry collection could bring lasting spiritual existence to its poet posthumously. Khayyam's other Arabic and Persian poems also provide significant clues about the origins, the nature, and the purpose of the Robaiyat as his lifelong project and *magnum opus*.

I argued that the thesis of Khayyam's Robaiyat as a secretive artwork of quatrains organized in an intended reasoning order as a 'book of life' serving to bring about his lasting spiritual existence can solve the manifold puzzles contributing to the riddle of his Robaiyat attributability. I posited that the lost quatrains comprising the original collection of Robaiyat have become extant over the centuries, such that we can now reconstruct, by way of solving their 1000-piece jigsaw puzzle, the collection as it was meant to be read as an ode of interrelated quatrains by Omar Khayyam.

The eighth book of the series was subtitled *Khayyami Robaiyat: Part 1 of 3: Quatrains 1-338: Songs of Doubt Addressing the Question "Does Happiness Exist?": Explained with New English Verse Translations and Organized Logically Following Omar Khayyam's Own Three-Phased Method of Inquiry.*

In Book 8, following a common introduction in which I shared the general guidelines about and an overview of the presentation of Khayyami Robaiyat in the series, I began by offering the first of a three-part set of 1000 quatrains I have chosen to include in the series from a wider set that have been over the centuries attributed to Khayyam. Part 1 included quatrains 1-338 for each of which the Persian original along with my new English verse translation and a transliteration for the same were shared. Each quatrain was then indexed according to the frequency of its inclusion in manuscripts, the earliest known date of its appearance in them, the extent to which it has "wandered" into other poets' works, and its rhyming scheme. Brief comments about the meaning of each quatrain in relation to other quatrains and works attributed to Khayyam were then offered along with any notes regarding its new translation as shared.

I showed that the quatrains 1-338, in the beginning 30 quatrains of which Khayyam offers an opening to his book of poetry as a secretive work of art, address the question "Does Happiness Exist?" The latter question is the first of a set of three methodically phased questions Khayyam has identified in his philosophical works as being required for investigating any subject. The order in which the quatrains were presented showed that the quatrains included in Part 1 follow a logically inductive reasoning process through which Khayyam delves from the surface portraits of unhappiness to their deeper chain of causes in order to answer his question. The thematic topics of the quatrains of Part 1 as shared in Book 8 were: I. Secret Book of Life; II. Alas!; III-Times; IV-Spheres; V. Chance and Fate; VI. Puzzle; VII. O God!; VIII. Tavern Voice; and IX. O Wine-Tender!

After the opening quatrains where Khayyam explained why he was composing a secretive book of poetry and what it aims to do, his inquiry started with doubtful existential self-reflections on his life, leading him to first blame his times, then the spheres, then matters of chance and fate, soon realizing that he really did not have an explanation for the enigmas of existence, concluding that the answer only lies with God. So, he appealed to God directly for an answer. It is then that he heard the voice of the Saqi from his inner "tavern," to whom he replied in a series of quatrains closing Part 1. It is in the course of the inquiry in Part 1 that the idea of using Wine as a poetic trope was discovered by him, a matter that is separate from his interest in drinking wine, which he never denied but is secondary to the Wine discovered and advanced in his book of poetry that in fact represents his poetry, the Robaiyat, itself and its promise in answering his questions.

The logical order of Khayyam's inquiry showed how seemingly contradictory views that have been attributed to him can in fact be explained as logical moments in the successively deeper inquiries he made inductively when addressing the question whether happiness exists in the created world. His inquiry is at once personal and world-historical, as two sides of expression of the human search for an answer. We should, therefore, judge each quatrain as a logical moment in Part 1's inquiry as a whole, in anticipation of the two remaining parts of his book of poetry to be shared in Books 9 and 10 of the series, respectively addressing the two follow-up questions: "What Is Happiness?" and "Why Does (or Can) Happiness Exist?"

The ninth book of the series was subtitled *Khayyami Robaiyat: Part 2 of 3: Quatrains 339-685: Songs of Hope Addressing the Question "What Is Happiness?"*:

Explained with New English Verse Translations and Organized Logically Following Omar Khayyam's Own Three-Phased Method of Inquiry.

In Book 9, following a common introduction in which I shared the general guidelines about and an overview of the presentation of Khayyami Robaiyat in the series, I continued by offering the second of a three-part set of 1000 quatrains I have chosen to include in the series from a wider set that have been over the centuries attributed to Khayyam. Part 2 included quatrains 339-685 for each of which the Persian original along with my new English verse translation and a transliteration for the same were shared. Each quatrain was then indexed according to the frequency of its inclusion in manuscripts, the earliest known date of its appearance in them, the extent to which it has "wandered" into other poets' works, and its rhyming scheme. Brief comments about the meaning of each quatrain in relation to other quatrains and works attributed to Khayyam were then offered along with any notes regarding its new translation as shared.

I showed that the quatrains 339-685 address the question "What Is Happiness?" The latter is the second of a set of three methodically phased questions Khayyam has identified in his philosophical works as being required for investigating any subject. The order in which the quatrains were presented showed that the quatrains included in Part 2 follow a logically deductive reasoning process through which Khayyam advances in the causal chain of moving from methodological to explanatory and practical quatrains, by way of addressing the question noted above. The thematic topics of the quatrains of Part 2 as shared in Book 9 were: X. The Drunken Way; XI. Willfulness; XII. Foes and Friends; XIII. Wealth; XIV. Today; XV. Pottery; XVI. Cemetery; and XVII. Paradise and Hell.

Khayyam began with reflections on God's created world, suggesting that its unitary existence cannot be understood using either/or dualistic lenses where the ways of knowing by the head, the heart, and senses are pursued separately. Instead, he advocated, building on the idea of the Wine trope discovered in Part 1, a "Drunken way" by which he meant a unitary way of knowing symbolized by the spiritual indivisibility of Wine in contrast to the fragmentations of the grapes. He then embarked on a deductive method of emphasizing human willfulness, also created by God, offering humankind a chance to play a creative role in shaping its world. He then continued to apply such an explanatory model in dealing with practical social matters having to do with foes, friends, and wealth, leading him to advocate for the practical significance of "stealing" the chances offered in our todays to transform self and society in favor of happier and more just outcomes.

Using the tropes of visiting the jug-maker's shop and the cemetery, Khayyam then emphasized the need to maintain a wakeful awareness of the inevitability of one's physical death in order to use the opportunity of life to cultivate universal self-awareness before it is too late, positing that paradise, hell, and judgment days are not otherworldly, but realities of our here and now living. He thus transcended the sentiment of a promised future hope by advising us to create a happy life in the cash of the present, his own poetry itself being a means toward that end. Part 2 must then be understood in consideration of the other two parts of his book of poetry, one shared in Book 8 addressing the questions "Does Happiness Exist?" and the next to follow in Book 10 addressing the question "Why Does (or Can) Happiness Exist?"

The tenth book of the series was subtitled *Khayyami Robaiyat: Part 3 of 3: Quatrains 686-1000: Songs of Joy Addressing the Question "Why Can Happiness Exist?": Explained with New English Verse Translations and Organized Logically Following Omar Khayyam's Own Three-Phased Method of Inquiry.*

In Book 10, following a common introduction in which I shared the general guidelines about and an overview of the presentation of Khayyami Robaiyat in the series, I continued by offering the third of a three-part set of 1000 quatrains I have chosen to include in the series from a wider set that have been over the centuries attributed to Khayyam. Part 3 included quatrains 686-1000 for each of which the Persian original along with my new English verse translation and a transliteration for the same were shared. Each quatrain was then indexed according to the frequency of its inclusion in manuscripts, the earliest known date of its appearance in them, the extent to which it has "wandered" into other poets' works, and its rhyming scheme. Brief comments about the meaning of each quatrain in relation to other quatrains and works attributed to Khayyam were then offered along with any notes regarding its new translation as shared.

I showed that the quatrains 686-1000 address the question "Why Does (or Can) Happiness Exist?" The latter question is the third of a set of three methodically phased questions Khayyam has identified in his philosophical works as being required for investigating any subject. The order in which the quatrains were presented showed that the quatrains included in Part 3 continue the logically deductive reasoning process started in Part 2, but serve as practical examples of how humankind can turn the activity of poetry writing itself as a source of joy in life when confronting the topics of death, survival, and spiritual fulfillment. The thematic topics of the quatrains of Part 3 as shared in Book 10 were: XVIII. Garden; XIX. Wine; XX. Love; XXI. Night; XXII. Death and Survival; XXIII. Liberation; and XXIV. Return.

Khayyam's overall sentiment in pursuing the inquiry in the third part of his book of poetry was expressive of joy. He began by showing, using the example of his own poetry, how strolling in a garden offers opportunities to enjoy life even when writing about the transient nature of the roses and greens. He then offered in the longest section of his book of poetry a set of quatrains in praise of Wine, disguising therein a praise of the joy of writing his own poetry, Wine's metaphorical double-meanings offering chances in the here-and-now of "stealing" joyfulness even amid feelings of helplessness in confronting physical death. He then turned to the topic of spiritual Love, signifying the role the sentiment of Love in search of the Source of creation plays in the evolutionary movements back and forth of the succession order of the created existence as discussed in his philosophical and theological writings.

Khayyam then turned to the topic of death and the possibility of lasting spiritual survival and existence by practically encouraging the Drinkers of the Wine of his poetry itself to help bring about that end. He ended the Wine of his poetry by expressing how it has helped free himself from the prior (in Part 1) doubtfully expressed inevitability of physical death in favor of not just hopefulness (in Part 2) but the certainty of having initiated a lasting spiritual existence by way of the bittersweet Wine of his poetry itself, celebrating a return to the spiritual Source of all existence as woven into the 1000-threaded wick of the candle of his Love for God. We should therefore judge each step of the third part of Khayyam's poetic inquiry in consideration of the two other parts of his book of poetry, those shared in Books 8 and 9 addressing the questions "Does Happiness Exist?" and "What Is Happiness?"

The eleventh book in the series was subtitled *Khayyami Robaiyat: Re-Sewing the Tentmaker's Tent: 1000 Bittersweet Wine Sips from Omar Khayyam's Tavern of Happiness*. In Book 11, following a common introduction in which I shared the general guidelines about and an overview of the presentation of Khayyami Robaiyat in the series, and having shared the three parts of the Robaiyat attributed to Khayyam in the Books 8, 9, and 10 of the series, I offered the entire set of the 1000 quatrains, including the Persian originals and their new English verse translations. The poems, comprising Khayyam's songs of doubt, hope, and joy, were organized according to the three-phased method of inquiry he introduced in his philosophical writings, respectively addressing the questions: "Does Happiness Exist?"; "What Is Happiness?" and "Why Can Happiness Exist?"

When Khayyam discussed the three-phased method of inquiry in his treatise *"Resalat fi al-Kown wa al-Taklif" ("Treatise on the Created World and Worship Duty")*, he noted an exception to the rule of asking, when studying any subject, whether it exists, what it is, and, why it exists (or can exist). He distinguished between things objectively existing independent of the human mind, and those created by the human mind. The normal procedure applies to the former, but for products of the human mind, he advised, the procedure must be modified to asking first what something is, then, whether it exists, and, then, why it exists or can exist. This is because, for products of the human mind, such as created works of art, we would not know whether something exists and why it exists unless we first know what it is. To illustrate his point, he used the example of the mythical bird ʿAnqāʾ (standing for Simorgh in Persian or the Phoenix in English). He argued that only when we know what the metaphor stands for, would we be able to say whether it exists (say, in a work of art, or even as a person represented by it), and why it exists or can exist.

Khayyam's elaboration implies that one has to make a distinction between objective and human objectified realities, which implies that for some objects, such as happiness, we in fact confront a hybrid reality where aspects of it may be externally conditioned, but other aspects being dependent on the human will. Once we realize the significance of Khayyam's point, then, we appreciate that his Robaiyat can also be regarded as a way of poetically portraying *and* advancing human happiness, its poetic Wine being not just reflective but also generative of the happiness portrayed. By way of his poetry, therefore, Khayyam has offered a severe critique of the then prevalent fatalistic astrological worldviews blaming human plight on objective conditions, in favor of a conceptualist view of reality in which happiness can be achieved despite the odds, depending on the creative human agency, itself being an objective force.

I further showed that the triangular geometry of the logic governing Khayyam's Robaiyat—the numerical values of whose three sides (that is, of the number of quatrains each side contains) are proportional to the Grand Tent governing Khayyam's birth chart (as studied in Books 2 and 3 of the series)—is expressive of the fact that for him his Robaiyat poetically represented the tent of which he regarded himself to be a tentmaker, revealing another key source of his pen name. I showed that the metaphor of the Robaiyat as Simorgh songs is hidden in the deep structure of Khayyam's 1000-piece solved puzzle, the same way he embedded his own triangular golden rule in the design of the North Dome of Isfahan, as shown in Book 7 of the series. Khayyam's Robaiyat are his Simorgh's millennial rebirth songs served in his tented tavern as 1000 sips of his bittersweet Wine of happiness.

The last (12th) book of the series was subtitled *Khayyami Legacy: The Collected Works of Omar Khayyam (AD 1021-1123) Culminating in His Secretive 1000 Robaiyat Autobiography*. It condensed the series and its findings in a single volume. This was the first time since Omar Khayyam's passing that all his extant works were compiled in a single publication series and volume and studied integratively, accomplished for the millennium of his true birth date and the ninth centennial of his true date of passing. It included two forewords, one by Winston E. Langley, Professor Emeritus of Political Science and International Relations and former Provost of UMass Boston, and another by Jafar Aghayani Chavoshi, Professor of History of Science and Mathematics at Sharif University of Technology in Tehran.

The original texts were included with their new English (and where needed, updated or new Persian) translations. The preface recapped how a method in quantum sociological imagination helped solve the riddles of Khayyam's life and works in the series. The introduction delineated the series' findings toward a scientifically reliable biography of Khayyam, including a critical commentary on how Edward FitzGerald's *Rubaiyat* colonially distorted Khayyam's Robaiyat and Islamic legacy. Three other chapters were also shared: one on how Khayyam's true dates of birth and death were discovered and reconfirmed in the series, including further notes on Swāmi Govinda Tīrtha's errors in studying Khayyam's birth horoscope for the purpose; another on integratively viewing astronomy and its relation to astrology amid all of Khayyam's works; and a third on the role he played in the design of Isfahan's North Dome.

More specifically, the section subtitles of the introduction were the following: 1. The Collected Works of Omar Khayyam: The Organization of This Last Book of the Series; 2. The Scientific Requirements for the Study of Omar Khayyam's Biography; 3. Delineating the New Findings of This Series That Make Possible a Textually and Historically More Reliable Biography for Omar Khayyam; 4. The Islamophobic and Islamophilic Colonialities of Edward FitzGerald's "Rubáiyát":

Decolonizing How He World-Famously Distorted Omar Khayyam's Robaiyat; and 5. Now We Know: Lifelong, Omar Khayyam Was Secretively Writing the Robaiyat as His Poetic Autobiography for Posthumous Release.

The subtitles of Section 3 above delineating the new findings of the series were as follows: 1) Omar Khayyam's True Date of Birth (AD 1021) Discovered; 2) Omar Khayyam's Historically Known True Date of Passing (AD 1123) Reconfirmed; 3) Omar Khayyam's Horoscope: A Possible Biographical Source of His Personal Interest in Astronomy and Critical Attention to Astrology; 4) The Biographical Significance of the Stated Feature of Samimi (Cazimi) in Omar Khayyam's Horoscope: Possible Source of a Personal Trouble and Motivation, and a Trope in His Robaiyat; 5) The Biographical Significance of the Silent Features of Triplicities and Venus Secrecy in Omar Khayyam's Horoscope: Inspirations for His Pen Name and for the Trope "Sewing Tents of Wisdom"; 6) Omar Khayyam's Three-Classmates Childhood Story Could Have Been True, Even Though Differently Told; 7) Omar Khayyam's Personally Attended Teachers Reaffirmed: al-Movaffaq, al-Anbari, and Ibn Sina (Avicenna); 8) The Biographical Significance of Khayyam's Relation to Abu Taher: What Was Khayyam Doing Before His Work in Isfahan?; 9) Omar Khayyam's Friends or Foes: Nezam ol-Molk, Abu Said abol-Kheyr, Moshkavi, Moayyed ol-Molk, Fakhr ol-Molk, Soltan Sanjar, and Muhammad Ghazali; 10) The Key Biographical Significance of the Secretiveness of Khayyam's Robaiyat for Solving Many Riddles of His Life and Works; 11) Omar Khayyam's Relation to Sufism Clarified; 12) Omar Khayyam's Alleged Character Traits Refuted; 13) The Othersystemic Utopystics of Omar Khayyam's Creative Social Activism by Way of His Pen's Secretive Poetics.

The section subtitles of Chapter I in which I offered further comments (beyond Books 2 and 3 of the series) about the errors made by Swāmi Govinda Tīrtha in studying Omar Khayyam's reported horoscope were the following; 1) Introduction; 2) Omar Khayyam's True Dates of Birth and Passing (AD 1021-1123): A Brief Summary of the Findings of Books 2 and 3 of This Series; 3. Further Explaining and Demonstrating the Errors Made by Swāmi Govinda Tīrtha in Studying Omar Khayyam's Reported Birth Horoscope: 1) The Essential Elements of Tīrtha's Approach, 2) Julian or Gregorian Calendar?; 3) How is the Gemini Degree Translated?; 4) What Gemini Degree is Translated?; 5) Do Tīrtha's Findings Fulfill the Horoscope's "Third Degree of the Gemini" Requirement?; 6) Do Tīrtha's Findings Fulfill the Horoscope's Samimi (Cazimi) Requirement?; 7) Do Tīrtha's Findings Fulfill the Horoscope's Ascendant Degree Requirement?; 8) Do Tīrtha's Findings Fulfill the Horoscope's Jupiter-Observing Feature Requirement?; 9) Tīrtha's Errors in His First Try; 10) Tīrtha's Errors in His Second Try; 11) Tīrtha's More Errors in His Second Try; 12) Tīrtha's Odd Birth Chart Figures; 13) How and Where Russian Scholars and Astronomers Went Wrong In Evaluating and Confirming Swāmi Govinda Tīrtha's Mistaken Date of Birth for Omar Khayyam; 14) Conclusion.

Khayyam's studied writings included in the last volume were: his treatise on the science of the universals of existence; his annotated Persian translation of Avicenna's "Splendid Sermon" on God's unity and creation; his treatise on the created world and worship duty; his three-part treatises on existence (1-on the necessity of contradiction, determinism, and survival; 2-on attributes; and 3-on the light of intellect on 'existent' as the subject matter of universal science); his treatise on soul's survival, necessity of accidents, and nature of time; his treatise in music on tetrachords; his two treatises on balance; his treatise on circle quadrant for achieving a certain proportionality; his treatise in algebra and equations; his treatise on Euclid's postulation problems; his literary treatise "Nowrooznameh"; and his secretive autobiography, the Robaiyat, comprised of 1000 quatrains logically organized based on his own three-phased method of inquiry.

By way of conclusion, I stated that the series had found the answer to its question about the origins, nature, and purpose of the Robaiyat in Khayyam's life and works. Lifelong, he was secretively writing his Robaiyat as his "book of life," his autobiography, for posthumous release. His pen name "Khayyam" ("tentmaker") had been inspired by his birth chart. By re-sewing in the series his autobiographical tent of wisdom as a Tavern serving the spiritual Wine of his poetry, we advanced from knowing little about his life to reading his most intimate autobiography. But the Robaiyat is not just a private autobiography; it is also a sociologically imaginative and poetic public telling of humanity's search for a universal healing.

Iran's appreciation of Omar Khayyam's legacy can be best judged not by the *physics* of his burial sites, traditionally humble or artistically modern, but by the role Iranians themselves have played since his time in safeguarding his works especially in the poetic bricks and mortars of the human architecture of his own secretly designed and designated everlasting tomb.

A major problem in Khayyami studies has been the treatment of the accounts shared by others about him as facts, even when evidence and new findings prove such opinions wrong. Aside from any variations and corruptions that the manuscripts have suffered, such accounts should always be treated as opinions, their truthfulness being subject to critical examination based on his own primary works.

The series had been, since the beginning of its first book publication in 2021, like an incomplete book with chapters being written over the course of several years, the 12th book bringing it to its close. I decided to publish the series first in English, since Khayyam's life and works are today no longer just Iranian cultural phenomena. Much of the opinions held about him transcend geographical boundaries, being formed and maintained not just in Iran, but globally, even reacting back and influencing Khayyami studies being undertaken in Iran. I hope that I will find the time to translate the entire series into Persian, but at the very least, I made sure that all of Khayyam's works shared in the series included the Persian and Arabic originals, Arabic texts also being shared with their Persian translations, newly made or shared from other most reliable Iranian scholars' efforts throughout the decades.

I did not expect the series to be immediately read, given its length and gradual publication over the years. But there have been and still remain many obstacles for its reaching the hearts and minds Khayyam's legacy deserves to reach. Thoughts also need time to migrate across such obstacles, facing formidable habits of the mind and the heart formed globally across decades and artificial borders of prejudice shaped in colonial contexts over many centuries. However, Khayyam has been a good teacher, illustrating how patient one has to be for his legacy to be rediscovered. Khayyam believed that body and physical existents are essentially divisible and therefore time-bound and transient, but intellect and soul, that is self-reflective knowledge, are essentially spirit, indivisible, lasting, and ultimately reunifying. Despite all the obstacles it has faced over centuries, his spiritual legacy has demonstrably endured.

There is no reason to dismiss the idea that the movement from doubt to hope and to joy characterizing the logic of the spiritual Wine of his Robaiyat can be also a telling of the three stages of Khayyam's life and his spiritual journey. In the introduction to his treatise in algebra, we find Khayyam reflecting back on a period of his life that was personally troubling and despairing for him, while his expressed respect for Abu Taher shows a new found hope in his life's work. Clearly, Khayyam may have as well experienced periods of satisfaction or despair during his 18-year stay in Isfahan, toward the end of the period finding himself again on the troubled public grounds of not knowing where to the post-Malekshah Iran was heading.

However, his *Nowrooznameh* and treatise on the universals of existence, and the secretive brushes he was now painting on his Robaiyat' canvas in the last third of his life, tell of a self-confident Khayyam whose happy Jupiter was now in his view observing his Sun-Mercury Samimi (Cazimi), having learned to remain joyful despite new troubling times, being content with what he had, having festive meetings such as that in Balkh with Esfezari and Nezami Arouzi, or in his garden, and his remaining friends. He was still mindfully turning simple moments of a child Beyhaqi's visit to teaching moments, testing him about his knowledge of circle arc types (perhaps geometrically representing lifetimes, of his own long one soon to close, or the child's short one just being drawn by him and his accompanying father) and also about a long epic Arabic poem from centuries past (Abu Tammam's *al-Ḥamāsah*), perhaps being secretly curious to learn whether his own epic autobiographical Robaiyat in Persian would also be remembered properly centuries later by another child.

Now, for the first time since his own time, we can read all of Khayyam's extant original works in a series and its last volume, separately published from this book, accompanied by their English (and, where needed, updated or new Persian) translations, a legacy culminating in his secretive 1000 Robaiyat autobiography, organized logically according to his own three-step method of inquiry about human happiness, all shared as poetic bricks and mortars of the human architecture of his own secretly designed and designated everlasting tomb. It was for the purpose of making his Robaiyat accessible to readers as a stand-alone book that I decided to share in this book his spiritual Wine, one that is organized as a tent whose numerical geometry is proportional to that of the Triplicities in his true birth date chart.

The Robaiyat of Omar Khayyam:
Part 1 of 3: Songs of Doubt
Addressing the Question "Does
Happiness Exist?"

رباعیات عمر خیام: بخش اول از سه بخش: آوازهای تردید
در پاسخ به سؤال «آیا سعادت وجود دارد؟»

I. Secret Book of Life (راز دفتر عمر)

1. When It Unveils (چون پرده بر افتد)

You and I don't know what God eternally veils.
You and I can't unveil yet what *this* book enveils.
In its veiled tent will talk in secret, I and you.
You and I won't remain by the time it unveils.

اسرار ازل را نه تو دانی و نه من
وین حرف معمّا نه تو خوانی و نه من
هست از پس پرده گفتگوی من و تو
چون پرده بر افتد نه تو مانی و نه من

2. Can't Be Told (نتوان گفتن)

The world secrets, as portrayed in *this* book of ours,
Can't be told since talk bodes ill in these times of ours.
Since there is no one trustworthy now in this world,
Cannot be disclosed all that's on these minds of ours.

اسرار جهان چنانکه در دفتر ماست
گفتن نتوان که آن وبال سر ماست
چون نیست در این مردم دنیا اهلی
نتوان گفتن هر آنچه در خاطر ماست

3. No Eye, Tongue, or Ear (بی چشم و زبان و گوش)

In the inner world of soul, one must stay Awake.
But in world affairs, one must silently partake.
So long as his eyes, ears, or tongue remain, he must
Live these times as if he saw not, heard not, nor spake.

در عالم جان بهوش می باید بود
در کار جهان خموش می باید بود
تا چشم و زبان و گوش بر جا باشند
بی چشم و زبان و گوش می باید بود

4. Sunset in Clay (غروب در گل)

I can't let the wisdom's Sun be set in grave's clay,
But the secrets of my time I can't now relay.
Beneath my thought's ocean rhymes, wisdom nursed a Pearl
That, I'm afraid, I cannot pierce yet for display.

خورشید به گل نهفت می نتوانم
و اسرار زمانه گفت می نتوانم
از بحر تفکرم برآورد خرد
دری که ز بیم سفت می نتوانم

5. Falcon from the Secret World (باز از عالم راز)

Like a falcon from the world of secrets I flew,
Raising from their depths to heights everything I knew.
But I encountered none here worth my secret's trust.
So, from the same door I had come in, I withdrew.

بازی بودم پریده از عالم راز
تا بو که پرم دمی ز شیبی به فراز
اینجا چو نیافتم کسی محرم راز
زان در که در آمدم برون رفتم باز

6. Indescribable State (حال شرح ناپذیر)

I can't just 'tell' the secret, be folks bad or good.
I would expand beyond brief verses, if I could.
I speak from a state of heart that I can't describe.
My secret can't be 'retold' to be understood.

با هر بد و نیک راز نتوانم گفت
کوته سخنم دراز نتوانم گفت
حالی دارم که شرح نتوانم داد
رازی دارم که باز نتوانم گفت

7. Telling Like Nightingales (بیان چو بلبلان)

From all the untrusted *this* secret one must hide,
And like nightingales *its* secrets to folks confide.
See what God's creature bird does to our human souls.
From humans the same way of telling must be eyed.

راز از همه ناکسان نهان باید داشت
و اسرار چو بلبلان بیان باید داشت
بنگر که به جان مردمان وی چه کند
چشم از همه مردمان همان باید داشت

8. What's This Symbolic Portrait? (چیست این نقش مجاز؟)

You asked what *this* symbolic portrait tries to say.
Its truth will take a long time for me to convey.
Let's just say a Pearl emerged from a shell at sea,
Then rolled down to the bottom of that sea to stay.

می پرسیدی که چیست این نقش مجاز
گر بر گویم حقیقتش هست دراز
نقشی است پدید آمده از دریائی
و آنگاه شده به قعر آن دریا باز

9. Perfected Pearl (درّ تمام)

Does it not seem to be quite offhandedly clear
Why meaning and form joined the way you find it *here*?
When the Pearl is perfected and its shell opens,
On the corner of the King's crown it will appear.

معلوم نمی شود چنین از سر دست
کاین صورت و معنی ز چه در هم پیوست
گوهر چو تمام شد صدف نیز شکست
در طرف کله گوشهٔ سلطان بنشست

10. More Hidden than the Phoenix (نهفته تر ز عنقا)

Any secret that is in a sage's heart sealed
Must be, even more than Simorgh, from all concealed,
Since it's from shell-hiddenness that becomes a Pearl
That drop where the ocean heart's secret is congealed.

هر راز که اندر دل دانا باشد
باید که نهفته تر ز عنقا باشد
کاندر صدف از نهفتگی گردد درّ
آن قطره که راز دل دریا باشد

11. Diving Technique (هنر غواصی)

Dive into the ocean, if it's the Pearl you seek.
Needed for the diving is a fourfold technique:
Rope held in your Lover's hand, let life go as is,
In breathless silence, with a head-walking physique.

غوّاصی کن گرت گهر می باید
غوّاصی را چار هنر می باید
سر رشته بدست یار و جان بر کف دست
دم نازدن و قدم ز سر می باید

12. Book of Love (دفتر عشق)

The topic of *this* book's world of meanings is Love.
These life songs' theme, from their youth beginnings, is Love.
O you who don't know about the world of Love, still!
Just know that the essence of life's yearnings is Love.

سر دفتر عالم معانی عشق است
سر بیت قصیدهٔ جوانی عشق است
ای آنکه خبر نداری از عالم عشق
این نکته بدان که زندگانی عشق است

13. Hundred-Toothed Comb (شانهٔ صد شاخ)

No one reached a Rosy Cheeked in this lasting world,
Who was not hurt by the thorns his times unfurled.
See the comb, how it endures a hundred-toothed split
Before it can groom a Beauty's Long Hair uncurled.

در دهر کسی به گلعذاری نرسید
تا بر دلش از زمانه خاری نرسید
در شانه نگر که تا به صد شاخ نشد
دستش به سر زلف نگاری نرسید

14. Droplet's Efforts (رنج قطره)

It's through conscious self-efforts that humans go free,
As the droplet goes pearl in its shell in the sea.
Although the pearl's wealth is lost, the secret's survives;
To be filled with it, the Cup must first go empty.

از رنج کشیدن آدمی حرّ گردد
قطره چو کشد حبس صدف درّ گردد
گر مال نماند سر بماند به جای
پیمانه چو شد تهی دگر پر گردد

15. Knowing-Not to Not-Knowing (از بیخبری تا بیخبری)

If you think you know, then, go and seek unknowing,
To Drink *this* Wine that's from the lasting Drunks flowing.
Don't you know that unknowing does not come easy?
Not all know-nots can reach the state of not knowing.

رو بیخبری گزین اگر باخبری
تا از کف مستان ازل باده خوری
تو بیخبری بیخبری کار تو نیست
هر بیخبری را نرسد بیخبری

16. Guideless Love (عشق بی سالاری)

There are no heads in which some secrets do not hide.
The heart does not care how 'much and little' divide.
Every crowd claims to be guiding you on its path;
But on the path of Love there cannot be a guide.

در هیچ سری نیست که اسراری نیست
دل را خبر از اندک و بسیاری نیست
هر طایفه ای روند راهی در پیش
الّا ره عشق را که سالاری نیست

17. Head to Heart (قال به حال)

Secrets of truth can't be revealed just through questions,
Nor by ridding self of wealth, or such pretensions.
You must labor to exhaustion for fifty years
To find from words a path to heartfelt dimensions.

اسرار حقیقت نشود حل به سؤال
نه نیز به در باختن نعمت و مال
تا جان نکنی خون نخوری پنجه سال
از قال تو را ره ننمایند به حال

18. Juiceless Love (عشق بی آب)

A love that's just symbolic, does not have the juice;
Like a dying fire, to ash its flames reduce.
Lovers seek love for months and for years, night and day,
Not letting sleep's and eating's lack be an excuse.

عشقی که مجازی بود آبش نبود
چون آتش نیم مرده تابش نبود
عاشق باید که به سال و ماه و شب و روز
آرام و قرار و خورد و خوابش نبود

19. Freethinking Way (راه قلندری)

Without a freethinking seekers' line, it won't work!
Without splashing face with heart's tears-brine, it won't work!
Why be deluded? Like those who're gut-wrenched lovers,
Without freeing self from selfish 'mine' it won't work!

تا راه قلندری نپویی نشود
رخساره بخون دل نشویی نشود
سودا چه پزی که تا چو دلسوختگان
آزاد به ترک خود نگویی نشود

20. My Jamsheed Cup (جام جم من)

I searched around the world looking for Jamsheed's bowl.
Restless days and sleepless nights I spent for the goal.
Then I heard its secret from the teacher and learned
That Jamsheed's world-reflecting bowl was my own soul!

در جستن جام جم جهان پیمودم
روزی ننشستم و شبی نغنودم
ز استاد چو راز جام جم بشنودم
آن جام جهان نمای جم من بودم

21. Dust to Dust (خاك به خاك)

For *this* Wine that selflessly Cheers the heart, I yearned.
From my life's low grounds, the heights of the spheres I earned.
From the blot of the body, I was cleared at last.
How to come from dust but go with *this* Dust, I learned.

ما کز می بیخودی طربناک شدیم
وز پایهٔ دون بر سر افلاک شدیم
آخر هم از آلایش تن پاک شدیم
از خاک بر آمدیم و با خاک شدیم

22. That Day (آن روز)

When they will wonder a thousand times on that day
Whether I was a foe, friend, or just a myth's play,
Had I not tried to compose *these* verses, they would
Still be making decanters or cups from my clay.

روزیکه هزار خویش و بیگانه کنند
وز هستی من از یاد به افسانه کنند
آیا که من از این سخن نیارم گفتن
تا از گل من سبو و پیمانه کنند

23. Wine on the Greens Paradise (بهشت می بر سبزه)

Suppose you don't solve *this* book's riddle in your tries,
And still not grasp *this* point, a sly way of the wise.
On the greens with *this* Wine build *this* paradise *now*
Since you may or not reach *that* supposed paradise.

گیرم که به سرّ این معمّا نرسی
در نکتهٔ زیرکان دانا نرسی
از سبزه و می خیز بهشتی بر ساز
کانجا که بهشت است رسی یا نرسی

24. 'Two-Worlds' Secret (سرّ دو جهان)

Pours from *this* Drunkards' Cup the secret of 'two worlds,'
As the full Moon's cup the Sun's lasting light upholds.
This point that is hidden in *this* heart of the world,
If only you knew how, in *this* Wine Glass unfolds.

سرّ دو جهان از قدح مستانست
خورشید ازل جام مه تابانست
این نکته که در قلب جهان پنهانست
در شیشه می اگر بدانی آنست

25. Fire in Harp-Tuned Water (آتش در آب چنگ)

Wake up! Let heart's flame boil *this* harp-tuned flowing song,
So that Cup's Revelation later comes along.
Steal from life a breath *now* since this dark blue wheel has
Stolen from the world, of people like you, a throng.

خیز آتش دل در آب چنگ افکن زود
کان جام ظهور دیرتر خواهد بود
بربای دمی ز عمر کین چرخ کبود
بسیار چو تو ز دست گیتی برربود

26. Erased from the Book of Life (پاک شدن از دفتر عمر)

From one's book of life one will be surely erased
And in the clutches of the angel of death placed.
O Wine-Tender, O Beauty, don't remain idle;
Bring *this* Wine before I am in the dust defaced.

از دفتر عمر پاک می باید شد
در چنگ اجل هلاک می باید شد
ای ساقی خوش لقا تو فارغ منشین
شرابی در ده که خاک می باید شد

27. Nightingale Singing (غلغل بلبل)

Tender! Serve me *this* Wine! Let's start our chirping toil!
Let's ourselves with *these* thousand nightingale tweets spoil!
Had the Drinking of Wine been allowed without songs,
This Wine would not have come in *this* Glass to its boil.

می بر کف من نه و بر آور غلغل
با نالهٔ عندلیب و صوت بلبل
بی نغمه اگر روا بدی می خوردن
می از سر شیشه مینکردی قلقل

28. Nightingale and Dove (بلبل و قمری)

Now is the time for the rose to unveil its face,
For the nightingale to zestfully chirp its case,
For the dove on the cypress, like prayer-criers,
To sing again every morning *this* song with grace.

وقتست که گل پرده ز رخ برگیرد
بلبل ز طرب شور و شعف درگیرد
بر سرو سهی بسان مقری قمری
هر صبحدم این ترانه از سر گیرد

29. Wine Alchemy (کیمیای می)

Drink *this* Wine to free your heart from the 'more or less,'
And fuse mind's seventy-two-sect dividedness.
Don't abstain from *this* alchemy, each of whose Sips
Heals a thousand causes of your unhappiness.

می خور که ز دل کثرت و قلّت ببرد
و اندیشهٔ هفتاد و دو ملّت ببرد
پرهیز مکن ز کیمیایی که از او
یک جرعه خوری هزار علّت ببرد

30. Return! Return! (باز آ باز آ)

Return! Return! O whatever you are! Return!
Rogue! Idolator! Pagan from afar! Return!
This book is not a door to despair; if you break
Your vows a hundred times, there is no bar! Return!

باز آ باز آ هر آنچه هستی باز آ
گر کافر و رند و بت پرستی باز آ
این درگه ما درگه نومیدی نیست
صد بار تو گر توبه شکستی باز آ

II. Alas! (افسوس)

31. Youth Letter (نامهٔ جوانی)

Alas! My youth's letter has long been sent away,
And that fresh spring of life is now a winter's day.
The singing bird of joy that's called 'the prime,' alas,
Came and left with the scroll. When? I can't even say!

افسوس که نامهٔ جوانی طی شد
وآن تازه بهار زندگانی دی شد
آن مرغ طرب که نام او بود شباب
افسوس ندانم که کی آمد کی شد

32. Slipped from Hand (ز کف بیرون)

Alas! My prime's wealth of life slipped soon from my hand,
While so many guts bled at the angel's command,
And no one came from that world, from whom I could ask,
"What happened to the passengers who left this land?"

افسوس که سرمایه ز کف بیرون شد
وز دست اجل بسی جگرها خون شد
کس نامد از آن جهان که پرسم از وی
کاحوال مسافران دنیا چون شد

33. Sky's Sickle and Mill (داس و آسیای سپهر)

Alas! How uselessly did our lives wither by,
Downed and crushed by the sickle and mill of the sky!
O what pains and regrets to bear, then, in a blink,
Not being self-fulfilled, become nothing to die!

افسوس که بی فایده فرسوده شدیم
وز داس سپهر سرنگون سوده شدیم
دردا و ندامتا که تا چشم زدیم
نابوده به کام خویش نابوده شدیم

34. Empty Mesh (غربیل خالی)

The days ended but not a single goal was met.
Life's up with not a single wish fulfilled, as yet.
At pains, with such a crafty mesh, I sieved the world;
Yet not a single grain did the sieving beget.

شد روز فرود و یک غرض بر نامد
شد عمر برون و آرزو در نامد
دردا که به غربیل حیل عالم را
سرسر کردیم و هیچ بر سر نامد

35. Remained Untold (ناگفته ماند)

All that remains from me in these times is chaos,
While of any hundreds of my Pearls, pierced none was.
Alas! How a hundred thousand precise meanings
Remained untold due to the folks' folly ethos!

رفتیم و ز ما زمانه آشفته ماند
بی آنکه ز صد گهر یکی سفته ماند
افسوس که صد هزار معنی دقیق
از بیخردی خلق ناگفته ماند

36. Nothing, Nothing (هیچ هیچ)

See all that I took away from the world: Nothing!
And what of life in my hands did unfold? Nothing!
A joyful night's candle, I'm, when melted, nothing!
Broken down, I'm a Jamsheed's Cup to hold nothing!

بنگر ز جهان چه طرف بر بستم هیچ
وز حاصل عمر چیست در دستم هیچ
شمع طربم ولی چو بنشستم هیچ
من جام جمم ولی چو بشکستم هیچ

37. Sewed Tents of Wisdom (خیمه های حکمت می دوخت)

The Khayyam who sewed his tents of wisdom, many,   خیام که خیمه های حکمت می دوخت
Fell in grief's pyre, burned, without a warning, any.   در بوتهٔ غم فتاد و ناگاه بسوخت
The angel of death's scissors cut short his life's line;   مقراض اجل طناب عمرش ببرید
The dealer of luck sold his for not a penny!   دلّال قضا به رایگانش بفروخت

38. Don't Go! (نرو)

My back is bending more from the weight of my time.   بر پشت من از زمانه تو می آید
Works from me are no longer tending to be prime.   وز من همه کار نانکو می آید
My soul resolved it was time to go. I said, "Don't!"   جان عزم رحیل کرد و گفتم مرو
He replied, "Well, what's my choice? See how homewrecked I'm!"   گفتا چه کنم خانه فرو می آید

39. Arrow to Bow (تیر به کمان)

Gone are my life's prime days with their horses and staff.   ایّام شباب رفت و خیل و حشمش
The feasts' aftertastes remain as a bitter laugh.   تلخست مرا عیش ولی می چشمش
The arrow that was my tall height is now a bow.   این قامت همچو تیر من گشته کمان
The string is now a staff, pulling on my behalf.   زه کرده ام از عصا و خوش می کشمش

40. Nearing Destruction (رو به خرابی)

My old head and limbs are all losing their functions,   پیری سر و برگ ناصوابی دارد
And my red face displays now pale blue complexions.   گلنار رخم رنگ آبی دارد
My body's roof, doors, and four elemental walls,   بام و در و چار رکن دیوار وجود
Are all breaking down and nearing their destructions.   ویران شده و رو به خرابی دارد

41. Flimsy Tent (خیمهٔ سست)

If your bones have been hoisted as some life-grown beams,   گر شاخ بقا ز بیخ تخت رستست
And life has sewn you a skin, stitched along the seams,   ور بر تن تو عمر لباسی چستست
On such flimsy four-nailed tent offering a shade   در خیمهٔ تن که سایبانی ست ترا
Beware not to lean, for it'd be unwise, it seems.   هان تکیه مکن که چارمیخش سست است

42. Wheel's Benefit? (سود گردون؟)

From bringing me here, the sphere benefited not!   ز آوردن من نبود گردون را سود
From taking me, its majesty grew not a lot!   وز بردن من جاه و جلالش نفزود
And these, my two ears, never heard from anyone   وز هیچ کسی نیز دو گوشم نشنود
This bringing and then taking of me were for what!   کاوردن و بردن من از بهر چه بود

43. Was for What? (چه بود مقصود؟)

In sheer anxiety, I was brought to this world.   آورد به اضطرابم اول به وجود
Nothing was added but wonder about this world.   جز حیرتم از حیات چیزی نفزود
I leave this world reluctantly, still not knowing   رفتیم به اکراه و ندانیم چه بود
Why I came and stayed here and why I leave this world?   زین آمدن و بودن و رفتن مقصود

44. Fire to Water, Wind to Dust (آتش به آب، باد به خاك)

Sinless we came from the void, then became sinful.   پاك از عدم آمدیم و ناپاك شدیم
Full of sadness we are now, though we were joyful.   شادان به در آمدیم و غمناك شدیم
Waters of tears we shed over a heart on fire,   بودیم ز آب دیده در آتش دل
Then became dust from a lifetime's wind, gone wasteful.   دادیم به باد عمر و در خاك شدیم

45. None Inherit (به كس نماند)

All these people who are young and those who are old,   آنها كه كهن شدند و اینها كه نو اند
All of whom run after the ambitions they hold,   هر یك به به مراد خویش یك یك بدوند
All of them came and will go, pass away and leave,   این كهنه جهان به كس نماند باقی
Not even one inheriting this ancient world.   رفتند و رویم و دیگر آیند و روند

46. How Is He Doing? (احوالپرسی او)

The leek and coriander farmer did not last.   كارندهٔ گندنا و گشنیز نماند
The chamber and its hallway builder did not last.   سازندهٔ آستان و دهلیز نماند
About anyone I asked, "So, how's he doing?"   از حال دل هر كه خبر پرسیدم
They said, "May *you* live long! He *too*, sir, did not last!"   گفتند تو را بقا كه او نیز نماند

47. Childhood Teacher (به كودكی به استاد)

When young I attended a teacher in the past,   یك چند به كودكی به استاد شدیم
Then gladly I too became a teacher at last.   یك چند ز استادی خود شاد شدیم
But now hear the last word on what happened to us: پایان سخن شنو كه ما را چه رسید
Like water we came and then like a breeze we passed.   چون آب بر آمدیم و چون باد شدیم

48. So What? (آخر چه؟)

Suppose you achieved all your goals of life, so what?   دنیا به مراد رانده گیر آخر چه
Suppose has been read all *this* book of life, so what?   وین نامهٔ عمر خوانده گیر آخر چه
Suppose a hundred years of your life were fulfilled.   گیرم كه به كام دل بماندی صد سال
Suppose passed a hundred more years of life, so what?   صد سال دگر بمانده گیر آخر چه

49. Heart Unfulfilled (دل ناكام)

Neither did the hand of my thirst reach any bowl,   هم دست من تشنه به جامی نرسید
Nor did my longing's foot find rest in any role.   هم پای تمنا به مقامی نرسید
And the heart that had remained so much unfulfilled   وآن دل كه بمانده بود در ناكامی
Did not reach any fulfillment of any goal.   هم عاقبت الامر به كامی نرسید

50. Which Plot? (چه جای؟)

They planted my life's seed from the water of naught.   از آب عدم تخم مرا كاشته اند
They raised my spirit from the fire of grief's lot.   از آتش غم روح من افراشته اند
I'm moving around the world like wind, bewildered.   سرگشته چو باد می روم گرد جهان
Who knows where they will dig, searching for my grave's plot?   تا خاك من از چه جای برداشته اند

51. Night Reached (به شب رسیده)

My heart not having reached out to join any feast,
My lips not having reached wine cups in joy at least,
Alas, days reached nights with my heart still not fulfilled,
The days of my life reaching the night I'm deceased.

52. World of Rest? (عالم آسایش؟)

How can I talk to a confidant, when there's none?
How can I grieve with an intimate, when there's none?
They tell me, "Why don't you go and rest for a while?"
How can I have some rest in this world, when there's none?

53. If I Had a Say (گر به من بدی)

If I had a say in life, I wouldn't have come here!
Nor would I leave the world now, if I could stay here!
In this ruined house, would it not have been the best
Not to have come, to be leaving, having lived here?

54. Sphere's Music (آواز فلک)

The sphere did not tune my work, for even a day.
For me, not a single music did the sphere play.
There was not a day that I inhaled happiness
Without exhaling a hundred sorrows to pay.

55. 'Death-Spared' Illusion (وهم از مرگ رستگی)

I'm leaving since remaining in this unjust world
Has led to nothing but air that no hand can mold.
But he should be happy for my passing away
Who can himself escape from the death angel's hold.

56. Latecoming Soon-Departed (دیرآمدگان زودرفته)

Since the tasks of our lives won't end as we desire,
How will the fulfillments of our life goals transpire?
We always sit and regretfully ask ourselves,
"Why did we come to life late, then so soon expire?"

57. A Dream Seen (خوابی دیده)

If resting with ease was your life's theme, all your life,
Or tasting this world's joys your life's scheme, all your life,
You will find out at the end, when your time arrives,
That they had been like a tranced life's dream, all your life.

58. Soul's Job? (کار جان؟)

O heart! Your share in all of this is the bleeding,
Yet life is what your beating pulses are feeding.
But why did *you* enter this, my body, O soul,
If you were, after all, to exit proceeding?

ای دل چو نصیب تو همه خون شدن است
احوال تو هر لحظه دگرگون شدن است
ای جان تو درین تن به چه کار آمده ای
چون عاقبت کار تو بیرون شدن است

59. Who Told You? (که گفتت؟)

Who told you, O heart, to bleed for this world in grief,
Or ride this flirtatious sphere for a time so brief?
You know what to do when there's nothing permanent:
Suppose you'd not come and go where's lasting relief.

ای دل ز غم جهان که گفتت خون شو
یا ساکن عشوه خانهٔ گردون شو
دانی چه کنی چو نیست سامان مقام
انگار درون نیامدی بیرون شو

60. Needless to Needless (بی نیازی به بی نیازی)

O one who had no sleep and no subsistence needs,
And now all your four elements needfulness breeds!
Each element will take back what it gave to you,
So that your existence to nothingness recedes.

آنی که نبودت به خور و خواب نیاز
کردند نیازمندت این چار انباز
هر یک به تو آنچه داد بستاند باز
تا باز چنان شوی که بودی زآغاز

61. They Thought Too (آنها نیز پنداشته اند)

Those who looked for fulfillment, as their hearts desired,
Left unfulfilled, without anything they'd acquired.
Do you think you'll remain forever in this world?
They thought the same also before they too expired.

آنها که به کام دل جهان داشته اند
ناکام جهان به جای بگذاشته اند
تو پنداری که جاودان خواهی ماند
پیش از تو هم ایشان چو تو پنداشته اند

62. Known Way (راه مشهور)

All my friends are gone now, by that way people know.
Some were burned in the pyres, some buried below.
I'm all that's left in this wasteland of vanity,
Like a dying mule, with heavy loads, far to go!

یاران همه رفتند به راه مشهور
که سوخته حرمند و گه ساخته گور
ما مانده درین بادیهٔ پر ز غرور
چون لاشهٔ خر بار گران منزل دور

63. Up and Down (فراز و نشیب)

I was led day and night to gallop to and fro.
I was taught to stand up and then go down below,
With no fruits to bear but lots of life's suffering,
Nothing ahead of me, yet a long way to go.

مائیم فتاده روز و شب در تک و تاز
برخیزه نهاده روی در شیب و فراز
نه هیچ ره آورده به جز رنج دگر
نه هیچ پس افکنده به جز راه دراز

64. Life Wasted Away (عمر بیهوده)

Alas! How it all passed, a life wasted away,
Between my sinful bites and sordid breaths in sway!
The commandments, not followed, led to my disgrace.
About the followed prohibitions, 'woe' I say!

افسوس که عمر رفت بر بیهوده
هم لقمه حرام و هم نفس آلوده
ناکردن فرموده سیه رویم کرد
فریاد ز کرده های نافرموده

65. Endless Lore (افسانه بی پایان)

O what pains my heart endured, yet no cure was found!
My life reached its end, and yet no Soulmate was found!
Life came to its end without any knowledge gained.
My lore of God's Love began, but no end was found!

66. Gut's Wine (می جگر)

This so wretchedly pained and maddened heart of mine
Did not Wake up to meet that Soulful Love of mine.
The day they were serving His Wine of Loving joy,
They must have tapped it from this bleeding gut of mine.

67. Wine-Server's Deceit (حیلۀ ساقی)

Until when should I endure this deceitful life
And drink what its saqi serves that's with pain so rife?
It's due to such deceitful servings that I've wished
To pour on earth what's left of my life, full of strife.

68. Walking A Dead-End Way (طمع محال پیمودن)

If the truth of it is that we'll go, why then stay?
Why greed after walking along a dead-end way?
Since, for expediency's sake, they won't let us in,
Why not be free of this "go or stay," I would say?

69. Being's Disgrace (ننگ وجود)

Today, I'm caught in the tight jailhouse of being,
Keener for the death's smell than the stains of being.
A hundred prostrations I'd do there to thank for
Freeing my name from all this disgrace of being.

70. Jail Break? (شکستن قفس؟)

I become so depressed in this jail, now and then,
So ashamed of the bricks and mortars of its den,
That I tell myself I should break out of the jail.
But my faith unsaddles my foot, time and again.

71. No Soulmate But This (نه همدمی جز این)

Finding friends for this talk has been of no avail.
My trusted soulmate has become *these* lines that wail.
Since my wet eyes cannot stay without any tears,
One way or another will finish this sad tale.

72. Trapped Birds (مرغان دام)

We are like the birds who have long been trapped as prey,   مائیم در اوفتاده چون مرغ به دام
In hard times become heartsick, yet for a while stay,   دلخستهٔ روزگار آشفته مدام
Dazed in a circular trap, with no roof or door,   سرگشته درین دایرهٔ بی در و بام
Not flown in at will, nor fulfilled flying away.   نا آمده بر مراد و نی رفته به کام

73. Solitude's Friendship (یاری عزلت)

Would it not be best that I befriend solitude,   به زان نبود که یار عزلت سازم
Ignoring what good or bad people may exude,   چشم از بد و نیک خلق پیش اندازم
Examining my own life and where it's leading,   تا آخر کار خویش معلوم کنم
Before dealing with the tales of the multitude?   آنگه به حدیث دیگران پردازم

III. Times (زمانه)

74. Humankind's Secret (راز آدم)

Where's a secret-trusted friend so I can disclose,
In a single breath, from what humankind arose?
He was born from the beginning of sorrow's clay,
One who comes, suffers living in the world, and goes.

کو محرم راز تا بگویم یك دم
کز روز نخست خود چه بودست آدم
محنت زاده سرشته ای از گل غم
یك چند جهان بگشت و برداشت قدم

75. What I See (چه می بینم)

Sleepwalkers on the Earth bred are all that I see.
Corpses under the earth spread are all that I see.
As I look around this desert of nothingness,
The unborn of the Earth dead are all that I see.

بر مفرش خاك خفتگان می بینم
در زیر زمین نهفتگان می بینم
چندان که به صحرای عدم می نگرم
ناآمدگان و رفتگان می بینم

76. Almond Cake (لوزینه)

The world is troubled in these times, so you beware!
Don't sit down, feeling safe, since its sharp sword is bare!
If it puts an almond cake in your mouth, realize
That it's poison! So, don't swallow it! Don't you dare!

هشدار که روزگار شورانگیز است
ایمن منشین که تیغ دوران تیز است
در کام تو گر زمانه لوزینه نهد
زنهار فرو مبر که زهر آمیز است

77. Agile Hands (دستان چابك)

Living based on reasoning that you try to do
May be possible but you cannot in my view.
It's because your master is the swift-handed times
Who hits your head hard and says, "Do as *I* tell *you*!"

بر موجب عقل زندگانی کردن
شاید کردن ولی نتانی کردن
استاد تو روزگار چابك دست است
چندان به سرت زند که دانی کردن

78. Sour Sand (شورستان)

Because humankind's harvest from this sour sand
Is nothing but grief before their deaths are at hand,
Happy at heart is the one who left this world soon.
Calm is he who did not even enter this land.

چون حاصل آدمی در این شورستان
جز خوردن غصّه نیست تا کندن جان
خرّم دل آنکه زین جهان زود برفت
و آسوده کسی که خود نیامد به جهان

79. Misery's Weight (بار عنا)

Hey, you, who are worn out from your misery's weight!
Why are you so uselessly grieving the world's state?
Do not seek relief from so much suffering since
It seems your sufferings those of others abate!

ای بار عنا شخص تو را فرسوده
چندین چه خوری غم جهان بیهوده
آسایش خود ز رنج بسیار مجوی
از رنج تو دیگری شود آسوده

80. Free-Riders (رایگان خوران)

The more I examine the affairs of this world,
The more I see that it's in the free riders' hold.
Glory be to God! But the more I look at things,
The more I see how my unfulfillments unfold.

81. Anonymous Living (زندگی گمنام)

When you're famous, you're treated as the town's vile man.
When withdrawn, you're seen as the obsessed of the clan.
Is it not best, then, as did Elijah or Kheżr,
To live life as anonymously as you can?

82. Perfect Yet Lacking (کامل و کم)

We are happy-natured, yet, too, mines of sorrow.
We seek justice, yet, too, in oppression wallow.
We're like Jamsheed Cups, yet become rusted mirrors.
We are high and perfect, yet, too, low and shallow.

83. Times' Plight (بلای زمانه)

O one who is worried about life, day and night,
Aren't you thinking about your last day not in sight?
Come to yourself and for a moment take a look
At how humankind is treated by our times' might!

84. Get Up, Let's Go! (برخیز و بیا)

Why should one who is wise, in this grim house below,
Maintain some hope, for God's sake, be it high or low?
As soon as he settles down to live in this world,
The angel says, pulling his hand, "Get up! Let's go!"

85. Sit and Watch (بنشین به تماشا)

Listen to me, you, O my distinguished old friend!
Don't mind this sphere that has no beginning or end.
Sit content in a corner of this world and watch
How the puppets of the wheel ascend and descend.

86. O Eye, See! (ای دیده، ببین)

O eye, see the graveyard, if you are not so blind!
See how the world is toward sedition inclined!
See all the kings, viziers, leaders, beneath the clay!
See all the Moon-likened faces, chewed in ants' grind!

87. Don't Seek the Crown (شاهی مطلب)

Are you seeking the crown? A breath will end your years!
You'll join the dusts of Jamsheed, Kayqobād, and peers!
You'll learn that the world, passing life, and existence,
Are just made of some daydreams, fancies, tricks, and smears!

88. Old Caravansary (کهنه رباط)

This old caravansary that's been called 'the world,'
Where the piebald horse of day and night has long strolled,
Has held palace feasts for a hundred Jamsheeds' bones,
Where a hundred Bahrāms found their graveyard foothold.

89. Bahrām's Game (گور بهرام)

In that palace wherein Jamsheed held high his grail,
The deer held calm, and the fox gave birth to its frail.
But Bahrām held wild ass hunting games all his life.
See how he died, held in his games' quicksanded trail?

90. Animal's Footprint (جاپای حیوان)

The sand that lies underneath an animal's feet
Was a lover's hand or face, so graceful and sweet!
Every brick that's in any courtyard's battlement
Was a king's head, or a finger of his elite.

91. Bokhari's Dust (خاک بخاری)

This road's dust is rising from that Bokhari Sage
Who was honored as the noblest of his age.
Everywhere you step on, know that it's surely been
The hand of a kindly man in his carriage.

92. Face's Dust (گرد رخ)

Every particle that's been lying on the ground,
A Sun-faced king or a Venus-beauty's ring crowned.
Clean the dust gently from your dear beloved's face,
Since it too was long ago a dear's face, renowned!

93. Veiled Lip (لب مستور)

This water jug that quenches a soldier in need,
Was a king's eye, or his vizier's heart when in lead.
The wine cup on a drunkard's palm was another's
Face, or the lips of his lover, veiled for her creed.

94. Bird's "Alas!" (افسوس مرغ)

I once saw an owl on the battlement of Ṭoos,
Sitting and chatting with the skull of Kaykāvoos,
Shaking its head, saying, "O king, alas, alas,
Where are your battle drums and your bells after truce?"

مرغی دیدم نشسته بر بارهٔ طوس
در پیش نهاده کلّهٔ کیکاووس
با کله همی گفت که افسوس افسوس
کو بانگ جرسها و کجا نالهٔ کوس

95. Who, Who? (کو؟ کو؟)

In that palace whose roof as high as the sky grew,
And to its gate headed many kings, quite a few,
Asking for their whereabouts, I saw on its fort
A cuckoo bird often reply, "Who, who? Who, who?"

آن قصر که بر چرخ همی زد پهلو
بر درگه او شهان نهادندی رو
دیدیم که بر کنگره اش فاخته ای
بنشسته همی گفت که کوکو کوکو

96. Sift Gently! (نرمک می بیز)

Wake up earlier at dawn, O dear wise old friend,
And to that child sifting the dust watchfully tend.
Advise him, "O boy, sift more gently! Can't you see
That now Kayqobād's brain and Parveez's eye blend?"

ای پیر خردمند پگه تر برخیز
و آن کودک خاک بیز را بنگر تیز
پندش ده و گو که نرم نرمک می بیز
مغز سر کیقباد و چشم پرویز

IV. Spheres (افلاك)

97. Counts for Nothing (هیچ است)

O heedless! This solid form here counts for nothing!
And this circle and tented plane counts for nothing!
Beware! In this circle of risings and declines
We're tied to one breath, and that too counts for nothing!

ای بیخبر این شکل مجسّم هیچ است
وین دایره و سطح مخیّم هیچ است
دریاب که در دایرهٔ کون و فساد
وابستهٔ یک دمیم و آن هم هیچ است

98. Nothingness Horizons (آفاق هیچ)

In the world that you've seen, what you saw is no more.
Whatever you said or heard also is no more.
Is no more, what you ran for across horizons.
Arriving home, also, what you brought is no more.

دنیا دیدی و هر چه دیدی هیچ است
وآن نیز که گفتی و شنیدی هیچ است
سرتاسر آفاق دویدی هیچ است
وآن نیز که در خانه خزیدی هیچ است

99. Let the Myth Go (بگذر از این خیال)

Outside this dome, there is no vestibule or hall.
There's no distinction but what you and I recall.
Let go of what you have fancied to be something
Since, laughably, it's no longer a thing at all!

زین سقف برون رواق و دهلیزی نیست
جز با من و با تو هیچ تمییزی نیست
هر چیز که وهم کرده ای کآن چیزی است
خوش بگذر از این خیال کآن چیزی نیست

100. Real Dolls (لعبتکان حقیقی)

The sphere is a doll-player and we, puppet dolls,
Real, not just symbolic, dolls that the sphere enthralls.
For a while we were played with on the being's stage,
Then returned, one by one, to a chest full of nulls.

ما لعبتکانیم و فلک لعبت باز
از روی حقیقتی نه از روی مجاز
بازیچه همی کنیم بر نطع وجود
افتیم به صندوق عدم یک یک باز

101. Tricks Box (حقّهٔ شعبده)

From the Earth's box of tricks I popped up, then vanished!
From the time's stand a sip I drank up, then vanished!
I sprang from the chest of the sphere magically!
On being's stage a doll-dance I stirred up, then vanished!

از حقّهٔ خاک سر برآوردم و رفت
وز جام زمانه جرعه ای خوردم و رفت
چون شعبده آمدم ز صندوق فلک
بر نطع وجود رقصکی کردم و رفت

102. World Without Us (جهان بی ما)

In a short while we won't be, but the world will be.
Our names and signs of today you'll no longer see.
Before this, we were not here; the world didn't care.
And the world will be the same without you and me.

ای بس که نباشیم و جهان خواهد بود
نی نام ز ما و نی نشان خواهد بود
زین پیش نبودیم و نبد هیچ خلل
زین پس چو نباشیم همان خواهد بود

103. Sphere's Game (بازی فلک)

Although my sorrows and toils have for long endured
And your joyfulness seems to be for long assured,
Lean on neither because the sphere's trickery plays
A thousand games in which you've been for long allured.

گر چه غم و رنج من درازی دارد
عیش و طرب تو سرفرازی دارد
بر هر دو مکن تکیه که دوران فلک
در پرده هزار گونه بازی دارد

104. Whose Spheres? (فلک کهٔ؟)

Were the spheres to the bringing of justice assigned,
Were the spheres entirely for goodness aligned,
Were the spheres whirling around for fairness's sake,
Why would the seekers of science suffer in mind?

گر کار فلک به عدل سنجیده بدی
احوال فلک جمله پسندیده بدی
ور عدل بدی به کارها در گردون
کی خاطر اهل فضل رنجیده بدی

105. Lasting Regret (دهر حسرت)

In this lasting time, when for a while we remained,
Nothing except affliction and sadness we gained.
Alas! Not one problem of our lives was resolved.
We left while our hearts a thousand regrets retained.

زین دهر که بود مدتی منزل ما
نامد بجز از بلا و غم حاصل ما
افسوس که حل نگشت یک مشکل ما
رفتیم و هزار حسرت اندر دل ما

106. Where's the Weft? (پودی کو؟)

We are coming and going, but the gain is where?
If life's being is the warp, then the weft is where?
In this whirling kiln so many innocent lives
Burn away into ashes, but the smoke is where?

از آمدن و رفتن ما سودی کو
وز تار وجود عمر ما پودی کو
در چنبر چرخ جان چندین پاکان
می سوزد و خاک می شود دودی کو

107. Lips and Hairs (لبها و زلفها)

He who established the Earth, the wheel, and the spheres,
Seared many sad hearts for the losses of their dears.
So many ruby lips and dark musk-scented hairs,
He buried in coffins below their loved ones' tears.

آن کس که زمین و چرخ و افلاک نهاد
بس داغ که او بر دل غمناک نهاد
بسیار لب چو لعل و زلفین چو مشک
در طبل زمین و حقهٔ خاک نهاد

108. Not Eaten You? (نخورده است تو را؟)

The whirling of the heaven's wheel, we mastered not.
From eating humans, the Earth filled up not a lot.
Are you boasting now that you've not been eaten yet?
Your turn will sooner or later come, hurry not!

بر چرخ فلک هیچ کسی چیر نشد
وز خوردن آدمی زمین سیر نشد
مغرور به آنی که نخورده ست تو را
تعجیل مکن هم بخورد دیر نشد

109. Cat's Parenting (بچه داری گربه)

This world is like an old white-haired, is it not true?
I don't find it to be reliable, do you?
It's just like a cat treating her kittens as such:
Bear them, eat them, lick the mouth, and then start anew!

دنیا به مثل چو کهنه زالیست درست
از پیر کهن چرا وفا باید جست
مانندهٔ گربه ایست بر بچهٔ خویش
پرورد و بخورد و روی مالید و بشست

110. So Hungry Are They (بس گرسنه اند)

From all the six directions, they surround our lives,
By way of four elements and senses in fives.
So hungry are they for eating us in this world
That they roam all the twelve months, all the seven skies.

در شش جهت آنچه گرد ما گستردند
در پنج حواس و چار طبع آوردند
بس گرسنه اند و عالمی را خوردند
این هفت که در دوازده می گردند

111. Raw Overflowing (خام لبریز)

Since the reason you have come here you do not know,
Does it benefit you that you've come here below?
Why bother with enduring the flames of the times,
If from the sphere's pot, still raw, you will overflow?

چون نیستی آگاه که چون آمده ای
سودت نکند فزون که دون آمده ای
در آتش روزگار کی پخته شوی
کز دیگ فلک خام برون آمده ای

112. Blood-Run Mill (آسیاب خونریز)

This Earthly floor, whose ceiling is the whirling sphere,
Can't be described well, though perhaps this much is clear:
To make a long story short, it's like a millhouse
Whose seeds are the humankind, blood running its gear.

این فرش زمین که سقف او گردون است
شرحش نتوان داد که حالش چون است
کم کن تو حدیث آسیایی کو را
مردم همه گندمند و آبش خون است

113. Mill's Immeasurable Appetite (اشتهای بی اندازهٔ آسیاب)

This wheel, just like a millhouse's grindstone, rests not!
It does not rest from rotating, its stone wears not!
Oh, so many tiny seeds the times send its way
That they're immeasurable; its belly fills not!

این چرخ چو آسیا بر آسوده نشد
آسوده نگشت و آسیا سوده نشد
چندانکه زمانه دانه پیمود در او
او سیر نگشت و دانه پیموده نشد

114. Torch-Bearing Thief (دزد شعله دار)

Every morning at dawn when the Sun's flame rises,
One more night of our lives again finalizes.
Every dawn, some more cash of our lives is stolen,
When the Sun, oh, that torch-bearing thief, surprises!

هر روز که آفتاب بر می آید
یک شام ز عمر ما به سر می آید
هر صبح که نقد عمر ما می دزدد
دزدیست که با شعله در می آید

115. Buds too (غنچه ها هم)

How much blood was it that this reckless wheel shed?
How many roses grew from the ground, then were shred?
O boy! Don't be proud of your youth and handsome face!
Look! So many unblossomed buds are also dead!

بس خون کسان که چرخ بی باک بریخت
بس گل که بر آمد ز گل و پاک بریخت
بر حسن و جوانی ای پسر غرّه مشو
بس غنچهٔ ناشکفته بر خاک بریخت

116. Torn New Shirt (چاک نوپیراهن)

So many shirts of life did the spheres sew at night
And then soon tore them apart, not being contrite!
So many happy and sorrowful did the times
Raise from some droplets and then bury out of sight!

بس پیرهن عمر که هر شب افلاک
بر دوخته و کرده گریبانش چاک
هر روز بسی زمانه شاد و غمناک
از آب بر آورد و فرو برد به خاک

117. If They Know (گر بدانند)

The spheres increase nothing but sadness, running deep.
As they add a life, they steal many in a heap.
Those who have not yet arrived would not ever come,
If they knew the grief that from this old world we reap.

افلاک که جز غم نفزایند دگر
ننهند بجا تا نرباینـد دگر
نا آمدگان اگر بدانند که ما
از دهر چه می کشیم نایند دگر

118. Heart's Sear (داغ دل)

Magnificently cruel is this heavenly wheel!
Ends no hardships as a rule, this heavenly wheel!
Wherever it finds a heart that's been seared in grief,
Adds to the burning more fuel, this heavenly wheel!

این چرخ جفاپیشۀ عالی بنیاد
هرگز گره کار کسی را نگشاد
هر جا که دلی دید که داغی دارد
داغ دگری بر سر آن داغ نهاد

119. Your Old Art (شیوۀ دیرینۀ تو)

O wheel! It was from your spite that the Earth went wrong!
Injustices have been your old art all along!
O Earth, if they split your chest, they will surely find
That many lost human jewels to your heart belong!

ای چرخ فلک خرابی از کینۀ توست
بیدادگری پیشۀ دیرینۀ توست
ای خاک اگر سینۀ تو بشکافند
بس گوهر قیمتی که در سینۀ توست

120. Are You Blind? (کوری؟)

O whirling sphere! Your deeds are evil, through and through,
From which against the free nothing but might ensue!
At least see who is human and who inhuman!
You're dark blue, O sphere, but you're not *that* blind! Are you?

ای چرخ فلک بجز شر و شور نه ای
با مردم آزاده بجز زور نه ای
به رأی بشناس مردم از نامردم
گیرم که کبودی فلکا کور نه ای

121. Lowbred Raiser (ناکس پرور)

O wheel, you raise none but the unwise, do you not?
You make the low lives rich, you realize, do you not?
You feed no one cultivated in arts with bread,
Without pouring blood tears from their eyes, do you not?

ای چرخ بجز تربیت دون نکنی
جز ناکس را با به سال قارون نکنی
نانی نخورد ز دست تو پرهنری
تا خون دلش ز دیده بیرون نکنی

122. O Wheel, Tell the Truth! (ای چرخ، راست بگوی)

O wheel, what have I done to you? Tell me the truth!
Why do you make me so much seek after the truth?
Why do you make me beg for bread, from road to road,
Then dishonor me for drinking sips from the truth?

ای چرخ چه کرده ام تو را راست بگوی
پیوسته فکنده ای مرا در تک و پوی
نانم ندهی تا نبری کوی به کوی
آبم ندهی تا نبری آب ز روی

123. Peace Missions Rejected (ردّ صلح جویی)

O wheel, why are you always waging war with me?
You cure others but cause pains ever more with me.
So many peace missions I sent along your way,
Yet you spared not a war ploy to explore with me!

ای چرخ همیشه در نبردی با من
درمان دگر کسی و دردی با من
از صلح چه ماند کان نکردم با تو
وز جنگ چه بود کان نکردی با من

124. Time Gone Senile (دهر خرف)

Don't you now confess to your crime, O lasting time? ای دهر به ظلمهای خود معترفی
Don't you see your cruelties sometime, O lasting time? در خانقه جور و ستم معتکفی
You enrich the misers, by burdening the poor! نعمت به خسان دهی و نقمت به کسان
Have you gone mad or dumb in time, O lasting time? زین هر دو برون نیست خری یا خرفی

125. Wrong Impelling? (چرخ اشتباهی؟)

O wheel! Why are you treating the misers so well, ای چرخ چه شد خسیس را چیز دهی
Giving them all the mills, baths, and houses to dwell? گرمابه و آسیا و دهلیز دهی
The free pay ransom for their nightly bread; I ask, آزاده به نان شب گروگان بنهد
Should not the free's fortunes be what your spheres impel? باید که بر اینچنین فلک نیز دهی

126. Miser Wheel (چرخ خسیس)

O miser sphere! In your lowbred hilding breeding, ای چرخ خسیس خس دون پرور خس
Have you ever heard any heart's earnest pleading? هرگز نروی تو بر مراد دل کس
Is not turning somebodies to nobodies and چرخا فلکا تو را همین عادت بس
Nobodies to somebodies enough proceeding? ناکس تو کسی کنی و کس را ناکس

127. O Wimp-Grower! (ای مخنّث پرور)

O wheel! Have you lost your mind, or also your art? ای چرخ فلک نه عقل داری و نه هنر
Can't you look at least once at a freethinker's chart? هرگز نکنی به کار آزاده نظر
You throw all wealth and jewels at the cowards' feet! نامردان را دهی همه گنج و گهر
Well-done, O wheel! O you, chief wimp-breeder at heart! احسنت زهی چرخ مخنّث پرور

128. Salt on Wound (نمک بر زخم)

O wheel! Your oppressions will go on until when? تا کی ز جفاهای تو ای چرخ فلک
For God's sake, please slow down; you're vexing until when? از بهر خدا جور کن آهسته ترک
I burn all over from your whirling all the time, من سوخته ام همین هر لحظه تو نیز
Yet you are throwing salt on my wounds; until when? بر سوخته می پراکنی سوده نمک

129. Better Weaving Wheel (چرخ زنی به)

O whirling sphere, so ungrateful you are of me ای چرخ فلک نه نان شناسی نه نمک
That like a plain fish you disrobe me constantly! پیوسته مرا برهنه سازی چو سمک
The weaver's wheel dresses up two people quite well! از چرخ زنی دو شخص پوشیده شوند
Then, the weaving wheel is better than you, I see! پس چرخ زنی به از تو ای چرخ فلک

130. Wind to Fire, Water to Dust (باد به آتش، آب به خاک)

O wheel! Why are you bringing me so much sorrow, ای چرخ دلم همیشه غمناک کنی
Tearing up the shirt of happiness I borrow, پیراهن خرّمی من چاک کنی
Turning into fire the wind you've sent my way, بادی که به من وزد تو آتش کنیش
Turning into mere dust the water I swallow? آبی که خورم در دهنم خاک کنی

131. Not Getting It (پند ناپذیر)

I am not at all pleased with your whirling, O wheel!
What you are advising I'm not getting, O wheel!
Given who *you* take to be trustworthy and wise,
An unwise, untrustworthy, I'm being, O wheel!

ای چرخ ز گردش تو خرسند نیم
پندم چه دهی که قابل پند نیم
گر میل تو با بی خرد و نا اهلست
من نیز چنان اهل و خردمند نیم

132. Wasted Wheel (چرخ بد مست)

O wheel! You're wasting me! Are you a wasted drunk?
Don't you still know my height, and how low you have sunk?
Am I not already, from poverty and grief,
So downhearted that to nothingness I have shrunk?

ای چرخ مرا مکش به بدمستی خویش
بشناس بلندی من و پستی خویش
من خود ز غم خویش و تهی دستی خویش
پیوسته ملول باشم از هستی خویش

133. It'd Be Odd (عجب است)

If the sphere wages no war with us, it'd be odd!
If it catapults no stones at us, it'd be odd!
If the judge using his endowment to buy wine
Plants no opium in schools for us, it'd be odd!

با ما فلک ار جنگ ندارد عجب است
گر بر سر ما سنگ نبارد عجب است
قاضی که خرید باده و وقف فروخت
در مدرسه گر بنگ نیارد عجب است

134. Lowbred Raiser Times (زمانۀ دون پرور)

From the times' recycles of these hildings' lot,
In hundreds of pains and griefs, my life has been caught.
I am a depressed bud in the world's flowerbed,
A lasting garden's tulip, blood filling its gut.

از گردش این زمانۀ دون پرور
با صد غم و درد میبرم عمر به سر
چون غنچه به گلزار جهان با دل تنگ
چون لاله ز باغ دهر با خون جگر

135. Eyelash Storm (سیل مژه)

From the bleeding of my gut a hundred homes flood.
Yet hundreds of fears nip all my crying in bud.
Blood is pouring from the spouts of my lashes such
That if I blink the world's hit by a storm of blood.

صد خانه ز خوناب دلم ویران است
وز گریه زار بیم صد چندان است
از هر مژه ناودان خون است روان
گر من مژه را به هم زنم طوفان است

136. Miser Raiser (خس پرور)

From the miser sphere's mirror-like oppressive quest
Of these times' breeding of these misers at no rest,
I have a face like a cup that brims with eyes' tears
And a heart like decanter, full of blood in chest.

دارم ز جفای فلک آینه گون
وز گردش روزگار خس پرور دون
از دیده رخی همچو پیاله پر اشک
وز سینه دلی همچو صراحی پر خون

137. Even Supposing (حتی گیرم)

Let's suppose that the sphere goes somewhat trustworthy,
The disagreeable times somewhat praiseworthy.
Wherefrom can our loved ones come back to us again,
To bring back a life that was somewhat noteworthy?

گیرم که فلک همدم و همراز آید
ناسازی دهر بر سر ساز آید
یاران موافق از کجا جمع شوند
وین عمر گذشته از کجا باز آید

138. Creativity's Dust (گرد حدوث)
The deeds of the sphere kicked around so much my clay
That the creative dust from my heart blew away.
I fear my house will become empty of my soul
before I find, to solving our problem, a way.

139. Here Comes the Moon (ماه می آید)
The dome that is whirling above is like a bowl
That gyrates ceaselessly, without a base or goal.
All it wants is to reap your life to waste. Now, look!
Here comes the new Moon's sickle, looking for your soul!

140. Grand Tent's Sigh (آه خرگاه)
From the alley of the ruins a Moon appeared!
On the high fort of the spheres a Grand Tent was geared!
A sigh came from the Grand Tent saying suddenly,
"This world's not even worth a straw to be revered!"

141. Time to Avenge (فرصت تلافی)
A long stretch of my life in hope I gave away.
I was not happy in my times, not for a day.
Now I'm afraid my life may not last long enough
To avenge the times, so it can, for its faults, pay.

142. Expectations from the Times (انتظار از زمانه)
O heart! Expect no good from our time and its lures.
Expect no life from it that is sound, that secures.
If you seek a cure from it, what you gain is pain.
Live with the pain, and don't seek from it any cures.

143. Fed Up Latecomers (دیرآمدگان سیر)
We are latecomers in the circle of being,
Yet we have sunk lower than a human being.
Because our lives are not going on as we wish,
Since we are fed up, why not seek our nonbeing?

144. What's the Point? (چه فایده؟)
Of the joy of the Sweetheart the sphere is empty.
Who, I wonder, is in this world calm and happy?
No one is feeling safe from the sudden death's strike.
So, in this useless life what is the use to be?

145. Hands Tied (دست بسته)

Since the time I could tell my two feet from my hands,
They were tied by this wheel that on wretchedness stands.
Alas! They'll count those days of life that passed without
Wine and the Beloved that truly understands.

146. Cup of Sediments (قدح دُرد)

Since I can't reach out to the outskirts of desire,
And being served fulfillment's cup won't transpire,
Then bring the sedimented wine since the Pure Wine
Won't be served in this glass sky of turquoise attire.

147. Betraying Jolly House (خوش سرای بی وفا)

This world is wearing a nice dress; it does, for sure.
It is dear to people's hearts, and it does endure.
To be fair, this world seems to be a jolly place.
Alas, it also betrays what it does assure!

148. Breathing World (دنیای نفس کش)

This world is a breath, and my soul a breath in it.
Its breathing allows me to take some breaths in it.
It asks us to thank it for breathing life in joy.
But unfaithfully it exhales all those in it.

149. Fate's Sheriff (شحنۀ تقدیر)

Sent me away to this exile, the ancient sphere,
Such that I no longer know where to my life steer.
See how I am now dragged around from town to town,
How I'm chained by the fate's sheriff, year after year.

150. What Would You Do? (چه کنی؟)

If the sphere's menacing to you, what can you do?
If a star-burned's crying to you, what can you do?
If you are sad all night, your hands held in prayer,
But your lot's berating to you, what can you do?

V. Chance and Fate (قضا و قدر)

151. Middle of Nothings (میان دو هیچ)

O unaware! You play no part in world affairs.
You're just based on wind, and all you do is blow airs.
You are caught in the middle of the two nothings,
While nothing surrounds you and nothing in you flares.

ای بیخبر از کار جهان هیچ نه ای
بنیاد تو باد است و ز آن هیچ نه ای
شدّ حدّ وجود تو میان دو عدم
اطراف تو هیچ و در میان هیچ نه ای

152. Deal Without You (قرارداد بی تو)

Relax! They concocted your deal a while ago,
While letting go of how you'd feel, a while ago.
What more can I say? Well, without your consent,
They fixed your tomorrow's ordeal a while ago.

خوش باش که پخته اند سودای تو دی
فارغ شده اند از تمنّای تو دی
قصّه چه کنم که بی تقاضای تو دی
دادند قرار کار فردای تو دی

153. Bring One, Take One (بیار و بر)

They bring one in but then take another away.
Why they do so is a secret they don't betray.
Our destinies then appear as chance accidents.
And it is our cups of life falling off the tray.

آرند یکی و دیگری بربایند
بر هیچ کسی راز همی نگشایند
ما را ز قضا جز این قدر ننمایند
پیمانهٔ عمر ماست می پیمایند

154. Familiar Stranger (غریب آشنا)

O rose! You appear to be a heart-stealing friend.
And wine! You're a ruby-like, life-enhancing blend.
But you, O combative luck, every time you come
As a stranger yet as familiar pretend!

ای گل تو به روی دلربایی مانی
وی مل تو به لعل جانفزایی مانی
ای بخت ستیزه کار هر دم با من
بیگانه تری به آشنایی مانی

155. Glad for Sadness (شاد غم)

He who gave the fortunate well their smiling lips
Gave the unfortunate unwell their bleeding ribs.
If no lots were given to me of joy, that's fine.
I am glad for a thousand tears of grieving drips.

آن کس که به خوبان لب خندان دادست
خون جگری به دردمندان دادست
گر قسمت ما نداد شادی غم نیست
شادیم که غم هزار چندان دادست

156. You Make, Then Break? (سازی و شکنی؟)

At times it composes the forms, mine and ours, straight.
At times it lets our charming bodies decimate.
"Why do you make us and then break us to pieces?"
Is what no one asks the master of our luck's slate.

گه راست کند صورت مائی و منی
گه بشکند این طلسم جانی و تنی
کس نیست که استاد قضا را گوید
از بهر چه سازی و چرا می شکنی

157. Luck's Spin (دوران قضا)

This turquoise dome and its golden bowl of the Sun
Will turn for a long time, as they have always done.
So, for a while, per the demands of our luck's spin,
We have arrived like others and soon will be gone.

این گنبد لاجوردی و زرّین طشت
بسیار بگشتست و بسی خواهد گشت
یك چند ز اقتضای دوران قضا
ما نیز چو دیگران رسیدیم و گذشت

158. Written Tablet (لوح نوشته)

Why light candles in a mosque, synagogue, or shrine,
Fearing for hell or hoping heaven's lot is mine?
Look at our chances' tablet, where eternally
The master of time wrote much of our storyline.

تا کی ز چراغ مسجد و دود کنشت
تا کی ز زیان دوزخ و سود بهشت
رو بر سر لوح بین که استاد قلم
اندر ازل آنچه بودنی بود نوشت

159. Untrappable Chance (قضای تله ناپذیر)

Regarding God's will, consent is all one can do,
But other than hypocrisy folks don't pursue.
I devised all sorts of schemes my mind could devise,
But I failed, since chance also decides what comes true.

با حکم خدا بجز رضا در نگرفت
با خلق بجز روی و ریا در نگرفت
هر حیله که در تصوّر عقل آید
کردیم و لیك با قضا در نگرفت

160. Saddled Horse (اسب زین شده)

When they saddled the heavens' Wild Horse on the day
The Pleiades joined Jupiter for their display,
They also wrote down our share from the book of chance.
What is *our* fault, then, if that's what our lots portray?

آنروز که توسن فلك زین کردند
و آرایش مشتری و پروین کردند
این بود نصیب ما ز دیوان قضا
ما را چه گنه قسمت ما این کردند

161. Hunter's Blame (بهانهٔ صیّاد)

The hunter, the death angel, who lays seeds as baits,
Traps the hunted, and their names 'human' designates.
Any good or evil that goes on in the world
It does but their blame to humankind relegates.

صیّاد اجل دانه چو در دام نهاد
صیدی بگرفت و آدمش نام نهاد
هر نیك و بدی که می رود در عالم
او میکند و بهانه بر عام نهاد

162. Regressive Blame (تسلسل تقصیر)

Any noble soul that illuminates a road
Knows that whatever happens starts from an abode.
Your suffering comes from the turning of the Moon,
Who is blameless for the motion it's been bestowed.

هر جان شریف کو شناسای رهست
داند که هر آنچه آید از جایگهست
رنجی کی رساند به تو از دور مهست
کو نیز ز هر چه می رود بی گنهست

163. Fate of Earth and Sky (تقدیر زمین و آسمان)

So long as there is an Earth underneath the sky,
Where all its animals and plants arise and die,
So long as the stars conjunct again in the wheel,
World affairs must basically with their fates comply.

تا روی زمین و آسمان خواهد بود
حیوان و نبات را مکان خواهد بود
تا چرخ قران اختران خواهد کرد
تقدیر خلاصهٔ جهان خواهد بود

164. Did They Consult? (مشورت کردند؟)

When they established the foundation of my life,
They did not ask me how I wished to live my life.
Since they set my life on course without asking me,
I know they did not mix my wishes with my life.

چون قاعدهٔ وجود ما بنهادند
در مشورتم پیام نفرستادند
چون کار مرا قرار بی من دادند
دانم که مراد من درو ننهادند

165. Judgment Day? (روز حساب؟)

Love comes with its troubles; it's a Godly command.
But why blame humans if our lives have all been planned?
If what's good or bad in people are destined traits,
What's a judgment day for? This, I don't understand!

عشق ار چه بلاست آن بلا حکم خداست
بر حکم خدا ملامت خلق چراست
گر نیک و بد خلق به تقدیر خداست
پس روز پسین حساب بر بنده چراست

VI. Puzzle (معمّا)

166. I've Not Mastered (استاد نیم)

Not even for one day am I free in this world.
Joyless is when any of my breathings unfold.
I apprenticed the times for a very long time,
But I'm not a teacher of the world, truth be told.

یك روز ز بند عالم آزاد نیم
یك دم ز زدن از وجود خود شاد نیم
شاگردی روزگار کردم بسیار
در کار جهان هنوز استاد نیم

167. Nobody Knows (هیچکس آگاه نشد)

Inside the chance's veil no one could ever go,
Nor could anyone the destiny's secrets know.
All have tried to say something by analogy.
But their tale did not end, nor did my knowledge grow.

کس را پس پردۀ قضا راه نشد
از سرّ قدر هیچکس آگاه نشد
هر کس ز سر قیاس چیزی گفتند
معلومم نگشت و قصه کوتاه نشد

168. I Know I Don't Know (می دانم نمی دانم)

My heart was never deprived of all that's been known.
I thought just a few secrets are left to be known.
But having now looked at it more reasonably,
I realize that nothing has been really known.

هرگز دل من ز علم محروم نشد
کم ماند ز اسرار که مفهوم نشد
با این همه چون بنگرم از روی خرد
معلومم شد که هیچ معلوم نشد

169. I Don't Know (هیچ معلومم نیست)

I do not know why the wheel should be turning such
That the times torment unimaginably much.
The more I see my work, the more I discover
A life gone by, yet the truth not closer to touch.

از گردش چرخ هیچ مفهومم نیست
جز رنج زمانه هیچ موهومم نیست
هر چند به کار خویش در می نگرم
عمری بگذشت و هیچ معلومم نیست

170. By and Large Slow (غم خوش خوش)

For a long time I explored the plains, high and low,
But my search did not help even a task, I know.
Despite all the hardships, I guess I must be glad
That my sorrows grew at a pace by and large slow!

بسیار بگشتیم به گرد در و دشت
یك کار من از گردش من نیك نگشت
خرسندم از آن که عمر من با همه رنج
گر خوش نگشت باز خوش خوش بگذشت

171. Miser Self (خسّت خود)

I am constantly sad about the sphere's turning.
I resent keeping to myself what I'm learning:
Not a knowledge that makes me stand up to the world,
Nor one that makes me lax about truth-discerning.

پیوسته ز گردش فلك غمگینیم
با طبع خسیس خویشتن در کینیم
علمی نه که از سیر جهان برخیزم
عقلی نه که فارغ ز جهان بنشینیم

172. Cup Full of Illusions (کاسهٔ پرسودا)
That Cup-maker who made all the Cups of our brains,
The Cup-maker who in our Cups His artwork trains,
On our being's table laid an inverted Cup
That can hold myths from which nobody ever gains.

173. Who Knows? (واقف کیست؟)
O boy! Who's not in awe about this world, tell me?
Who's come to really understand this world, tell me?
Did anyone live a happy day in his life
Without crying the next day in this world, tell me?

174. Happy Lies (دروغهای خوش)
All the world's seekers have so highly raised their cries
That, instead of tears, blood is running from their eyes.
Whenever they fail to unravel a secret,
Being so helpless, they happily tell their lies.

175. Magic Lantern (فانوس خیال)
This heavenly wheel that's for us so surprising,
Is like a magic lantern, of us comprising.
The Sun shines its candlelight in the world's lantern
For a whirling shadow-show of us, just browsing.

176. Not Sure They Knew (آگاه نیم که آگه بودند)
Those who searched for truths with this world beneath their feet
And thought crossing both worlds made their knowledge complete,
I'm not sure how far they succeeded at learning
The truths of a world that is with riddles replete.

177. Ocean of Being (بحر وجود)
This ocean of being emerged from what's concealed.
There is no one who has the pearl of its truth drilled.
Each of them said something out of desperation.
What it really is, no one has ever revealed.

178. Ant and Cow (مور و گاو)
Under this rotating ancient dome, we are still
Like some ants circling to enter an ant-hill.
Not knowing where we're going, in hope or in fear,
Like a blindfolded cow we're turning a cow-mill.

179. Secrets' Tent (پردهٔ اسرار)

There is no one who has entered His secrets' tent.
Beyond speculations on life, no one went.
Beyond the heart of the grave, there will be no home.
Alas in making these myths there will be no end.

در پردهٔ اسرار کسی را ره نیست
زین تعبیهٔ جان هیچ کس آگه نیست
جز در دل خاک هیچ منزلگه نیست
افسوس که این فسانه ها کوته نیست

180. Circle of Coming and Going (دایرهٔ آمد و رفت)

In the circle around which we all come and go,
No one knows where it ends or where began its flow.
And no one has let out any straight truths about
Where this coming's from and where goes this to-and-fro.

در دایره ای کآمدن و رفتن ماست
او را نه بدایت نه نهایت پیداست
کس می نزند دمی در ین معنی راست
کاین آمدن از کجا و رفتن به کجاست

181. Bedtime Story (فسانهٔ خواب)

All who gained the knowledge and manners of the wise,
And outshined in science their brilliant allies,
Could not lead to a daylight this thickness of night.
They uttered some myths and went asleep in surprise.

آنانکه محیط فضل و آداب شدند
در کشف علوم شمع اصحاب شدند
ره زین شب تاریک نبردند برون
گفتند فسانه ای و در خواب شدند

182. Chin Movers (زنخ زن ها)

All those who pierced the pearls of meanings, all the wise
Who in telling about God's essence made their tries,
About the source of the secrets said nothing much.
First, they moved their chins, and finally shut their eyes.

آنانکه به حکمت درّ معنی سفتند
در ذات خداوند سخن ها گفتند
سر رشتهٔ اسرار ندانست کسی
اول زنخی زدند و آخر خفتند

183. Hundred Kisses (صد بوسه)

There's a human Cup that the intellect praises,
While bringing a hundred kisses to its faces!
Such a tender Cup, however, I wonder why,
The lasting Potter makes and then quickly razes?

جامی است که عقل آفرین میزندش
صد بوسه ز مهر بر حسن میزندش
این کوزه گر دهر چنین جام لطیف
می سازد و باز بر زمین میزندش

184. Whose Love, Whose Hate (مهر که؟ کین که؟)

Breaking a wine cup whose parts are so intertwined
Would not be condoned by drunkards or so inclined.
Who joined in love, then, and who broke so hatefully,
The dear heads and feet of many a humankind?

ترکیب پیاله ای که در هم پیوست
بشکستن آن روا نمی دارد مست
چندین سر و پای نازنین از سر دست
از مهر که پیوست و به کین که شکست

185. Whose Fault? (عیب کراست؟)

When God cast the mixtures of natures by design,
Why did He let them fall short and again decline?
If these forms fell short, on whom one can place the blame?
And why did they decline if they'd turned out so fine?

دارنده چو ترکیب طبایع آراست
باز از چه سبب فکندش اندر کم و کاست
گر نیک نیامد این صور عیب کراست
ور نیک آمد خرابی از بهر چراست

186. Before-the-Judge-Throwing (به داور خواندن)

If they move the pen of chance without my knowing,
Why do they blame *me* for its good or bad flowing?
Yesterday, today, passed despite my say or yours.
Why then have tomorrow's before-the-judge-throwing?

بر من قلم قضا چو بی من رانند
پس نیک و بدش ز من چرا میدانند
دی بی من و امروز چو دی بی من و تو
فردا به چه حجّتم به داور خوانند

187. Impossible to Decline (پرهیز محال)

About something that's impossible to decline
He ruled, "Do not commit it! Leave it, I Opine!"
Caught helplessly between the commands and refrains,
A whole world remain living on a borderline.

حکمی که از او محال باشد پرهیز
فرموده و امر کرده کز وی بگریز
آنگاه میان امر و نهیش عاجز
درمانده جهانیان که کج دار و مریز

188. Knew From the Start (از ازل می دانست)

I drink, and one who is of my drinking aware
Would know easily about my life's wine affair.
God knew eternally that I would be drinking.
If I don't drink, "I was wrong," then, must He declare?

من می خورم و هر که چو من اهل بود
می خوردن من به نزد او سهل بود
می خوردن من ز حق به ازل می دانست
گر می نخورم علم خدا جهل بود

189. When Forbidden? (حرام کی؟)

God said that wine won't be in heaven forbidden.
When did He declare it's in both worlds forbidden?
When Hamzeh drank too much and then killed a camel,
Did our prophet say it's just *for him* forbidden?

ایزد به بهشت وعده با ما می کرد
پس در دو جهان حرام می را کی کرد
حمزه به عرب اشتر مردی پی کرد
پیغمبر ما حرام می بر وی کرد

190. Why the Burning? (سوختن برای چه؟)

When God was fashioning my clay below the sky,
He knew well the deeds that would arise from my try.
Against His commandments, no sins can come from me.
Then what is the hell's burning for, just wonder I?

ایزد چو گل وجود ما می آراست
دانست ز فعل ما به بر خواهد خواست
بی حکمش نیست هر گناهی که مراست
پس سوختن قیامت از بهر چراست

191. Whose Want? (خواست چه کسی؟)

If God has not wanted all that I've been wanting,
Then, how can be achieved all that I've been wanting?
If what He wanted for me is all that's proper,
Then, have they all been wrong, all that *I've* been wanting?

ایزد چو نخواست آنچه من خواسته ام
کی گردد راست آنچه من خواسته ام
گر جمله صواب است که او خواسته است
پس جمله خطاست آنچه من خواسته ام

192. Prohibition Enough (منع بس)

The Creator made us from some water and clay,
Rendering us content with our griefs of the day.
You're often prohibiting me from drinking wine;
My empty hand's enough prohibition, I'd say!

از آب و گل آفرید صانع ما را
کرده به غم زمانه قانع ما را
پیوسته مرا ز می همی منع کنی
خود دست تهی بس است مانع ما را

193. Problem Unsolved (مشکل حل نشده)

I will leave this world that has so betrayed my heart. زین عالمِ خاک بی وفا خواهم رفت
Not having solved the problem, I'll helplessly start حل ناشده مشکل به فنا خواهم رفت
To go into nothingness, still reflecting on عاجز گشتم درین تفکّر عاجز
Why I came to this world and where to I depart. کز بهر چه آمدم کجا خواهم رفت

194. Polo Ball (گوی چوگان)

O luck's polo ball, who've been moving dazedly! ای رفته به چوگان قضا همچون گو
Go left and right, and stop guessing why it may be, چپ می رو و راست می رو و هیچ مگو
Since the reason He tossed you to this back and forth کان کس که تو را فکند اندر تک و پو
Is something only He knows, He knows, He knows, He! او داند و او داند و او داند او

VII. O God! (خدایا)

195. O Book of Secrets' Opening! (ای سردفتر اسرار)

O One whose essence opens being's secrets page,
All being doors and wall signs, Your attribute's gauge!
O One behind Divine veil hidden from our eyes,
Yet so present in the bazaar of being's stage!

ای ذات تو سردفتر اسرار وجود
نقش صفتت بر در و دیوار وجود
در پردهٔ کبریا نهان گشته ز خلق
بنشسته عیان بر سر بازار وجود

196. O Absolute Survivor! (ای باقی محض)

O Absolute survivor! Finite, You are not!
You have no place, but where is it that You are not?
O One in essence free from direction and place!
But where are You and where is there that You are not?

ای باقی محض با فنائی که نه ای
در جای نه ای کدام جائی که نه ای
ای ذات تو از جا و جهت مستغنی
آخر تو کجائی و کجائی که نه ای

197. O Hidden Apparent! (ای پنهان آشکار)

At times we think that You hide, not showing Your face.
At times we see You in everything taking place.
In this, You are manifesting Yourself to You.
You're both the seen and the Self that sees His own grace.

گه گشته نهان رو به کسی ننمایی
گه در صور کون و مکان پیدایی
این جلوه گری به خویشتن بنمایی
خود عین عیانی و خودی بینایی

198. Ant's Eyes, Fly's Legs! (دیدهٔ مور، پای پشه)

In the slight eye of an ant is light from Your light.
In the slight leg of a fly is might from Your might.
It's *Your* essence that deserves what is Godliness.
May no poor description take a slight from Your height.

در دیدهٔ تنگ مور نورست ز تو
در پای ضعیف پشه زورست ز تو
ذات تو سزاست مر خداوندی را
هر وصف که ناسزاست دورست ز تو

199. O Sun's King! (ای شاه خورشید)

O One for whom twilight is the court of Your face!
The Sun has become the Moon servant of Your face!
Your Moon's eyebrow is like a foreheaded night guard's,
Who's tightened his belt to serve the King of Your face!

ای بارگه نور سحرگاه رخت
خورشید شده ست بندهٔ ماه رخت
ابروی تو حاجبی ست پیشانی دار
بربسته کمر به خدمت شاه رخت

200. O Author! (ای نگارنده)

O Author! On the lips of a sweetheart, You wrote.
It's the same on the violet's petals, to note.
The Sun tried to write You a line. Lacking paper,
On the Moon it wrote the line, "I Love You," to quote.

خطّی که خطت بر لب دلخواه نوشت
بر برگ گل بر بنفشه ناگاه نوشت
خورشید به بندگیش میداد خطی
کاغذ مگرش نبود بر ماه نوشت

201. O Candle of Delight! (ای شمع طرب)

Kissing You on Your feet, O candle of delight,
Bests kissing the lips of any beauty in sight.
I pass days, dreaming I could touch Your notion's robe.
My feet run after Your Love, during every night.

202. O Beauty! (ای زیبا)

O One whose beauty adorns all daffodil forms,
Whose face is etched in all of China's idol forms,
Your Loving wink gave the king of Babylon all
The designs of knight, rook, bishop, pawn, and queen forms!

203. O Unfathomable! (ای شناخت ناپذیر)

Neither can the intellect know Your glory, God,
Nor can our thoughts capture Your eternity, God.
No one can fathom the depth of Your perfection.
Who other than You can express Your beauty, God?

204. O Just! (ای عادل)

O God! All that exist on Earth or in the sky
You made out of nothing else, but Your wisdom's try.
To Your port of justice arrive, darvish or king.
Your house of mercy shelters all, sober or high.

205. O Sought After (ای مطلوب)

O One seeking whom the whole world is in uproar,
Yet both rich and poor must bare their souls to implore!
You are recalled in sayings, but their ears are deaf!
You are present to them, but their blind eyes ignore!

206. O Most Precious! (ای پربهاترین)

I won't trade away my Pearls that, too, come from You.
I trade all balms for the pains of exile from You.
I won't trade Your Door's dust for all of Jamsheed's lands.
I will give up both worlds, for just a hair from You.

207. O Outside Both Worlds! (ای برون از هر دو جهان)

Many hearts have bled and teary-eyed souls have wailed
To discover what Your truth is behind the veiled.
O One, to know whom intellects fail and spheres bend!
You are beyond both worlds; yet, from You they entailed.

208. O Beloved! (ای معشوق)

There's no gut that bleeds not from this exile, is there?
There's no wise that's not loving You meanwhile, is there?
Although You are not maddened about anyone,
There's no madness for You that's not worthwhile, is there?

209. Hills and Clouds the Same (که و مه یکسان)

O God, in Your worship, hills and clouds are the same.
Better than to serve You in both worlds, there's no aim.
You give us joy and take away calamity.
Giving and taking them both from Your wisdom came.

210. O Owner (ای مالك)

O God, what exists is what You in essence own.
Those who seek after You must try each on their own.
I speak to You using Your own created words:
"Nothing lasts but You, everlasting on Your own."

211. Seventy-Two Sects (هفتاد و دو فرقه)

Seventy-two sects are seeking after Your truth.
Each with a different tongue is teaching Your truth.
The tip of the thread is not in any sect's hands,
Yet each greets one as if only *it* knows Your truth.

212. Futile Chase (جستجوی بی حاصل)

Masters of knowledge sought after in many ways
Nothing other than Your door, searching through the maze.
But other than failure nothing was achieved.
So, all gave up such efforts in their futile chase.

213. Wandering Horse (براق سرگردان)

Those who have been the most learned of all humankind,
Ones who, riding intellect's horse, the spheres defined,
In knowing Your essence, like the heavenly spheres,
Have been bewildered, upturned, and to awe resigned.

214. O All Knower! (ای دانای همه چیز)

O God, the drug for all those who are pained, You know!
The way to cure those who've long ill remained, You know!
As I explain my gut-wrenching hardships for You,
A hundred thousand still to be explained, You know!

215. O Refuge (ای پناهگاه)

Here I am, taking refuge in Your compassion,
Freed from committing submission and transgression.
Where there comes to be Your favor, will be the same
Unexpressed in action and acted expression.

216. O Matchless! (ای بی مانند)

In this untrustworthy world that we populate,
I searched a lot in what is to me a known state.
There's no Moon as clear as Your Face, let me be clear.
No straight cypress can reach Your height, a truth told straight.

217. Eyes and Intellect From You! (چشم و عقل از تو)

O One who are the source of life, including mine!
I'm unable to know Your life that's so Divine.
But my eyesight's power is from You, so I see.
My intellect's power is from You, so I opine.

218. Wondering Design (نقش حیران)

You have cast a design for my being, O God,
That leaves me puzzled about my being, O God,
Asking, "How can I be better than I'm, given
The traits that *You* have cast on my being, O God?"

219. Why the Wondering? (چرا سرگشتگی؟)

If at first You intended that I know myself,
Why did You make me alienated from myself?
If You had not meant to exile me from day one,
Then why in this world I wonder about myself?

220. Why the Exile? (چرا هجر؟)

Amid my heart's grief, recalling You brought me bliss,
But exile instead diminished my joy in this.
I braved this world's bitterness to enjoy Your Love;
With the exile's pain, I've no use for its abyss.

221. Futile Effort (کوشش بی سود)

My search for You led to nothing but a flame's smoke.
No hope was left to heal my body that's gone broke.
I searched hard to find ways of reaching out to You.
My efforts were futile, with no luck to invoke.

222. Not Reaching You (بوصالت نرسیدن)

Neither did I in reaching Your presence succeed,
Nor can I endure a moment's exile, indeed,
Nor do I have the guts to tell my grief to one,
A life's problem, a new sadness, a joyful need.

نه سوی وصال تو مرا دست رسی
نه طاقت هجران تو دارم نفسی
نه زهره که باز گویم این غم به کسی
مشکل کاری طرفه غمی خوش هوسی

223. Don't Look? (منگر؟)

O God, the face of that spring month of lovely kind
You adorned with fragrant hyacinths and its kind.
Then, why is it that You command us not to look?
Is this one of those "tilt the cup but don't pour" kind?

یا رب تو جمال آن مه مهر انگیز
آراسته ای به سنبل و عنبر نیز
پس حکم همی کنی که در وی منگر
این حکم چنان بود که کج دار و مریز

224. Arise! Excite! (خیز، شور انگیز)

I was asleep in nothingness, You said, "Arise!
Go into the world! Explore it! Excite! Suprise!"
Now that I'm under Your command, the story was
"Tilt the cup but do not let it pour," I realize.

در کتم عدم خفته بدم گفتی خیز
رو به جهان دور جهان گرد شور انگیز
واکنون که به فرمان تو ام حیرانم
القصّه چنان بود که کج دار و مریز

225. Why Hell-Bound? (چرا دوزخی؟)

You are the Creator and so created me
That wine and poetry have captivated me.
If You made me eternally to be this way,
Then why have You to a hell relegated me?

خالق توئی و مرا چنین ساخته ای
هستم به می و ترانه دلباخته ای
چون روز ازل مرا چنین ساخته ای
پس بهر چه در دوزخم انداخته ای

226. Love's Trap (دام عشق)

It was my love for You that had trapped my old head.
Otherwise, why would my hand be to the wine led?
The vow that the head had once made the heart then broke,
And the clothing sewn of patience was in time shred.

پیرانه سرم عشق تو در دام کشید
ور نه ز کجا دست من و جام نبید
آن توبه که عقل داد جانان بشکست
وان جامه که صبر دوخت ایّام درید

227. Creation and Sin (آفرینش و گناه)

O One tending to us when we're alive or dead,
By Whose rules this wandering wheel is being led,
I'm not worthy, since this servant's master is You,
But how can one sin if existence from You spread?

سازندهٔ کار مرده و زنده تویی
دارندهٔ این چرخ پراکنده تویی
من گرچه بدم خواجهٔ این بنده تویی
کس را چه گنه که آفریننده توی

228. What Sin? (چه گناه)

What were the mercy and kindness from the start for?
What was keeping me in some comfort in part for?
Now You are trying me with the life's suffering.
What sinfulness am I being torn apart for?

چندان کرم و لطف ز آغاز چه بود
وان داشتنم در طرب و ناز چه بود
اکنون همه در رنج دلم میکوشی
آخر چه گناه کرده ام باز چه بود

229. Rebel? (عاصی؟)

You are setting thousands of traps for me, O God!
In every step warn that You will trap me, O God!
No dust in the universe is free from Your Will.
Why then "rebellious" do You call me, O God?

بر رهگذرم هزار جا دام نهی
گوئی که بگیرمت اگر گام نهی
یک ذرّه ز حکم تو جهان خالی نیست
حکمم تو کنی و عاصیم نام نهی

230. This Is A Payment (این مزد بود)

If I am a rebel, Your acceptance is where?
If I'm in darkness, Your illuminance is where?
For my obedience, You promise paradise.
That's just a payment, Your benevolence is where?

من بندۀ عاصیم رضای تو کجاست
تاریک دلم نور و ضیای تو کجاست
ما را تو بهشت اگر به طاعت بخشی
این مزد بود لطف و عطای تو کجاست

231. Forgiving Heals (کریمی مرمست)

O God, the Forgiver! Heals, the one who forgives!
Why outside the Éram Garden the sinner lives?
Forgiving is not for my obeying, is it?
Only a sinner hopes that forgiven he is.

یا رب تو کریمی و کریمی مرم ست
عاصی ز چه رو برون ز باغ ارم ست
با طاعتم ار عفو کنی نیست کرم
با معصیتم اگر ببخشی کرم ست

232. What's the Difference? (فرق چیست؟)

O God! Who is sinless in this world? Please tell me!
He who did not sin, how did he live? Or did he?
If I commit bad things and You badly punish,
Then, please tell me, God, what their difference may be.

ناکرده گناه در جهان کیست بگو
وآن کس که گنه نکرد چون زیست بگو
من بد کنم و تو بد مکافات دهی
پس فرق میان من و تو چیست بگو

233. Broke My Decanter (ابریق مرا شکستی)

You shatter this, my body's jug of wine, O God!
You cease my joy in all that is divine, O God!
You pour my red blood's wine to dust. Biting the dust,
I muse: Is *that* of drunkenness a sign, O God?

ابریق می مرا شکستی ربّی
بر من در عیش را ببستی ربّی
بر خاک بریختی می گلگون مرا
خاکم بدهن مگر که مستی ربّی

234. Questioning Back (پرسش متقابل)

On the day the high heavens will cleave asunder,
And when their brightnesses all the stars surrender,
I'll grab Your robe and amid Your questioning ask,
"O Idol! Who caused all the carnage, I wonder?"

روزیکه شود اذا السّماء النشقت
وآندم که شود اذا النّجوم انکدرت
من دامن تو بگیرم اندر سئلت
گویم صنما بایّ ذنب قتلت

235. Which Name? (کدام نام؟)

Calling You 'Punisher,' the ascetic shuns sin.
Calling You 'Forgiver,' in sin drowning I've been.
He calls You 'Punisher'; I call You 'Forgiver.'
Which name do You prefer, O One without a twin?

زاهد نکند گنه که قهّاری تو
ما غرق گناهیم که غفّاری تو
او قهّارت خواند و من غفارت
امّا به کدام نام خوش داری تو

236. Hope for Mercy (امید رحمت)

Even though I become sinful each day and night,
Of Your mercy, I am trustful each day and night.
I don't have a grain of hope left in the world's folks.
Of Your mercy, though, I'm hopeful each day and night.

هر چند اگر گناهکارم شب و روز
امید به رحمت تو دارم شب و روز
از خلق جهان جوی ندارم امید
از بخشش تو امیدوارم شب و روز

237. I'm Excused (معذورم)

You brought to being from nothing my existence.
You blessed me with everything beyond subsistence.
I'm subjected to Your Will, so long as I live.
So, I am excused in needing Your assistance.

آنم که ز هیچم به وجود آوردی
دانم که به من بسی نکوئی کردی
چون عاجز تقدیر تو ام معذورم
مادام که باقیست ز خاکم گردی

238. You Decide (چسان دار)

In my exile I can cry, if that's what You want.
I can enjoy reaching You, if that's what You want.
I'm not the one to tell You how to treat me, God.
Treat me as Your heart wishes, if that's what You want.

خواهی ز فراق در فغان دار مرا
خواهی ز وصال شادمان دار مرا
من با تو نگویم که چسان دار مرا
زان سان که دلت خواست چنان دار مرا

239. Worse Than Us (بتر از ما)

You see in just one breath a hundred sins in us.
Yet, from Your beneficence, tear no veils of us.
We may be worse than the worst of all folks, and yet,
You gracefully forgive regretfuls worse than us.

ای هر نفسی صد گنه از ما دیده
وز لطف و کرم پردهٔ ما ندریده
ای من بتر از هر که به عالم بترست
وی لطف تو از من بتر آمرزیده

240. Unveiling (پرده دری)

O One whose essence is one that is without fail,
In thousands of ways unveiled, yet lays behind veil!
Behind a veil I may commit a thousand sins.
But before Your mercy, my remorses unveil.

ای ذات منزّه تو از عیب بری
بیرون ز هزار پرده در پرده دری
در پرده هزار معصیت هست مرا
ایمن شده ام ز فضلت از پرده دری

241. What Can I Do? (من چه کنم؟)

O God! You have shaped this, my clay; what can *I* do?
You wove the clothes in which I pray; what can *I* do?
If each good or bad that came to being from me
You wrote on my head to relay, what can *I* do?

یا رب تو گلم سرشته ای من چه کنم
پشم و قصبم تو رشته ای من چه کنم
هر نیک و بدی که آمد از من به وجود
تو بر سر من نبشته ای من چه کنم

242. Forgive the Parts (رحمت بر اعضاء)

O God! On this, my enthralled heart, please have mercy.
On this chest where my sorrows start, please have mercy.
Please forgive my tavern-frequenting feet, O God!
On this hand, my cup-holding part, please have mercy.

یا رب به دل اسیر من رحمت کن
بر سینهٔ غم پذیر من رحمت کن
بر پای خرابات رو من بخشای
بر دست پیاله گیر من رحمت کن

243. No Road But Yours (فقط درگه تو)

O One whose favor's hand is sought when despots fail,
Whose mercy reaches all those disgraced, ones who wail,
Please forgive me! I am one who during his life
Has had no road to walk except on Your door's trail.

244. O Needless! (ای مستغنی)

O the One whose essence is unknown to the wise,
Needless of our worships, nor of our sinful sighs!
My sinful drinking, or hopeful sobriety,
Are both meant to invite Your mercy in disguise.

245. Torment? Where? (عذاب؟ کجا؟)

"I will torment you," I'm told that You will say!
But where will You do it, I wonder, if I may?
Wherever You are, torment can never exist!
Wherever You are not, can't exist any way!

246. Tavern's Altar (محراب نماز)

Speaking of truth to You in a ruined tavern
Is better than praying to an altar's pattern.
O my source, O my end, and all that's in-between,
Punish me or endear me in my life's sojourn.

247. O Repentance-Accepter! (ای عذرپذیر)

O God, You're the inner secrets knower of all,
Amid our frailty, the supreme helper of all!
Accept my repentance while knowing my reasons!
O the reasoned repentance accepter of all!

248. Breeze of Mercy (نسیم بخشش)

You give Solomon's throne to a miser at times,
Or the prophethood's crown to an orphan at times.
O God! What will it take for a cause You send me
A breeze from Your heaven of forgiveness at times.

249. Tell Him Who Does Not Know (به کسی گو که نشناسد)

Hermits don't know Your mercy as well as I do.
The lost don't know You nearly as well as I do.
You said that You will send me to hell if I sin?
Tell this to those who don't see as well as I do.

250. Far Far Far (دور دور دور)

Some folks with fanciful thoughts in vanity fell,
Living in hopes of heaven, or in fears of hell.
Will it be revealed, when the veil is pulled at last,
That they went far, far, far astray from where You dwell?

قومی ز گزاف در غرور افتادند
واندر طلب حور و قصور افتادند
معلوم شود چو پرده ها بردارند
کز کوی تو دور و دور و دور افتادند

251. Dark Listing (سیه نامه)

With all Your mercy, about sinning I won't think.
With Your assistance, about toiling I won't think.
If Your mercy clears my face of all wrongs, about
Even a dot in a dark listing I won't think.

با رحمت تو من از گنه نندیشم
با توشهٔ تو ز رنج ره نندیشم
گر لطف توام سپیدروی انگیزد
یک نقطه ز نامهٔ سیه نندیشم

252. Accept Me (بپذیرم)

O God! I take refuge in You, will You accept?
In Your eternal mercy's shade, can I be kept?
From Your Will's fate, nobody can ever escape.
Help me given that You are the Master Adept.

یا رب به تو در گریختم بپذیرم
در سایهٔ لطف لایزالی گیرم
کس را گذر از چارهٔ تقدیر تو نیست
تقدیر تو کرده ای بکن تدبیرم

253. Essence Knows Essence (ذات دانندهٔ ذات)

My wisdom deserves not the proof of You, O God!
My thoughts include nothing but praise of You, O God!
How can I account for Your necessity when
Only You can know the essence of You, O God!

کنه خردم در خور اثبات تو نیست
واندیشهٔ من بجز مناجات تو نیست
من ذات تو را به واجبی کی دانم
دانندهٔ ذات تو بجز ذات تو نیست

254. Wisdom Chain (زنجیر خرد)

Without Your blessing, I am deprived of wisdom.
Has lost his way onward, this old man of wisdom.
Do a favor and drawing on Your mercy tie
The wall of my nature to Your chain of wisdom.

بی لطف تو ضایع شده تدبیر خرد
گم کرد ره معاملهٔ پیر خرد
لطفی بکن و به لطف خود بسته بدار
دیوار طبیعتم به زنجیر خرد

255. Hearer of the Mute (شنوای لالان)

O God, the state of depressed hearts that cry, You know.
The grief of those who've lost their wings to fly, You know.
If I sing to You from a sobbing heart, You hear.
My silent tongue, like the mute ones who sigh, You know.

آنی تو که حال تنگ حالان دانی
احوال همه بی پر و بالان دانی
گر خواهم از سینهٔ نالان شنوی
ور دم نزنم زبان لالان دانی

256. What About the Shame? (با شرم چه کنم؟)

I've been always at war in me. What can I do?
My acts cause lots of pain in me. What can I do?
Even if You forgive what I have done before,
About the shame You saw in me what can I do?

با نفس همیشه در نبردم چه کنم
وز کردهٔ خویشتن به دردم چه کنم
گیرم که ز من در گذرانی به کرم
زین شرم که دیده ای چه کردم چه کنم

257. One, Not Two (یک، نه دو)

Although I did not pierce my duty's Pearls for You,
Nor could I sweep to hide my dust of sins from You,
I'm not despaired of the reach of Your forgiveness,
Since I've always believed that One, not two, are You.

گر گوهر طاعتت نسفتم هرگز
ور گرد گنه ز رخ نرفتم هرگز
نومید نیم ز بارگاه کرمت
زیرا که یکی را دو نگفتم هرگز

258. Open the Door (باز کن در)

Show me a door, since the key to this maze is You.
Show me a way, since the guide for all ways is You.
I do not extend hands to folks for charity
Since they are finite and the One who stays is You.

بگشای دری که در گشاینده توئی
بنمای رهی که ره نماینده توئی
من دست به هیچ دستگیری ندهم
کایشان همه فانی اند و پاینده توئی

259. Offer a Hand (دست گیر)

My poor heart is downed under Your feet from much grief.
O God, why not give a helping hand, even brief?
If there's been any neglect in my deeds for You,
Your mercy surely exists for my heart's relief.

در پای غمت شد دل مسکینم پست
یا رب چه شود اگر مرا گیری دست
گر در عملم آنچه تو را باید نیست
اندر کرمت آنچه مرا باید هست

260. Hope for Forgiveness (امید عفو)

If I've committed in this world a transgression,
I have always been hopeful in Your discretion.
You've said that in hard times You will lend me a hand,
No harder can be than this time of depression.

گر من گنهی روی زمین کردستم
عفو تو امیدست که گیرد دستم
گفتی که به روز عجز دستت گیرم
عاجزتر از این مخواه که اکنون هستم

261. Each Dawn (هر پگاه)

Every dawn I come and in *this* Ruin I dwell,
Like all those who freely talk and those who rebel.
Since only You know my secret and hidden thoughts,
Help me to offer in *these* lines my prayers well.

هر روز پگاه در خرابات شوم
همراه قلندران به طامات شوم
چون عالم سرّ و الخفیّات توئی
توفیقم ده تا به مناجات شوم

262. I Seek Your Door (نیاز به درگه تو)

Each dawn I give You my secret prayer, that's *this*:
"Powerless and in need, I seek Your door of bliss!
O the graceful One, free of need for our worship,
Help me correct where I've gone helplessly amiss!"

در هر سحری با تو همین گویم راز
بر درگه تو همین کنم عجز و نیاز
بی منّت بندگانت ای بنده نواز
کار من بیچارهٔ سرگشته بساز

263. Take Back Your Gift (گوهرت نثارت)

O One for whom Jesus was a breath, out and in!
Giving life is for You just a Divine routine!
Life is a prime gift You give. Here, I give back mine!
You'll be taking back the treasure that Yours has been.

آنی که دم مسیح یارت شده است
بخشیدن جان همیشه کارت شده است
جان بخشش تست اگر فدای تو کنم
هم گوهر گنج خود نثارت شده است

264. I Am at Wit's End (سیر آمده ام)

I am now at the wit's end of my life's being.
I'm depressed and just an empty human being!
You bring all beings out of non-being, O God!
Bring me, then, out of this feeling of non-being!

سیر آمدم ای خدای از هستی خویش
وز تنگدلی و از تهیدستی خویش
از هر نیست تو هست میکنی بیرون آر
زین نیستیم به حرمت هستی خویش

VIII. Tavern Voice (ندا از میخانه)

265. Tavern Voice (ندا از میخانه)

That morning at dawn a voice from our Tavern came:
"O our Rogue Ruins-dweller who Maddened became!
Wake up! Let's fill the Cup with *this* Wine when alive
Before they fill our Cup when it won't be the same!"

آمد سحری ندا ز میخانهٔ ما
که ای رند خراباتی دیوانهٔ ما
برخیز که پر کنیم پیمانه ز می
زان پیش که پر کنند پیمانهٔ ما

266. Wine Lasso (کمند شراب)

"The Sun lassoed the roof, casting morning ray's rope.
The day's king cast *this* Wine in Cup, as in Kay's trope.
Drink *this* Wine since the early birds' prayer-crier
Cast the song 'O Drink *this* Wine' in everyday's scope!"

خورشید کمند صبح بر بام افکند
کیخسرو روز باده در جام افکند
می خور که منادی سحرگه خیزان
آوازهٔ اشربوا در ایّام افکند

267. Why Grieving? (ماتم چیست؟)

"O Khayyam, what's all this, your grieving for a sin?
Of what use, more or less, your being sad has been?
Were there no sins, there would not have been forgiveness.
If not for sins, why else did forgiving begin?"

خیام ز بهر گنه این ماتم چیست
وز خوردن غم فایده بیش و کم چیست
آنرا که گنه نکرد غفران نبود
غفران ز برای گنه آمد غم چیست

268. Rooster's Crow (نوحهٔ خروس)

"Do you know why, when the twilight is in the sky,
The morning rooster sings and crows aloud its cry?
It means they've revealed in the mirror of the dawn
That one more night has passed and still Asleep you lie!"

هنگام سپیده دم خروس سحری
دانی که چرا همی کند نوحه گری
یعنی که نمودند در آیینهٔ صبح
کز عمر شبی گذشت و تو بیخبری

269. Just a Fly? (مگسی بود؟)

"It was a water drop, *yet joined the sea* in pour.
A tiny dust in air became *one with the floor*.
You came to this world for what reason, do you think?
Like a fly that flew by, but then is there no more?"

یک قطرهٔ آب بود با دریا شد
یک ذرهٔ خاک با زمین یکتا شد
آمد شدن تو اندر این عالم چیست
آمد مگسی پدید و ناپیدا شد

270. Drop and Sea (قطره و بحر)

"A drop cried, 'Oh I just fell apart from the sea!'
The sea laughed: 'No, you and I are drops of a we!
There is nothing else but God, to tell you the truth.
We split but whirl around the center that is He!'"

قطره بگریست که از بحر جدائیم همه
بحر بر قطره بخندید که مائیم همه
در حقیقت دگری نیست خدائیم همه
لیک از گردش یک نقطه جدائیم همه

271. Lantern, Reed, Jug (صراحی، نی، فانوس)

"Humans are like Jugs and Wine their spirit inside.
The body's a reed; a voice comes from it inside.
O Khayyam, do you know what Earthly humans are?
They are lanterns *themselves* with sunlight lit *inside*."

آدم چو صراحی بود و روح چو می
قالب چو نیی بود صدایی از پی
دانی چه بود آدم خاکی خیام
فانوس خیالی و چراغی در وی

272. Primordial Intellect (عقل قدیم)

"We're from the primal intellect, nursed by the world.
All the existents from our existence unfold.
All places and entire beings depend on us.
World is our shadow, and we're *its* essence, behold!"

ما عقل قدیمیم و جهان دایهٔ ماست
موجود به جملگی همه مایهٔ ماست
قائم به وجود ما همه کون و مکان
ما ذات جهانیم جهان سایهٔ ماست

273. All the Same Substance (سرتاسر از یک گل)

"All this world is made of the same substance as ours.
Angelic souls live in hearts, the same way as ours.
The spheres, four elements, plants, and animals are
Lucid beings reflecting the same ray as ours."

سرتاسر آفاق جهان از گل ماست
منزلگه روح قدسیان از دل ماست
افلاک و عناصر و نبات و حیوان
عکسی ز وجود روشن منزل ماست

274. Ring Crown (نگین انگشتر)

"The sole reason for this whole creation is us!
Its core substance, from a wise point of view, is us!
This world is a circle, like a ring on His hand.
There's no doubt that its crown jewel design is us!"

مقصود ز جمله آفرینش مائیم
در چشم خرد جوهر بینش مائیم
این دایرهٔ جهان چو انگشتریست
بی هیچ شکی نقش نگینش مائیم

275. See the Friend (دوست ببین)

"See the soul as our truth's heart, the body its shell.
In your spirit you will see God, if you look well.
See that whatever has a sign of existence
Is either He or wherever His light rays dwell."

جان مغز حقیقتست و تن پوست ببین
در کسوت روح صورت دوست ببین
هر چیز که آن نشان هستی دارد
یا پرتو نور اوست یا اوست ببین

276. Not Within, Then Where? (با خود نه، کجا؟)

"O one who the goal of a lasting life pursue!
Recalling Him takes you above an Earthly view!
God is with you; the greatest sphere is in your heart!
If you cannot find them there, then where else could you?"

ای در طلب آنکه بقا خواهی یافت
وقت ذکرش فوق سما خواهی یافت
با تست خدا و عرش اعظم دل تست
با خود چو نیابیش کجا خواهی یافت

277. Ten to One (ده تا یک)

"Ten intellects, in nine spheres and eight heavens, told
My seven stars through notes from directions, six-fold,
That from five senses, four pillars, and three spirits
God in two worlds designed no one like you, behold!"

ده عقل ز نه رواق و از هشت بهشت
هفت اختر از شش جهت این نامه نوشت
کز پنج حواس و چار ارکان و سه روح
ایزد به دو عالم چو تو یک کس نسرشت

278. Adam's Part (جزو آدم)

"The Beloved bestowed to Adam His own grace,
As if hiding His secret in a secret place.
Any cash the King had in the world's treasure-house
He gifted generously to the human race."

محبوب جمال خود به آدم بخشید
سرّ حرمش به یار محرم بخشید
هر نقد که در خزانهٔ عالم بود
سلطان به کرم به جزو آدم بخشید

279. You Are It! (تو آنی)

"O one searching for a gem in mine, *you're* the mine!
O one after a scent of Divine, *you're* divine!
In a nutshell, hear from me the Absolute's truth:
If you have been looking for His sign, *you're* the sign!"

ای در طلب جوهر کانی کانی
وی زنده به بوی وصل جانی جانی
فی الجمله حدیث مطلق از من بشنو
هر چه که در جستن آنی آنی

280. All Is Humankind (همه انسان است)

"What really exists is for becoming human.
Not all can grasp this point without some acumen.
Drink a Sip of *this* Wine of Wakefulness to know
What distinguishes the human from nonhuman."

موجود حقیقی بجز انسان نبود
بر فهم کسی این سخن آسان نبود
یک جرعه از این شراب بی غش در کش
تا خلق خدا پیش تو یکسان نبود

281. Wine's Evolution (تکامل شراب)

"The matter that by nature accepts many forms,
Taking on many animal and plant-based forms,
Unless you suspect it can become Drunken too,
You'll miss that it describes *your* achievable forms."

آن مادّه که قابل صورهاست به ذات
گاهی حیوان همی شود گاه نبات
تا ظن نبری که مست گردد هیهات
موصوف به ذات توست گر هست صفات

282. Oneness (توحید)

"God breathes life into the universe's body,
And all angel-kinds are senses of this body.
The spheres, elements, and compounds are its organs.
That's all what His Unity's meanings embody."

حق جان جهانست و جهان جمله بدن
واصناف ملائکه حواس این تن
افلاک و عناصر و موالید اعضا
توحید همین است و دگرها همه فن

283. This and That (این و آن)

"*That* precious Ruby is from a different mine.
And *this* Pearl, so unique, has a different shine.
It's you and I who think 'this' is apart from 'that.'
Love's lore uses the tongue of a different line."

آن لعل گرانبها ز کانی دگرست
وین درّ یگانه را نشانی دگرست
اندیشهٔ این و آن خیال من و تست
افسانهٔ عشق از زبانی دگرست

284. Separation Illusion (بی اصلی فصل)

"They say things in this world are separately made.
Don't listen to them! From the right view don't be strayed!
Drink *this* Wine at dawn so that from long nights you let
One more pleat of your life's robe to its whole pervade."

در کار جهان ساخته هر یک فصلی
رو گوش مکن که آن ندارد اصلی
می خور به صبوح تا ز شبهای دراز
بر دامن عمر خود فزایی وصلی

285. You Make You (هر چه خواهی تویی)

"O one made after His image free, that is you!
O one who mirrors the King's beauty, that is you!
There is nothing outside you in all that exists.
You make yourself what you wish to be. *That* is you!"

286. Guest (مهمان)

"The spirit that's free of Earth's corruptible plight
Is a guest from the pure world, who's here to enlight!
Help it by your morning Sips from *this* Cup of Wine
Before it tells you unexpectedly 'good night!'"

287. Between Two Nothings (بین العدمین)

"Do not sit so quietly, O Omar! Beware!
Your life exists between the two nothings to bear.
While of the first you were not yet around to know,
The next can be a hundred times sadder affair."

288. Tent Furnisher (فرّاش خیمه)

"Khayyam! Your body is just like a tent. Besides,
Your spirit's the king; lasting, is where it resides.
In order to move the king to that house, this tent
Is dismantled when the death's furnisher decides."

289. Drink and Enjoy to Know (نوش و خوش باش تا بدانی)

"Know that from your spirit your body splits apart
And goes beyond the secrets' veil, into doom's heart!
Drink *this* Wine *now*, or you'll never know where you're from!
Enjoy *now*, since you don't know where to you'll depart!"

290. Wine's Benefit (سود می)

"Drink *this* Wine to forget your low selves to ascend!
It makes even your foe a bleeding-hearted friend!
Beware! The body has no other use than this:
It makes you sad about the fact that it will end."

291. Wine Meditation (باده نشینی)

"Meditate with *this* Wine; it's the true heaven's ground!
Hear how *its* harp tunes like the prophet David's sound!
Don't bother with what has passed or not yet arrived.
Now's *joy* is where the reasons for being abound!"

292. Times' Treachery (زمانۀ غدّار)

"*Today*, when your roses of happiness still thrive,
Why don't you try and *now* for *this* Cup of Wine strive?
Drink *this* Wine *now*, since the times are treacherous foes.
Another day like this may no longer arrive."

293. Wine's Bitterness (تلخی می)

"In the morning hours when the sky turns to blue,
You must hold a Cup of *this* Wine that's pure in brew.
It has been said that the truth is always bitter.
Well, it must be, and that's why Wine is bitter too!"

294. Cup's Verse (آیۀ پیاله)

"The Quran, they say, is the best word of all time,
Yet it is read not by all, or from time to time.
But on *this* Cup's Rim Line, there is a verse so plain
That they call it 'Wine' everywhere, read all the time."

295. Don't Sit Depressed (ننشین دلتنگ)

"O Khayyam, the times shame those who sit down idly,
Being depressed about how everyday may be.
Therefore, Drink *this* Wine from *this* Jug while the harp cries,
Before your Jug shatters on the stone suddenly."

296. Wine Prayer (دعای می)

"Fasting, praying, going to the mosque, until when?
Drink *this*, too, in Taverns of darvishhood again.
Oh Khayyam! Drink *this* Wine or else the Earth will make
You a cup, a pitcher, or a jug, now and then."

297. Decline's Reason (دلیل کم و کاست)

"If a mixture of natures did never decline,
It would take the form of a form-giving divine.
He formed it to decline so you know correctly
That just One Mighty King is behind world's design."

298. Why Depressed? (چرا دلتنگ؟)

"Why be depressed? So long as the human world stands,
Your name and signs will endure throughout all the lands.
So long as the wheel treks along ether and stars,
You grant *this* gist of how the world self-understands."

299. Myths Choice (انتخاب افسانه)

"Even if you live for five hundred years or more,
You will become at last a myth others explore.
So, if you're to become a myth, O the wise one,
Be a myth of those whom people love, not abhor."

300. From Dead Bone (از استخوان رمیم)

"In the Kind Giver who can from nothing create
Lose no hope if your sins have been little or great.
If you die Ruined in *this* Drunkenness today,
From your spoiled bones new tomorrows He'll germinate."

301. Wheel's Grand Tent (خرگاه چرخ)

"Khayyam! Even though your Grand Tent of the blue wheel
Was fastened but its door to talk remained in seal,
Like the Wine's froth in being's Cup, the Wine-Tender
Will eternally a thousand Khayyams congeal."

302. Tent of Needlessness (خیمهٔ بی نیازی)

"When your birth-chart's Grand Tent Needlessness is recalled,
Hundreds of ascetic shrines will be overhauled.
Shaded by His mercy's tent, Khayyams of the times
Become like the four poles of the Earth, unequaled."

303. Who'll Bear the Fruit? (که را بار دهد؟)

"The life force, from whose tree-branches results so fruit,
And the shell's royal pearl comes from whose art, so mute,
Will attract to His door many seeking Lovers.
Who knows whose soul will unveil your fruit, so astute?"

304. Imagine Not to Be to Be (انگار نباش تا باشی)

"Khayyam! If you're now Drunk from *this* Wine, be happy!
Sitting with a tulip-faced divine, be happy!
Since this world's end is nothingness, then imagine
You're nothing, to appreciate the line: *Be* happy!"

305. Everlasting Life Is This (عمرجاودانی این است)

"Drink *this* Wine, since your everlasting life is *this*!
The ultimate fruit of your youth in life is *this*!
In the season of roses, amid Drunken friends,
Enjoy *this* moment's Drinking since your life is *this*!"

IX. O Wine-Tender (ای ساقی)

306. Wine for that Heart (می برای آن دل)

Last night, from the purest depths of my truthful heart,
An uplifting self in my heart's Tavern said, "Start!
Drink *this* Cup of Wine I've brought!" I said, "I don't drink!"
He said, "Will you, for my heart, that's of yours a part?"

دیشب ز سر صدق و صفای دل من
در میکده آن روح فزای دل من
جامی به من آورد که بستان و بخور
گفتم نخورم گفت برای دل من

307. Where Were You? (از کجا برخاسته ای؟)

O dear! From what horizon did you manifest,
To put to shame a beauty such as the Moon's crest?
The world's charmers groom themselves well for festive days.
But instead *this* festive day is by your charm blessed!

جانا ز کدام دست برخاسته ای
کز طلعت خویش ماه را کاسته ای
خوبان جهان به عید رو آرایند
تو عید به روی خویش آراسته ای

308. Who Can Help? (که رسد فریاد؟)

Wine-Tender! In forgiveness, you're recalling me!
Who but you can cure the sadness befalling me?
If you don't lend me a hand when I'm sad at heart,
Who else can be for joyfulness enthralling me?

ساقی به کرم تو می کنی یاد مرا
غیر از تو که می رسد به فریاد مرا
گر در غم دل تو دستگیرم نشوی
سوی که روم که می کند شاد مرا

309. More Worn Out Than the Dead (ز مرده فرسوده تر)

My heart has been more worn out than those underground
Whose hearts are more restful than mine is on the ground.
Wine-Tender! I wash my robe with blood tears, yet find
It's soaked in more tears than tears in my eyes abound.

ساقی دل من ز مرده فرسوده ترست
کو زیر زمین ز من دل آسوده ترست
هر چند به خون دیده دامن شویم
دامان ترم ز دیده آلوده ترست

310. Can I Be So Lucky? (هرگز بود این بخت؟)

The turquoise wheel left me behind without your Wine.
So, I have to be always begging for your Wine.
Could I be so lucky to Drink from your own hand,
In the Bowl of my head, a Jug full of your Wine?

با ما نگذاشت چرخ پیروزه شراب
زآن روی همی کنیم دریوزه شراب
هرگز بود این بخت که از دست شما
در کاسهٔ سر کنیم یک کوزه شراب

311. Winter's Spring (بهار زمستان)

Wine-Tender, my sadness has become widely known!
But now my Drunkenness has beyond limits grown!
Despite my winter-white hair, from your Line of Wine
My heart's spring seeds in my old head are being sown.

ساقی غم من بلند آوازه شدست
سرمستی من برون ز اندازه شدست
با موی سپید سرخوشم کز می تو
پیرانه سرم بهار دل تازه شدست

312. See I'm Happy (ببین خوشم)

Tender! Look! My heart's happy to see you, for sure!
Your seeds I'm happy to grow, harvest, and procure.
My conscience is now hearing your unspoken heart.
Lovers' Jamsheed Cup is your heart that is so pure.

ساقی نظری که دل خوش از دیدن تست
جان شاد ز خوشه چینی خرمن تست
ناگفته دلت ضمیر ما میداند
جام جم عاشقان دل روشن تست

313. Your Mindful Heart (دل آگاه تو)

O mindful heart behind the joys of festive days!
O beauty whose full Moon's face graces festive days!
To attain its marks of glory, honor, and joy,
From His blessings came forth from your door festive days!

ای خرّم و شاد از دل آگاه تو عید
آراسته باد از رخ چون ماه تو عید
تا کسب سعادت کند و عزّ و شرف
آمد به مبارکی به درگاه تو عید

314. Your Face Bests Jamsheed's Cup (رخت ز جام جمشید بهتر)

Wine-Tender, your face is finer than Jamsheed's grail!
Dying in your way bests an immortal life's sail!
Your step's dust enlighten paths so brightly for eyes
That beside each, hundreds of thousands of Suns pale!

ساقی که رخت ز جام جمشید به است
مردن به رهت ز عمر جاوید به است
خاک قدمت که چشم من روشن از اوست
هر ذرّه ز صد هزاران خورشید به است

315. Our Soul (جان ما)

Wine-Tender! Your Moonlit face lights the souls of all.
It is my sweetheart and the heart-stealer of all.
It's like the Sun, not like its water reflection.
It belongs not to me but to the hearts of all.

ساقی مه رخسار تو جان همه است
دلدار منست و دل ستان همه است
خورشید صفت نه مهر در آب خوشست
تنها نه از آن من که ز آن همه است

316. Rooster's Wine (بادۀ خروس)

I've been sad and at my wit's end, indeed, Tender,
With my gut wrenched from folks and their misdeed, Tender.
Sing your morning rooster songs from *this* Cup's mouth.
Its Wine is red like the rooster-eye seed, Tender.

جانم به غم آمده ستوه ای ساقی
در دل گره است ازین گروه ای ساقی
این بانگ خروس از دهن می پیش آر
از بادۀ چون چشم خروه ای ساقی

317. Past Wine Drinking (می خوری در گذشته)

My not drinking wine is not because I am strapped,
Nor because I'd be drunken or in scandal trapped.
I drank for my heart's joy; but since you've now settled
In my heart, from now on I'll let *your* Wine be tapped.

من می نه ز بهر تنگدستی نخورم
یا از غم رسوایی و مستی نخورم
من می ز برای خوشدلی می خوردم
اکنون که تو در دلم نشستی نخورم

318. New Food (قوت نو)

Tender! Your Ruby Wine now nourishes my soul.
Your face is the morning Sun's edifying whole.
Rise to my aid now, since dying to your feet brings
More joy than a thousand Noah lives can on roll.

ساقی می لعل قوت روح است مرا
دیدار تو خورشید صبوح است مرا
برخیز که در پای تو مردن نفسی
خوشتر ز هزار عمر نوح است مرا

319. Devoted I Stand (سر بفرمان)

Here I go, submitting to your Wine's new command!
Facing *this* Cup's laughing lips, devoted I stand,
The Decanter's throat held in your Wine-Tending grip,
Wine's life dripping from the lips of *this* Cup in hand.

ماییم نهاده سر به فرمان شراب
جان کرده فدای لب خندان شراب
هم ساقی ما حلق صراحی در دست
هم بر لب ما ساغر آمده جان شراب

320. New Praying (دعای نو)

My praying *this* Rogue way will now be underway.
I'll do *this* praying also five rounds every day.
Where there's a Cup, you will find that, like a Glass Jug,
My neck is stretched for *this* Wine in *this* Drunken way.

کردیم دگر شیوهٔ رندی آغاز
تکبیر همی زنیم بر پنج نماز
هر جا که پیاله ایست ما را بینی
گردن چو صراحی سوی او کرده دراز

321. Won't Leave (سفر نخواهیم گرفت)

O Wine-Tender! I will no longer leave your door.
Dying in your path will bring fear to me no more.
Even if you do not resurrect me from dust,
I won't leave your path that I've long been searching for.

ساقی ز درت سفر نخواهیم گرفت
گر هم بکشی حذر نخواهیم گرفت
گیرم که ز خاک بر نگیری سر ما
ما سر ز ره تو بر نخواهیم گرفت

322. Fill Up (پر کن)

O Wine-Tender! From the depths of my soul and creed
Fill my Cup since *this* is now my sweet life! Proceed!
Although Drinking *this* Wine is not these people's way,
Drinking your Cup's Sweetheart is now my way indeed!

ای ساقی از آن می که دل و دین منست
پر کن قدحی که جان شیرین منست
گر نیست شراب خوردن آئین شما
معشوقه به جام خوردن آئین منست

323. Hit the Veins (رگ بزن)

O Tender! Break my name that's been fame and shame prone.
Hit repentance and piety's jug to the stone.
O harp-player! You're the true healer, come on forth!
Hit the harp's veins and draw vials of *this* Wine's tone.

ساقی برخیز و نام بر ننگ بزن
قرابهٔ زهد و توبه بر سنگ بزن
مطرب تو طبیب راست قولی پیش آی
قاروره می گیر و رگ چنگ بزن

324. Brazenness (گستاخی)

O Tender! From *this* Wine that your Ruby lip tends,
My heart won't let go until all my breathing ends.
I'm brazen in meeting you because of your Wine,
A brazenness that from my wish's depth extends.

ساقی ز میی که لعلت آنرا ساقیست
دل بر نکنم تا دمی از من باقیست
مشتاقم از آن بدیدنت گستاخم
گستاخی من ز غایت مشتاقیست

325. Absent Wine (می غایب)

Wine-Tender! Look! Now, of thoughts, my heart is empty.
Its lions have left, my head's thicket is empty.
Every night the wheel's glass is brimming with some froth,
Now that it's my turn, again, *this* Glass is empty.

ساقی نظری که دل ز اندیشه تهی ست
شیران همه رفته اند و سر بیشه تهی ست
هر شب ز حباب کف زدی شیشهٔ چرخ
امروز که دور ما بود شیشه تهی ست

326. Healer of Pain (طبیب درد)

O Wine-Tender! My heart is full of your desire!
O come back and heal this Drunkards' pains with your fire!
Dying to hear your footsteps is my only hope.
While I'm living, it's all that I wish to acquire.

ساقی دل من سوخته از مشتاقیست
باز آ که طبیب درد مستان ساقیست
جان دادن امید است مرا در قدمت
تا جان بودم امیدواری باقیست

327. For God's Sake (بهر خدا)

Tender! Glance more at us lonely ones, for God's sake!
Break the fever of desiring ones, for God's sake!
We are dead fish and you're the elixir of life!
Make us into consummated ones, for God's sake!

ساقی نظری به بیکسان بهر خدا
بشکن تب ما بوالهوسان بهر خدا
ما ماهی مرده ایم و تو آب حیات
ما را به وصال خود رسان بهر خدا

328. Heart's Cure (مرهم دل)

O the cure that heals our broken hearts, come over,
Since our problem can be solved when you cross over.
Bring a Jug of your Wine such that we may assist,
Since for sure our clay will become jugs all over.

تشریف ده ای مرهم خون دل ما
کآسان به تو می شود همه مشکل ما
تا کوزهٔ می به خدمتت نوش کنیم
چون هست یقین که کوزه گردد گل ما

329. Letting Chatters Go (رها از گفتگو)

O Wine-Tender! Bring me *this*, your Musk-Scented Wine,
So I let the chatters go of this mind of mine.
Bring a Jug of *this* Wine, before the lasting time
Makes a pitcher of my dust that comes from your Line.

در ده می لعل مشکبو ای ساقی
تا باز رهم ز گفتگو ای ساقی
یک کوزهٔ می بده از آن پیش که دهر
خاک من و تو کند سبو ای ساقی

330. Wine's Chain (زنجیر می)

Lay your Cup of *this* wholesome Ruby on my hand.
Lay your Glass Jug that's a fine beauty on my hand.
Bring forth *this* Grapevine that is twisting like a chain.
I've gone Mad, come and tie it fully on my hand!

آن بادهٔ خوشگوار بر دستم نه
وان ساغر چون نگار بر دستم نه
وان می که چو زنجیر بپیچد بر خود
دیوانه شدم بیار بر دستم نه

331. Moment's Detachment (دمی رهایی)

Offer me *this* purple-hued Drink, O Wine-Tender,
Since from grief my life's on its brink, O Wine-Tender.
It will help me detach and be free for a while
From what my low selves and times think, O Wine-Tender.

در ده می همچو ارغوان ای ساقی
کز غصّه به لب رسید جان ای ساقی
تا بو که شوم بیخبر و باز رهم
از خویش و زمانه یک زمان ای ساقی

332. Arise (برجه)

Raise me, raise me, from the Sleep of mine, O Tender.
Serve me! Serve me from your pure Divine, O Tender.
Before they make a jug from a cup of my skull,
From your Jug to my Cup flow *this* Wine, O Tender.

برجه برجه ز جای خواب ای ساقی
در ده در ده شراب ناب ای ساقی
زان پیش که از کاسهٔ سر کوزه کنند
از کوزه به کاسه کن شراب ای ساقی

333. Bragging (لاف زنی)

My being blamed for trickery will reach its height.
Rise O Tender and bring your Wine that's pure and light!
I will pawn my prayer rug and robe for *this* Wine
To last, bragging that I could with you reunite.

334. Tend the Wine (در ده شراب)

Since the death angel does not offer us a chance,
Then from today on, your Cup of this Wine advance.
Futile grieving is not what the heart is made for,
Given these few days of our worldly existence.

335. Stealing A Breath (ربودن دمی)

O Tender! The morning cleared the black flag of night.
Rise and swiftly bring *this* Magi Wine that's so bright!
Let me steal one more breath of life, since this blue wheel
Has stolen from the hands of time many outright.

336. Hurry (بشتاب)

Since the times are passing so hurriedly, Tender,
Lay *this* Cup of Wine in my palm quickly, Tender.
Early dawn is the best time to unlock *this* Door.
Bring it since the Sun is rising swiftly, Tender.

337. Pure Wine (می ناب)

O Wine-Tender! Bring me your purest Wine at dawn
And let it, Cup after Cup, for Drunkards be drawn.
Drunkards are Ruined in the ruin of this world.
So, spread your Songs in this ruined world on and on.

338. Rise O Idol! (برخیز بتا)

Rise O idol! Come and for the sake of our heart,
To solve our problem at hand, your Beauty impart!
Bring a whole Jug of Wine so we may Drink before
They make many more jugs from our clay from the start!

The Robaiyat of Omar Khayyam:
Part 2 of 3: Songs of Hope
Addressing the Question "What Is
Happiness?"

رباعیات عمر خیام: بخش دوم از سه بخش: آوازهای امید در پاسخ به سؤال «سعادت چیست؟»

X. Drunken Way (راه مستی)

339. There's Nothing But God (جز هست خدا نیست)

There is nothing but God and what's from Him; I know.
I read it in the book of this heavenly show.
Ever since my heart's eye saw the true light of God,
Shades of faithlessness in my faith could never grow.

جز هست خدا نیست یقین میدانم
از دفتر کائنات این میخوانم
چون دیدۀ دل به نور حق بینا شد
شد ظلمت کفر محو در ایمانم

340. Shows His Grace Day and Night (جمال می نماید شب و روز)

Where's the heart that can lift, for once, a veil from Him?
Where's the ear that can hear, for once, a word from Him?
The Beloved shows His face every night and day.
Where's the eye that can see, for once, a sign from Him?

کو دل که بداند نفسی اسرارش
کو گوش که بشنود دمی گفتارش
معشوقه جمال می نماید شب و روز
کو دیده که تا برخورد از دیدارش

341. Where's That Heart? (آن دل کجاست؟)

Where's the heart that freed itself of 'love or vengeance,'
Or the eye that saw faiths and unfaiths' convergence?
Where's he who freed himself from "being's start or end"
And saw no light but His certitude's emergence?

آن دل که ز مهر و کینه ببرید کجاست
وآن دیده که کفر و دین یکی دید کجاست
آن کس که ز آغاز و انجام وجود
فارغ شد و جز یقین نوردید کجاست

342. Raw to Cooked (خام به پخته)

O heart! You have not tried even once to retreat,
Since you feared in knowing yourself you'll face defeat.
You've not felt the pain of even a night's exile!
How can your raw self converse with One so complete?

ای دل به مجرّدی نرفتی گامی
چون زهرۀ آن بود که جویی کامی
تو درد فراق نیم شب برده نه ای
در صحبت او کجا رسی تا خامی

343. Head Praying? (نماز سر؟)

If you rote-learn and profess some divine knowing,
How about the faithlessness that's in you growing?
When you lay down your forehead on the ground to pray
Leave there all the chatter that's in your head flowing.

گر علم لدنی همه از بر داری
با این چه کنی که نفس کافر داری
سر را به زمین چه می نهی بهر نماز
آنرا به زمین بنه که در سر داری

344. Prayer Game? (بازیچۀ نماز؟)

From among those who left, not even one returned
To share with you what from beyond the veil they learned.
It's through heartfelt prayers that worshiping succeeds.
Mindless prayers are games that just begin and end.

رفتند و ز رفتگان یکی نامد باز
تا با تو بگوید سخن از پردۀ راز
کارت ز نیاز میگشاید نه نماز
بازیچه بود نماز بی صدق و نیاز

345. Self-Critique (نقد خود)

Until when should I exhibit such shallowness
That has been due to my own state of mindlessness.
So, I will wear from now a Magian faith's belt
That is made, you know of what? Of *my* Muslimness.

تا چند کنم عرضهٔ نادانی خویش
بگرفت دل من از پریشانی خویش
زنّار مغانه بر میان خواهم بست
دانی ز چه چیز از مسلمانی خویش

346. Servitudes (بندگی ها)

Idol house and Ka'beh are both sites of worship.
The tolling of bells are all songs of worship.
The belt, the church, the bead rosary, and the cross,
Truly, they also all serve as signs of worship.

بتخانه و کعبه خانهٔ بندگیست
ناقوس زدن ترانهٔ بندگیست
زنّار و کلیسیا و تسبیح و صلیب
حقّا که همه نشانهٔ بندگیست

347. Heart Mecca (کعبهٔ دل)

In the holy paths, two ka'behs rose from the start:
One ka'beh in clay, and then one ka'beh in heart.
Do your best to make pilgrimage to people's hearts.
A thousand times better is the heart-touching art.

اندر ره دین دو کعبه آمد حاصل
یک کعبهٔ دلهاست و یک کعبهٔ گل
تا بتوانی زیارت دلها کن
کافزون ز هزار کعبه باشد یک دل

348. Mecca of Presence (کعبهٔ حضور)

In your quest for God, empathize with people's hearts.
Seeking His Presence, be present to people's hearts.
Do not equal one heart, a hundred clay ka'behs.
To go to your ka'beh try touching people's hearts.

در راه نیاز هر دلی را دریاب
در کوی حضور مقبلی را دریاب
صد کعبهٔ آب و گل به یک دل نرسد
کعبه چه روی برو دلی را دریاب

349. High Spirituality (رتبت ابرار)

If you seek a higher spiritual knowing,
Do not approve acts that are oppression-sowing.
Don't worry about your life, or your livelihood,
Since they both will be gone in just a breath's blowing.

خواهی که تو را رتبت ابرار رسد
مپسند که کس را ز تو آزار رسد
از مرگ میندیش و غم رزق مخور
کین هر دو به وقت خویش ناچار رسد

350. Be Arrow, Not Bow (تیر باش نه کمان)

Whether a Zoroastrian, Muslim, or Jew,
Let your soul from selfishness to wholeness debut.
Whatever sect you're from, be straight like an arrow,
Since otherwise you'll be bowing to a guru.

گر گبر و جهود و گر مسلمان باشی
از خود بگذر تا همه تن جان باشی
در هر ره کیش راست باشی چون تیر
ور نه چو کمان لایق قربان باشی

351. See For Yourself (از دیدهٔ کن روایت)

Don't boast of a hunting, if a hunter you're not.
Don't boast of a reading, if a reader you're not.
Even if a truthful elder guides you, learn from
Your own seeing, if a blind follower you're not.

صیّاد نه ای حدیث نخچیر مکن
چیزی که نخوانده ای تو تقریر مکن
چون پیر حقیقت از تو معنی طلبد
از دیده بکن روایت از پیر مکن

352. Fixed and Wandering Stars (ساکنان و سرگردانان)

The fixed-star masses that adorn this turning dome
Are the enlightened wise masters' frequenting home.
Beware not to lose touch with *their* intellect's thread,
Since the planet ones do in daze their whirling roam.

353. Intellect's Shackle (عقیلهٔ عقل)

Involved in science and intellect, I became.
I supposed that aware of secrets I became.
'Intellect' became a shackle, 'science' a veil.
Once I learned this, weary of them both I became.

354. Bull-Milking (گاو نر دوشی)

Those who use only their thinking powers to seek,
What they draw is the bull's milk, not cow's, when they speak.
It's best that they wear an asylum robe instead,
So that in intellect's trade, they don't sell their leek.

355. Knowing Not Knowing (دانستن ندانستن)

No one unveiled the secret of chance on its trail,
Nor did one ever destiny's secret unveil.
All said something based on their intellect alone.
So, nothing was learned about the end of the tale.

356. Knowing After Death? (دانستن پس از مرگ؟)

If the heart the life's secret, as it is, could know,
After death, its knowledge of God's secrets could grow!
Today, still with a self, you do not know this world!
What knowledge will your selfless tomorrow bestow?

357. Intellect Not Enough (عقل ناکافی)

The cause of the turning of the Sun's golden grail,
Or the end of this well-founded existence tale,
Cannot be known with just the intellect alone,
Nor can they be known on a comparison scale.

358. Ant or Wolf (مور یا گرگ)

O wise! If, as you wish, the world has not turned out,
"Seven or eight spheres" is not worth fretting about!
When you die your wishes, too, die away with you.
You'll be chewed up by ants or wolves without a doubt!

359. Whim to Breath (هوس تا نفس)

'Tomorrow' is a whimsical fiction, O wise!
About eternity, don't braggingly surmise!
These days the wise know that everything on this Earth
Is like a breath an existence that's born and dies!

ای مرد خرد حدیث فردا هوس است
در دهر زدن لاف سخنها خرس است
امروز چنین هر که خردمند کس است
داند که همه جهان چنان یک نفس است

360. Non-Dualism (دو نبینی)

To understand the world affairs, whoever came,
For him, joy, toil, or sorrow will all be the same.
The world's good and bad will certainly come and go,
Whether you are healed now or in much pain aflame.

آنرا که وقوف است بر احوال جهان
شادی و غم و رنج بر او شد یکسان
چون نیک و بد جهان به سر خواهد شد
خواهی همه درد باش و خواهی درمان

361. Take and Go (بردار و برو)

O sir! Know that this vainly-running-away wheel
Did many young or old folks, like you and me, steal.
Why worry about when the world began or ends?
Steal from life your share and run, since it's still a deal!

ای خواجه بدان کین فلک بیهده دو
همچون من و تو دید بسی کهنه و نو
آغاز و سرانجام جهان را چه کنی
از عمر نصیب خویش برادر و برو

362. A Day Bests A Century (روز به از صد سال)

Those who cannot tell what's a symbol from what's real
Will pass long nights praying to God in their appeal.
I'm free from that, since in *this* secret tent, a day's
Plea bests a hundred-year mindless prayer's ordeal.

آنها که ندانند حقیقت ز مجاز
مشغول نمازند به شبهای دراز
من فارغ از آنم که درین پردهٔ راز
یک روزه نیاز به ز صد ساله نماز

363. Fasting and Meditation (روزه و مراقبه)

Two things bring wisdom, they said a long time ago,
More than any traditions you may ever know:
Better than all the food you can eat is fasting.
Better than talking, meditation helps you grow.

دو چیز که هست مایهٔ دانایی
بهتر ز همه حدیث ناگویایی
از خوردن هر چه هست ناخوردن به
وز صحبت هر چه هست به تنهایی

364. A Mindful Breath (یک نفس)

A breath determines whether you're faithful or not!
A breath determines whether you're doubtful or not!
Mindfully cherish *this* dear breath that's passing, since
A breath determines whether you're fruitful or not!

از منزل کفر تا به دین یک نفس است
وز عالم شک تا به یقین یک نفس است
این یک نفس عزیز را خوش میدار
کز حاصل عمر ما همین یک نفس است

365. Self-Mirror (خودآینه)

The opinionated are each other's mirrors.
But they are not aware of themselves, like mirrors.
To become an enlightened mirror, self-reflect!
Reflecting you, they too may become self-mirrors.

صاحبنظران آینهٔ یکدگرند
چون آینه از هستی خود بیخبرند
گر روشنی ای می طلبی آینه وار
در کس منگر تا همه در تو نگرند

366. Self-Seeing (دیدن خودشمول)

The eye itself must also be seen when seeing,
While from world affairs meditatively freeing.
It's *you* who do not yet have the eye to see Him.
Otherwise, He's all, and we, His humans being.

در دیده و دیده دیده میباید بود
از جمله جهان بریده میباید بود
تو دیده نداری که ببینی او را
ور نه همه اوست دیده میباید بود

367. Wave or Ocean? (موج یا دریا؟)

Any sign that's expressed on existence's board
Is a form in which the One His artwork explored.
When the ancient sea manifests a wave anew,
It remains the sea, though its name 'wave' they accord.

هر نقش که بر تختی هستی پیداست
آن صورت آن کس است کان نقش آراست
دریای کهن چون چو زند موجی نو
گر چه موجش خوانند در حقیقت دریاست

368. Idol's Lesson (درس بت)

An idol told its worshiper, "O devotee!
Do you know why you are prostrating before me?
In me is reflected in the form of yourself
The face of the ever-watchful beauty that's He."

بت گفت به بت پرست کای عابد ما
دانی ز چه روی گشته ای ساجد ما
بر ما به جمال خود تجلّی کردست
آن کس که ز تست ناظر ای شاهد ما

369. Flimsy Branch (شاخی سست)

In time the roses of learning have never blown
Since no one has treated time as it must be known.
Let go of barren branches, since today's the time
That yesterdays are learned and tomorrows are sown.

در دهر بر نهال تحقیق نرست
زیرا که در این راه کسی نیست درست
هر کس زده است دست در شاخی سست
امروز چو دی شناس و چو فردا نخست

370. Meditate (سر کن در گریبان)

In the whirling robe of this old renewing wheel
A time to meditate to join with the Friend steal!
Your hand that has found no start or end to the times
Don't deprive of *this* Cup of Wine's long tale ordeal.

در دامن این چرخ نو انگیز کهن
با دوست تو سر ز یک گریبان پر کن
دستی که زمانه را نه سر یافت نه بن
کوته مکن از می که دراز است سخن

371. Open Heart's Eye (دیدهٔ دل بگشا)

Go close your head's eyes, so that your heart's eye opens.
Meditate, so your eye to a new world opens.
When your eyes rise above all the worldly penchants,
Your life's vision to more praiseworthy states opens.

رو دیده ببند تا دلت دیده شود
زان دیده جهان دگرت دیده شود
چون چشم تو از روی جهان گشت فراز
احوال تو سر به سر پسندیده شود

372. Selfishness for How Long? (خودپرستی تا کی؟)

For how long will you spend life in selfish routines,
Just thinking of what 'being' or 'non-being' means?
Sip *this* Wine: Is the life that's doomed to end best spent
In *this* Drunken Wakefulness or Sleep's dreamy scenes?

عمرت تا کی به خودپرستی گذرد
یا در پی نیستی و هستی گذرد
می نوش که عمری که اجل در پی اوست
آن به که به خواب یا به مستی گذرد

373. Let Go (بگذر)

One crowd assert that everything is there to take,   قومی گویند جمله برداشتنی است
That their house full of ease and riches they should make.   این خانه به ناز و نعمت انباشتنی است
But when it comes to my turn my intellect says,   نوبت چو به من رسید عقلم فرمود
"Drink *this* Wine in joy and let go, since Cups will break!"   خوش خور بگذر که جمله بگذاشتنی است

374. Created or Eternal (چه محدث چه قدیم)

Since we will not stay in this two-doored lodge of time,   چون نیست مقام ما در این دیر مقیم
Letting go of *this* Wine and Love would be a crime.   پس بی می و معشوق خطایی است عظیم
Why should I fear or be hopeful for the time's length?   تا کی ز قدیم و محدث امیدم و بیم
Who cares if it ends or not, if no longer I'm?   چون من رفتم جهان چه محدث چه قدیم

375. Fish and Duck (ماهی و بط)

Once from a duck asked agitatedly a fish: با بط میگفت ماهئی در تب و تاب
"Will the brook's water ever flow back, if we wish?"   باشد که به جوی رفته باز آید آب
The duck answered, "Who cares if it flows to the sea   بط گفت چو من و تو بگشتیم کباب
Or to its mirage, if we're grilled now for a dish!"   بود از پس مرگ ما چه دریا چه سراب

376. Pearl of Tear (دُرِ اشك)

There has not been a night in my wondering years   شب نیست که عقل در تحیّر نشود
That I've not been showered by *these* Pearls made of tears.   وز گریه کنار من پر از درّ نشود
But a maddened head's Cup not always fills with Wine,   پر می نشود کاسۀ سر از سودا
Nor does a downturned Cup fill again, it appears.   هر کاسه که سرنگون بود پر نشود

377. Drunken Awareness (مست هشیاری)

Now that truths and certainties are not yet at hand,   چون نیست حقیقت و یقین اندر دست
One should not let a lifetime on doubtfulness stand.   نتوان به امید شک همه عمر نشست
Beware not to lay down *this* Wine's Cup from your palm.   هان تا ننهیم جام می از کف دست
Know-nots neither learn nor Drunkenly understand.   در بیخبری ست مرد نه هشیار نه مست

378. Mystic Wine (شراب معرفت)

People who Drink the wisdom of *this* mystic Wine,   آنانکه شراب معرفت نوش کنند
Forget about all things except for the Divine.   از هر چه بجز دوست فراموش کنند
Those who have been given just the tongue lack vision,   آنرا که زبان دهند دیدن ندهند
And those given vision toward silence incline.   وآنرا که دهند دیده خاموش کنند

379. Wine and wine (می و می)

O heart! Don't become a drunken waste from *that* wine,   ای دل حذر از مستی و مخموری کن
And from befriending its heavy drinkers resign.   وز همدمی رطل گران دوری کن
This Wine brings health but *that* wine's drunkenness, distress.   از باده شفا خیزد و از مستی رنج
Don't avoid *this* healing, but *that* illness decline.   تو حذر شفا مکن ز رنجوری کن

380. Cooked or Raw? (پخته یا خام؟)

For the heart, it matters not if a seed's a bait.
As it faces the mosque, it can be a cup's mate.
That is why we seek the Beloved through *this* Wine.
Tavern-cooked is better than a convent-raw state.

دل فرق نمی کند همی دانه ز دام
رویش به مسجدست و رویش به جام
با این همه ما و می و معشوق مدام
در میکده پخته به که در صومعه خام

381. Wine and Raisin (انگور و میویز)

Obsessing about distinctions by mind alone
Does not make what exists or not fruitfully known.
O wise! Seek *this Juice* of the world's distinctive grapes,
Since the ignorants' unripe grapes are raisin prone.

آنان که اسیر عقل و تمییز شدند
در حسرت هست و نیست ناچیز شدند
رو با خبرا تو آب انگور گزین
کان بیخبران به غوره میویز شدند

382. Drunken Wisdom (خرد مست)

Losing my lower selves, I reach my true self more.
But when I seek after high ranks, I succumb more.
It's intriguing that from *this* Wine of existence
When I Drink, I begin to feel that I know more.

چندان که ز خود نیست ترم هست ترم
هر چند بلند پایه تر پست ترم
زین طرفه تر از آنکه از شراب هستی
هر لحظه که هشیارترم مست ترم

383. School and Minaret (مدرسه و مناره)

Unless Ruined is the false school or minaret,
Then Rebuilt by Drunkard freeseekers' work and sweat,
Unless faith and unfaith inform one another,
You cannot a true faithful from someone beget.

تا مدرسه و مناره ویران نشود
از کار قلندران بسامان نشود
تا ایمان کفر و کفر ایمان نشود
یک بنده حقیقتاً مسلمان نشود

384. Gnostic State (حال عارف)

What exists becomes known through images and signs.
Only he knows this who like mystics reads *these* lines.
Sit and Drink from *this* Wine in *this* Cup. Cheer the Sips!
Be free from all the impossible-dream confines.

این صورت کون جمله نقشست و خیال
عارف نبود هر که نداند این حال
بنشین قدحی باده بنوش و خوش باش
فارغ شو ازین نقش خیالات محال

385. Intellect's Chain (بند عقل)

It's best to enliven heart with *this* Cup of Wine
To become free from 'past and future' chatters' twine.
Let's unshackle our spirits that have been borrowed
And free them from the narrow intellect's confine.

آن به که به جام باده دل شاد کنیم
وز آمده و گذشته کم یاد کنیم
وین عاریتی روان زندانی را
یک لحظه ز بند عقل آزاد کنیم

386. Brawl, Drink, Agitate (خروش، نوش، جوش)

Oh, let's go to the convent and brawl there a bit,
Pass by the Tavern, to Drinking call there a bit!
Let us sell our turbans and our books for *this* Wine!
Let's go to the school, agitate all there a bit!

هان تا به خرابات خروشی بزنیم
بر میکده بگذریم و نوشی بزنیم
دستار و کتاب را فروشیم به می
بر مدرسه بگذریم و جوشی بزنیم

387. School to Tavern (مدرسه به میکده)

We hung piety's robe on *this* Barrel of Wine,
Abluting ourselves with Dust in *this* Ruin's shrine,
So that we may recover, from *this* Tavern's Dust,
The life that we so wasted in the school's confine.

ما خرقهٔ زهد بر سر خم کردیم
وز خاک خرابات تیمّم کردیم
باشد که ز خاک میکده دریابیم
آن عمر که در مدرسه ها گم کردیم

388. Heart's Eye (دیدهٔ دل)

If you do not open the eye of your heart's mind,
In this world a true vision you will never find.
Therefore, Sip *this* Wine *today*; Drink it *all*, Jug-full!
Don't let today's hope be to the next day consigned.

تا دیدهٔ دل ز دیده ها نگشایی
هرگز ندهند دیدهٔ بینایی
امروز ازین شراب جامی در کش
منشین تو بر امید پس فردایی

389. Why Beg? (دریوزه چرا؟)

Those who have heard the good news from God, the Divine,
They've shunned the entire cosmic spheres as a shrine.
Why should I seek Him through some middle-men's blessing,
When I can seek His blessing through His own Grapevine?

آنها که ز معبود خبر یافته اند
از جملهٔ کائنات رخ تافته اند
دریوزه همی کنم ز مردان نظری
مردان همه از قرب نظر یافته اند

390. Ways of Hearing (راههای شنیدن)

"When I hold in my arms the Stealer of my heart,
The good or bad of the times from my thoughts depart."
A Drunkard does not hear the mystic words I said,
But hears them like the wise trained in *this* Drinking art.

با دلبر خود دست در آغوش کنم
نیک و بد ایّام فراموش کنم
مست ار چه کلام عارفان کم شنود
این نکته بسان عاقلان گوش کنم

391. Better Run Away (بگریزی به)

From ascetic or school ways run away, indeed!
To caress the Beloved's Hair instead proceed.
Before the times shed your red blood on the low ground
Shedding *this* Glass Jug's red Blood in Cup must precede.

از درس علوم و زهد بگریزی به
و اندر سر زلف دلبر آویزی به
زآن پیش که روزگار خونت ریزد
تو خون صراحی به قدح ریزی به

392. Why Futile Stress? (چرا غم بیهوده؟)

Drinking *this* wholesome Wine for our nature is best
When done with the ill-famed wheel's star-burned and depressed!
Since the eternal past led us all to this point,
Why should we all be about its final end stressed?

آن به که به طبع بادهٔ خام کشیم
با سوختگان چرخ بدنام کشیم
چون در ازل آنچه خواست بودن بودست
بیهوده چرا غم سرانجام کشیم

393. Better Ruined (خراب اولیٰ تر)

With happy friends *this* Cup of Wine would be better,
When I feel shedding tears of mine would be better.
Since this world below the last sphere won't be loyal,
Drinking from *this* Sphere below nine would be better.

با یار خوشم جام شراب اولیٰ تر
وز دست غمش دیده پر آب اولیٰ تر
چون عالم دون وفا نخواهد کردن
در عالم دون مست و خراب اولیٰ تر

394. Thought's Obsession (وسوسهٔ فکر)

Let go of the mind's obsessive thought-chains, O heart!
Drink from *this* Cup *now* and let your boredoms depart!
Be free and single-purposed, cherishing *this* Wine
To become human through its soul-perfecting art!

بگذار دلا وسوسهٔ فکر محال
در کش قدح باده و بگذر ز ملال
آزاده شو و مجرّد و باده پرست
تا مرد شوی رسی به سر حدّ کمال

395. Brim-to-Brim (مالامال)

The talk-talk of the world's griefs and sorrows now end!
Awaken now, *now*, from Sleep to a joy-now trend!
When the Earth becomes green from its end to end, Drink
Gulp-gulp of the Sips poured from *this* Ruby-now blend!

چند از غم و غصهٔ جهان قالاقال
برخیز و به شادی گذران حالاحال
از سبزه چو شد روی زمین میلامیل
در کش می ز لعل از قدح مالامال

396. Wined Elderly (پیر مست)

I saw a restful old man, from *this* deeply Wined.
Swept of all thinking was his body's house of mind.
Excitedly, Wine-full, and resting Drunk, he was
Humming, "To His creatures, God would be surely kind!"

پیری دیدم به خواب مستی خفته
وز گرد شعور خانهٔ تن رفته
می خورده و مست خفته و آشفته
و اللّهُ لطیفٌ بعباده گفته

397. Retire to A Corner (کناره گیر)

For the wise who retreat to a corner, it's best
To learn from the ancients who're of wisdom abreast.
Drink *this* Wine and kiss such Ruby-natured idols
To find amid the turmoil of this world some rest.

آن به که خردمند کناری گیرد
وز خلق گذشته اعتباری گیرد
می خورد و لعل بتانی بوسد
در عالم شوریده قراری گیرد

398. We Are Marbles (رخامیم همه)

While my two hands hold *this* book, like a Jug, ajar,
Sometimes I am sin-free, and sometimes go too far.
We are just like marbles under this turquoise dome.
Neither full Muslims nor full pagans, each we are.

یک دست به مصحفیم و یک دست به جام
گه مرد حلالیم و گهی مرد حرام
ماییم در این گنبد فیروزه رخام
نه کافر مطلق نه مسلمان تمام

399. Go Drink This Wine (رو این باده خور)

All those who no longer remain, O Wine-Tender,
Fell asleep in their graves, still vain, O Wine-Tender.
Go and Drink *this* Wine and hear *this* truth I'm telling:
They blew air, again and again, O Wine-Tender.

آنان که ز پیش رفته اند ای ساقی
در خاک غرور خفته اند ای ساقی
رو باده خور و حقیقت از من بشنو
باد است هر آنچه گفته اند ای ساقی

400. His Pure Wine (می طهور او)

O Tender! *This* Cup of Wine that brings light to all
Fill since it brings His presence's insight to all.
Be glad since impurities will be forgiven
By the One who brings a Wine that's so bright to all.

ساقی قدحی که نور بخشد همه را
پر کن که دمی حضور بخشد همه را
خوش باش که هم ببخشد آلایش ما
آن کس که میی طهور بخشد همه را

401. Talk Until When? (تا چند حدیث؟)

How long talk of senses, elements, five and four?
Why fret about a problem or a thousand more?
O Wine-Tender! We are all dust, so play your harp!
We are all wind, Tender; bring *this* Wine to the fore.

تا چند حدیث پنج و چار ای ساقی
مشکل چه یکی چه صد هزار ای ساقی
خاکیم همه چنگ بساز ای ساقی
بادیم همه باده بیار ای ساقی

402. Allowed Wine (می حلال)

O love! Drink *this* Wine that is now settled and pure,
With Idol beauties who have heart-stealing allure.
This Wine is the Blood of Di-"vine" spirit, saying,
"I've allowed you to Shed my Blood! Enjoy *this* cure."

جانا می صاف نامشوّش میخور
بر یاد بتان نغز دلکش میخور
می خون رز است و رز تو را میگوید
خون بر تو حلال کرده ام خوش میخور

403. Fall Madly in Love (مجنون شو)

Madly fall in Love to seek the Beloved's heart,
Freed from the world and yourself, meditating start.
Connect with Lovers above when the way opens.
Retreat with your eyes closed and silently depart.

گر صحبت لیلی طلبی مجنون شو
وز خویشتن و جمله جهان بیرون شو
در خلوت عاشقان گرت راه دهند
بی دیده در آ و بی زبان بیرون شو

404. Transcending Twoness (عبور از دوئی)

Go along this path such that the twoness departs.
If there's twoness, efforts' pulling-throughness departs.
You will not become Him for sure, but if you try,
You will reach a point where all your you-ness departs.

چندان برو این ره که دوئی برخیزد
گر هست دوئی ز رهروی برخیزد
تو او نشوی ولی اگر جهد کنی
جائی برسی کز تو توئی برخیزد

405. O God, Intoxicate Me (یا رب، مستم کن)

O God! Free me from being judged worthy or not?
Busy me with You; free me from my me-me plot!
While just thinking, I'm caught in good-or-bad twoness.
Intoxicate! Free me from my good-or-bad lot.

یا رب ز قبول و از ردم باز رهان
مشغول خودت کن ز خودم باز رهان
تا هشیارم ز نیک و بد میدانم
مستم کن و از نیک و بدم باز رهان

406. Neither That, Nor This (نه آن، نه این)

One crowd are searching in religion for a way.
One crowd pursue the way of science, so *they* say.
I'm afraid that one day a voice will cry out loud,
"The way is neither this nor that, O gone astray!"

قومی متفکرند اندر ره دین
قومی به گمان فتاده در راه یقین
می ترسم از آنکه بانگ آید روزی
کای بیخبران راه نه آن است و نه این

407. State of Drunkenness (مرتبۀ مستی)

The appearance of what exists or not, I know.
The essence of what high and low's about, I know.
I would be ashamed of my knowledge, however,
If higher than *this* Drunkenness a thought I know.

من ظاهر نیستی و هستی دانم
من باطن هر فراز و پستی دانم
با این همه از دانش خود شرمم باد
گر مرتبه ای ورای مستی دانم

XI. Willfulness (اراده)

408. Symbol's Truth (حقیقت مجاز)

O heart! Since the world's truths are symbolic insights,
Why be sad about the world's long tormenting plights?
Let chance take its course and cope with the pains because
This pen, having written, never for you rewrites!

409. Won't Build A Shop (کارگاهی ننهند)

In the heavens equally whirling are the spheres,
Yet we are given unequal lots, it appears.
That's how it is, so go seek after contentment.
They won't build a new shop to sell your joy arrears!

410. Futile Worrying (غم خوردن بیهوده)

For a long time have existed all that exist.
Pen's writings of good and bad will always persist.
Fate has already given you what it must have.
Futile worrying and trying, you must resist.

411. Why Cry? (چرا فریاد؟)

It's so bewildering, the motion of the sphere.
Contemplating fails to grasp the depth of the sphere.
Since nobody is free from the sphere's tyranny,
Why cry over the Aries-Taurus of the sphere?

412. Wax in Hand (موم در دست)

If livelihood, like life, can't be made less or more,
Don't sadden your heart about seeking less or more.
Molding my life or yours, beyond a point like this
Wax in my hands, can't be done any less or more.

413. Life's Backgammon (تخته نرد زندگی)

In life's backgammon we tossed five-six; soul, two-one.
Whoever is born dies. Is there doubt, anyone?
Whatever food that is spread on the sphere's table
Turns out to be full of salt or ends up with none.

414. Chance's Arrow (تیر قضا)

Since your thumb does not control your luck-arrow's throw,
Be content if things, as you have wished, do not go.
Be happy since in your deeds, whether good or bad,
You hold the strings of neither past nor tomorrow.

چون تیر قضا گشاده از شست تو نیست
راضی شو اگر کار به بایست تو نیست
خوش باش که در تصرّف نیک و بدت
سر رشتهٔ روزگار در دست تو نیست

415. Not All Due to You (نه همه چیز از توست)

If things go well for you, they don't all due to you.
If you lose your head, too, you won't all due to you.
Let go and *choose* to be content and live in joy.
The world's good or bad are not so all due to you.

گر کار تو نیکست به تدبیر تو نیست
ور سر برود نیز به تقصیر تو نیست
تسلیم و رضا پیشه کن و شاد بزی
چو نیک و بد جهان به تسخیر تو نیست

416. See 'Now' (حالی بین)

Look at all the wrongful deeds of this whirling dome,
The empty place of all the loved ones gone from home.
Now see yourself living amid *this* moment's breath.
See *now*; to its before or after do not roam.

زین گنبد گردنده بد افعالی بین
وز جملهٔ دوستان جهان خالی بین
تا بتوانی تو یک نفس خود را باش
فردا مطلب دی منگر حالی بین

417. Planted and Reaped (کشت و درود)

The peasant of chance plants us so much in masses
That sorrow is futile when we're cut like grasses.
What goes on today has been going on before.
So, pour *this* Wine swiftly; let's Cheer up our Glasses.

دهقان قضا بسی چو ما کشت و درود
غم خوردن بیهوده نمیدارد سود
پر کن قدح می به کفم ده نه زود
تا باز خورم که بودنی ها همه بود

418. Lips on Lips (لب بر لب)

This sphere is like an upside-down bowl that's turning.
Its bright ones are helpless in its truth-discerning.
Now notice the friendship of *this* Glass with *this* Jug:
How their lips are joined, their Blood across sojourning.

این چرخ چو طاسیست نگون افتاده
در وی همه زیرکان زبون افتاده
در دوستی شیشه و ساغر نگرید
لب بر لب و در میانه خون افتاده

419. Wine-Hair Compass (پرگار می و زلف)

You live in a circle, its two-legged compass lost,
From which the body's chance of lasting life is tossed.
Grasp *this* Ruby Wine's Cup and the Beloved's Hair.
Try taking stock of *their* two-legged compass, you must!

چون نیست درین دایرهٔ بی پرگار
از مایهٔ عمر هیچکس برخوردار
هم در می لعل و زلف دلبر آویز
وین یک دو دم خویش غنیمت میدار

420. Dome's Circling Cup (جام سپهر به دور)

Deeply hidden in that rounded heavenly dome,
A Cup goes around feeding all during its roam.
When your turn comes, Drink *its* Wine in joy! Do not sigh!
It's a circle, so what goes comes brimful back home.

در دایرهٔ سپهر ناپیدا غور
جامیست که جمله را چشانند به دور
نوبت چو به دور تو رسد آه مکن
می نوش به خوشدلی که دور است به جور

421. Never Will (هرگز نشود)

Tender! This world depends on a breath. Pour *this* Wine!
Even one breath taken in joy would be divine!
Enjoy *now*, since what will come your way from this world
Will not always with your heart's desires align.

422. Breeze, Dust, Heat, and Mist (نسیم، گرد، شرار، و نم)

If your mixture of natures meets your moment's needs,
Be happy *despite* what's been cruel in heaven's deeds.
Take the wise as your friends since you are, after all,
Mostly a passing dust, heat, and mist that still breathes.

423. Even the Wheel Knows Not (چرخ هم بیخبر است)

Be happy and think, when you tend to agonize,
That sorrow and joy will have their turns to arise.
Beware not to feel too wounded by the wheel's acts,
Since even the wheel knows not why it whirls the skies.

424. It's Been Like This (آنچه بود بود)

The ascetic's benefits are not great, Tender,
Given what his outer *acts* indicate, Tender.
O Wine-Tender! Fill up my Cup with *this* Wine soon
Since from the start it's been like this our state, Tender.

425. Whole in You (کلّ در تو)

This, your being, is the being of another,
And your Drunkenness is the same of another.
Go and meditate on this to know that your hand
Is the sleeve for a hand acting for another.

426. Is What Is (هست آنچه هست)

Other than God there cannot be a judge as fit.
Existence can't a thing against His Will admit.
What exists is how it's supposed to be changing.
What is not how it should be, can't being befit.

427. Prince to Garlic (میر تا سیر)

One day I'm dressed by the sphere, as if I'm a prince.
One day I'm undressed like garlic, sent for the rinse.
I now care less about why its turns made me sad,
Than why *I've let* such futile sadness age me since!

428. Sphere's Secret Confession (گفت فلک پنهانی)

One day in my heart's ear the sphere secretly said,
"Do you think what happens by chance is by *me* led?
Had I had a hand on my own whirling around,
I would have freed *myself* from wandering instead!"

429. Field of Causes (صحرای علل)

Those who rush to explain a thing's field of causes,
Ignore the role the thing itself plays in causes.
So, as they blame the past for today, the next is
Unchanged since stayed the same its yesterday's causes.

430. Poorer Wheel (چرخ بیچاره تر)

The good and the bad that are found in humankind,
Or the joys and sorrows that are chanced or destined,
Don't blame on the wheel since, as far as wisdom goes,
The wheel has a thousand times less choice than your mind.

431. Don't Give In, Don't Beg (گردن منه، منّت مکش)

So long as there are in you bones, muscles, and veins,
Don't leave the fort that fate also built you: your brain's.
Don't cede even if your foe is Rostam of Zāl!
Don't beg even if Hatam Tai your friend remains!

XII. Foes and Friends (دوست و دشمن)

432. Foe Wrongly Said (دشمن به غلط گفت)

The foe wrongly said that a philosopher I am.
God knows I am not whatever he said I am.
But as I've come to this sorrow's nest, after all,
Why can I *myself* not know at least who I am?

433. My Faith (ایمان من)

Faithlessness, from one like me, cannot come easy.
There cannot be a faith stronger than that in me.
In all time there's one like me. If I was faithless,
There would not have been a Muslim eternally.

434. Be Fair (انصاف بده)

What you say about me arises from a spite.
Calling me a faithless man is your daily rite.
I confess to whatever I am; however,
To be fair, to judge me so, what gives *you* the right?

435. Woman's Question (سؤال زن)

A sheikh told a harlot, "You excessively drink!
Each time in the trap of yet another you sink!"
The woman replied, "O sheikh, what you say is true.
But are you who *you* pretend to be, do you think?"

436. Hundred Bites (صد لقمه)

If you don't drink, then don't taunt Drunkards, O sober!
Don't build your life on deceptiveness, moreover.
Don't be proud of your sobriety, since you are
To a hundred greater bites enslaved all over!

437. Foe's Mirror (آینۀ دشمن)

The foe who's always seeing me in a bad light,
Does so unwisely and for sure he is not right.
He looks inside and finds there a mirror and then,
Mistaking his dead soul for me, he thinks he's bright.

438. My Mirror (آینهٔ من)
Why bother with what he, who's a nobody, said,
When a fault in me is like a hundred portrayed?
I am a mirror, so whoever looks at me,
It is his own good and bad that become displayed.

439. Real Hell (دوزخ به یقین)
I'd die for someone who is a trustworthy friend.
A head for his sake would be easy to expend.
But if you wish to know what hell is, certainly,
It's the time that with the untrustworthy you spend.

440. They Hate Their Souls (از جان خود بیزارند)
These people in schools, holding their titles and roles,
From distress and anxiety hate their own souls.
When one's not like them enslaved to greed, notably
They treat him as if a non-human being strolls.

441. Defamers (بدنام کنندگان)
Those who have not burned at all any midnight oils,
Those who have not stepped out of their own selfish soils,
The ignoble who're dressed in fancy noble clothes,
Do nothing but defame a few men's noble toils.

442. Uncooked (خامان)
Wearing their patch-clothing of greed, raw men, a few,
Not walking the path of true and pure men, a few,
Having learned a few alphabets from Sufi talks,
All they do is stain the names of good men, a few.

443. Stone, Wax, Bow, Arrow (سنگ، موم، کمان، تیر)
If I'm strong, they smelt me just like an ore of stone.
If I'm soft, they melt me like wax without a bone.
If I bend, they try to pull me in like a bow.
If I walk straight, like an arrow, away I'm thrown.

444. Famed for Talking Nonsense (به کرخی معروفان)
Some who are known for their coarse, wool-garmented wraps,
And for begging handfuls of water and bread scraps,
Say they're from Junaydi or Shibli paths. They're not,
But being famous for talking nonsense? Perhaps.

445. Buy-Nothing Crowd (نخران)

What profits can come from this dumb buy-nothing crowd?
What science can you sell these ignorance endowed?
Not once do they offer a grain of salt each year,
Yet each day they shout a hundred insults aloud.

446. Reply to Takfiris (پاسخ به تکفیریان)

Toward these ignorant folks, who are just a few
And from ignorance assume all they know is true,
Act just like an ass since as asses that they are
They call all but asses infidels in *their* view!

447. Bulls and Asses (گاوان و خران)

There's the Pleiades on the Bull's hump in the skies!
There's another bull that the Earth on its back lies!
Now open your wisdom's eyes to certitude and
See how a handful of asses in between flies!

448. Who's Blood-Thirstier? (کدام خونخوارتر؟)

O rules-issuer! We are busier than you!
Despite *this* Drunkenness, we're soberer than you!
You drink human blood; we Drink the Blood of *this* Vine!
Be honest! Who is Blood-Thirstier: We, or you?

449. Aren't You Ashamed? (شرمت ناید؟)

Aren't you ashamed of behaving ill very much,
Of neglecting just rules of living very much?
Let's suppose that the entire world becomes all yours.
Beside letting it go, could you do very much?

450. Blame for How Long? (تا چند ملامت؟)

O the naive ascetic! How long will you blame
Us for tavern-going, for drinking, or the same?
Grieve your bead counts of hypocrisy and deceit,
And let us be with *this* Wine and Loving aflame.

451. Who Are You To Teach God? (حق را تو کجا آموختنی؟)

O the burned one, the burned out, and burnable one!
O one from whom the flames of hell must have begun!
How long will you ask for God's mercy for Omar?
Who are *you* to teach how God's mercy should be run?

452. Go Fix Your Eyes (رو چارهٔ دیده کن)

O sir! Let us live life to fulfill who we are.
Be quiet and let God judge us for who we are.
We walk a straight path, but you see it as twisted?
Go fix your own eyes; free us to be who we are.

ای خواجه یکی کام روا کن ما را
دم در کش و در کار خدا کن ما را
ما راست رویم و لیک تو کج بینی
رو چارهٔ دیده کن رها کن ما را

453. Zoo (باغ وحش)

Your soul is like a house dog that is often bound.
Nothing comes from it but an empty-bellied sound.
It has fox's attributes; sleeps like a rabbit;
Snarls like a leopard; its wolf-deceit is renowned.

نفست به سگ خانه همی ماند راست
جز بانگ میان تهی از او هیچ نخاست
روبه صفتست و خواب خرگوش دهد
آشوب پلنگ دارد و گرگ دغاست

454. Fire and Water (آتش و تر)

Would it not be a pity if a hand like mine
Holds an office or pulpit, instead of *this* Wine?
You're a dry ascetic and I'm a Wet Lover.
Have you heard that fire and water intertwine?

دست چو منی که جام و ساغر گیرد
حیفست که او دفتر و منبر گیرد
تو زاهد خشکی و منم عاشق تر
آتش نشنیده ام که در تر گیرد

455. Where Were They? (کجا بودند؟)

Those who said I'd burn in fire, where is its smoke?
If I piled up wealth, what profit records I broke?
He who said that I was just a wine-house dweller,
About which kind of wine-house did he so much spoke?

از آتش ما دود کجا بود اینجا
وز مایهٔ ما سود کجا بود اینجا
آن کس که مرا نام خراباتی کرد
در اصل خرابات کجا بود اینجا

456. Pupil's Disrespect (بی احترامی شاگرد)

One day with the right faith to a ruin I went,
Wearing there a Magian belt for the event.
Yet, a pupil there, fearing of my infamy,
Washed my seating after discarding my garment.

رفتم به خرابات به ایمان درست
زنار مغانه در میان بستم چست
شاگرد خرابات ز بدنامی من
رختم بدر افکند و خرابات بشست

457. Jug-Breaker (صراحی شکن)

A sordid-bodied man appeared from far away.
His shirt smelled as if he'd had a hell of a day.
He then broke *this* Jug so it would be shorter-lived,
Wasting such a tender Wine of my soul in play!

از دور پدید آمده ناپاک تنی
وز دود جهنم به تنش پیرهنی
بشکست صراحیم که عمرش کم باد
وانگه می چو لطیف مردی چو منی

458. Wasted Sheriff (محتسب دایم مست)

In the school, *these* Drinkings and music are debased,
Neither harp, nor reed, nor *these* heartful songs embraced.
Rogue Drunkards have quit drinking *that* wine for *this* Wine,
But the town's sheriff remains just a drunken waste!

در مجلس درس ساز مستی پست است
نی چنگ و نه نای و نه دم در دست است
رندان همه ترک می پرستی کردند
جز محتسب شهر که دایم مست است

459. Hello-Bye (سلام و کلام)

Invitation came from someone's forbidden land!
Whose friendship? What humanity? Whose helping hand?
The best in this world is to withdraw from them all.
So, from afar I said "hello-bye" to his brand.

460. Friend or Foe (دوست یا دشمن)

In these times, it's better to befriend people less.
Engaging them from afar brings more happiness.
In the person on whom you relied all your life,
Looking wisely, you'll find ill-will too in progress.

461. Changing Affection (لطف پویا)

The same moon you thought was a gracious angel's seat,
Looking back, you'll find it's with devilry replete.
The beauty's face that used to make your winter warm
Is today a woolen coat in the summer's heat.

462. Enough Already (بس است)

If rose wasn't my lot, thorns are enough already.
If light doesn't reach me, flames are enough already.
If sect, monastery, or sheikh, were not for me,
Church's bell and belt all are enough already.

463. Sufi Prayer (دعای صوفیانه)

May *this* Tavern be full of Drunkards constantly.
May ascetic robes be thrown in flames instantly.
May dark woolen cloaks, torn in a hundred pieces,
Carpet dusty roads for a pained man urgently.

464. Friendship or Ill-Intention (خویش یا بداندیش)

If he is trustworthy, a stranger is a friend.
Acting ill-intendedly, he's just a pretend.
If a bitter drug helps, it leads to a sweet cure.
If sweets harm you utterly, you'll bitterly end.

465. Sweet Poison, Poisonous Sweet (زهر نوش، نوش زهر)

Engage with those folks who are pure at heart and wise,
But run away for miles from untrusted allies!
If the wise pour you a cup's bitter advice, drink!
But the sweets from those who're untrustworthy despise!

466. Humble Rogue (رند پشت دست)

A man is not good if people know he is bad
But, fearing his wrath, treat him as a friendly lad.
A rogue man who reveals a benevolent hand
Will be treated by other rogues like a comrade.

مرد آن نبود که خلق خوارند او را
وز بیم بدی نیک شمارند او را
رندی که نمود روی دستی به کرم
رندان همه پشت دست دارند او را

467. Don't Drip (مچکان)

No matter how sad about the times you may be,
Sad about the wheel's oppression and tyranny,
Beware not to taste a drop offered by the vile,
Even if you are burning intolerably.

هر چند ز دست دهر غمکش باشی
وز جور و جفای چرخ ناخوش باشی
زنهار ز دست ناکسان آب زلال
بر لب مچکان اگر در آتش باشی

468. Life's Wine-Drinking Bench (مصطبهٔ عمر)

By *this* Wine-Drinking bench, facing infamy woes,
I'm at my wit's end from the slanders of raw foes.
Where is the strength in my feet to support my life
So I can walk away before the angel blows?

در مصطبهٔ عمر ز بدنامی چند
سیر آمدم از سرزنش خامی چند
کو قوّت پایی که مرا گیرد دست
تا پیش اجل برون نهم گامی چند

469. Bravo Grief! (آفرین بر غم)

I'd offer my life for those who're honest with me.
But of the low lives of the Earth, let there less be.
Due to my poverty no one remained a friend.
O grief! A thousand bravos for *your* company!

جانم به فدای مردم همدم باد
وز روی زمین سفله و ناکس کم باد
از بی درمی کسی مرا یار نشد
جز غم که هزار آفرین بر غم باد

470. Sea's Overflow? (سر رفتن دریا؟)

Tender! Were my heart in *this* Wine to overflow,
It could not, since it's ocean; where to overflow?
But that Sufi's thin jug is so full of nonsense
That one Sip of *this* Wine leads it to overflow.

ساقی می من ز دست اگر خواهد رفت
دریاست کجا ز خود به ته خواهد رفت
صوفی که چو ظرف تنگ پر از جهل است
یک جرعه اگر خورد به سر خواهد رفت

471. Worse Than Death (از مرگ بدتر)

Living for a hundred years in the heart of fire,
I would tolerate the burning that would transpire!
But I'd rather not deal with untrustworthy folks.
Death is better than their company to acquire.

صد سال در آتشم اگر محل بود
آن آتش سوزنده مرا سهل بود
با مردم ناهل مبادم صحبت
کز مرگ بتر صحبت ناهل بود

472. Ill-Wisher's Self-Abuse (خودآزاری بدخواه)

He who is an ill-wisher will not reach his goal.
One ill deed begets him a hundred ills on roll.
I'm wishing you well, but you wish me ill instead.
Your ill-wish does not hurt me, but you hurt your soul.

بدخواه کسان هیچ به مقصد نرسد
یک بد نکند تا به خودش صد نرسد
من نیک تو خواهم و تو خواهی بد من
تو نیک نبینی و به من بد نرسد

473. O Scarecrow! (ای که نه)

O scarecrow know-it-all! What's cloak-wrapped in your self!
The cloak causes neither hope nor fear by itself,
Whether you wear burlap on your body or head,
Whether it's a sack or a silk from the top shelf.

474. O Darvish (ای درویش)

Darvish! Tear from your body the clothing of form,
So that you don't give in to the clothing of norm.
Go and put on your poverty's ragged old klim,
And your royal drum under klim clothing perform.

475. Hairsplitting Knower (دانا مو به مو)

The Wise Knower of the spheres knows your secrets, all.
From hair to hair, and from vein to vein, He knows all.
Let's suppose that you can fool people with deceit.
What do you do with the One who knows each and all?

476. Deed Knowing (فعل شناسی)

Why should local storms frighten the surrounding sea?
Become human! Know it from what it seems to be.
Bad never comes from good, nor does good come from bad.
Distinguishing good from bad *in deeds* is the key.

477. Not My Fault (من نکردم از خود)

Working for some just to oppress others? Oh, don't!
Live with, don't abuse, folks who're your brothers. No, don't!
Tomorrow, you'll say, "I did it since I was asked!"
They won't hear your excuse, nor another's! So, don't!

478. How Ignorant! (عجب نادانی)

If you think you can be happy in life despite
Bringing sadness to a calm heart, a lot or slight,
You will mourn your entire life asking yourself,
"Why was I so ignorantly full of the spite?"

479. Suffer, Don't Cause Suffering (میرنج و مرنجان)

As far as you can, do not mistreat other souls.
Do not subject to your wrath's fire other souls.
If you want lasting peace, suffer helping others,
But do not induce suffering in other souls.

480. Friend to Foe, Foe to Friend (دوست به دشمن، دشمن به دوست)

With friends and foes, it's still good to be good in act. با دشمن و دوست فعل نیکو نیکوست
How can a good-natured man badly interact? بد کی کند آن که نیکیش عادت و خوست
If you act badly toward friends, they become foes. با دوست چو بد کنی شود دشمن تو
If you treat your foes well, they'll become friends in fact. با دشمن اگر نیک کنی گردد دوست

481. Be Good (خوب باش)

One should not treat badly the people who are good. با مردم نیک بد نمی باید بود
In wilderness, wild manners should not be pursued. در بادیه دیو و دد نمی باید بود
About one's livelihood, one should not be gloating, مفتون معاش خود نمی باید بود
Nor should one gloat over one's virtues accrued. مغرور به فضل خود نمی باید بود

482. Eye's Pupil (مردمک چشم)

It's a great fault to elevate to heights oneself, عیب است عظیم برکشیدن خود را
In the lives of people to single out oneself. وز جملۀ خلق برگزیدن خود را
One should try to learn from the pupil of the eye: از مردمک دیده بباید آموخت
To see others' needs, not selfishly just oneself. دیدن همه کس را و ندیدن خود را

483. Anonymous Living (زندگی گمنام)

Walk such that people don't bow to you on the street. در راه چنان رو که سلامت نکنند
Live such that people don't rise for you on their feet. با خلق چنان زی که قیامت نکنند
If you go to a holy place, enter it such در مسجد اگر روی چنان رو که تو را
That you're not seen as someone on a lofty seat! در پیش نخوانند و امامت نکنند

484. From Intellect to Wine (از خرد تا می)

Since wisdom is not appreciated in these days, چون نیست درین زمانه سودی ز خرد
No one but the ignorant folks in these days sways. جز بیخرد از زمانه بر می نخورد
Then serve me *this* Wine that washes away dull thoughts. پیش آر از آن که او خرد را ببرد
Perhaps the times may then accommodate *our* ways. تا بو که زمانه سوی ما بر نگرد

485. Bowl and Dices (طاس و کعبتین)

From all the loose-talker's nonsense do not go mad. از هرزه به هر دری نمیباید باخت
Endure the times' good and bad, and do not grow sad. با نیک و بد زمانه میباید ساخت
When fate-and-luck's double dices in the wheel's bowl از طاسک چرخ و کعبتین تقدیر
Come down, you must act asking, "What does the throw add?" هر نقش که پیدا شود آن باید تاخت

486. Time Robbery (زمان دزدی)

How long should I, enduring their oppressive ways, تا چند درین مقام بیدادگران
Bring the days to nights and then the nights back to days? روزی به شبی شبی به روزی گذران
Bring *this* Bowl of Wine, since it's in unawareness هین کاسۀ می که عمر در بیخبری
That life is robbed from our bags, O you gone-astrays! از کیسۀ ما می شود ای بیخبران

487. Denude From Abuse (جفا از تن در کش)

O friend! Rid your heart from the enemy's abuse.
Yourself with *this* bright Wine and a beauty amuse.
Don't deprive yourself of sitting with honest friends.
Denude from vanity and its baseness refuse.

ای دوست دل از جفای دشمن در کش
با روی نکو شراب روشن در کش
با ساده رخی نشین و مگذر از خویش
پیراهن کبر و پستی از تن در کش

488. Cup's Show (نمایش پیاله)

Drink *this* Wine, since the natures of your friends will be
Around *this* Cup, like a mirror, revealed; you'll see.
How long do you cry and say, "Oh, I broke a vow!"
This Glass of Wine is worth a life's vow-breaking spree!

می خور که حریفان جهان را در وی
بر گرد بنا گوش ز می بینی خوی
تا کی گوئی توبه شکستم هی هی
صد توبه شکسته به که یک شیشهٔ می

489. Don't Play Their Game (تو مگرای)

Although, for your eyes, a pleasing world they portray,
Do as the wise would do and its games never play.
So many like you arrive and many will go.
Steal your life's share *today* or be stolen away!

بر چشم تو عالم ار چه می آرایند
مگرای بدان که عاقلان نگرایند
بسیار چو تو روند و بسیار آیند
بربای نصیب خویش کت بربایند

490. Be Simorgh, not Owl (سیمرغ باش، نه بوف)

Happy at heart is he who was never renowned,
Did not himself in robes, gowns, or wool rags surround,
Simorgh-like flew to the peak empyrean sphere,
And sat not, like owls, on this ruined world aground.

خرّم دل آن کسی که معروف نشد
در جبّه و درّاعه و در صوف نشد
سیمرغ صفت به عرش پروازی کرد
در کنج خرابهٔ جهان بوف نشد

XIII. Wealth (ثروت)

491. Violet and Rose (بنفشه و گل)

The wise don't greed after wealth on the silver's trail,   سیم ار چه نه مایهٔ خردمندان ست
But, without some, the world's garden would be a jail.   بی سیمان را باغ جهان زندان ست
The empty-handed violet bows down to kneel,   از دست تهی بنفشه سر بر زانوست
But the rose laughs with golden pollens in its bale.   وز کیسهٔ زر دهان گل خندان ست

492. Free Wealth's Danger (خطر ثروت رایگان)

The food that you eat, or the clothing that you wear   آن مایه ز دنیا که خوری یا پوشی
Are worth all the efforts and the hardships you bear.   معذوری اگر در طلبش می کوشی
Shun the rest, though, even if they're offered for free,   باقی همه رایگان نیرزد هشدار
Since they will sell away your precious life, beware!   تا عمر گرانبها بدان نفروشی

493. Less is More (کمتر بیشتر)

If you earn a loaf of bread for a day or two,   یک نان به دو روز اگر بود حاصل مرد
And drink cool water from a jug that's not so new,   وز کوزه شکسته ای دمی آبی سرد
You won't need to be a servant of someone else   مخدوم کم از خودی چرا باید بود
And bow to others who are human just like you!   یا خدمت چون خودی چرا باید کرد

494. Content With a Bone (قانع به یک استخوان)

Being, even like vultures, content with a bone   قانع به یک استخوان چو کرکس بودن
Is better than relying on a stranger's loan.   به زانکه طفیل خوان ناکس بودن
Eating one's own dry barley bread is much better   با نان جوین خویش حقّا که به است
Than being defiled by the weeds misers have grown.   کآلوده به پالودهٔ هر خس بودن

495. Don't Be a Fly (مگس مباش)

Serving the misers and the ingrates, for how long?   تا چند کنی خدمت دونان و خسان
Whizzing like a fly on others' baits, for how long?   جان بر سر هر طعمه منه چون مگسان
Eat your guts for a day or two and be content!   نانی به دو روز خور مکش منّت کس
Eating someone else's bread or dates, for how long?   خون دل خود خوری به از نان کسان

496. Here I Am! (آید که منم)

Once in a while someone comes and says, "Here I am!"   هر یک چندی یکی بر آید که منم
Amassing gold and silver, he says, "Here I am!"   با نعمت و با سیم و زر آید که منم
When things begin to go well, one day suddenly   چون کارک او نظام گیرد روزی
The angel ambushes him and says, "Here I am!"   ناگه اجل از کمین در آید که منم

497. Fame to Slavery (شهرت تا غلامت)

They named imperial crowns and reigns after you.
They said high heavens, spheres, or shrines are seating you.
Now that they made you their chief leader or imam,
From end to end of horizons their slave is *you!*

498. Greedy Poppy (سگ بچهٔ مایل)

Alas for this poppy dog, just running around,
Moving as fast as the wind, just like a greyhound.
It was so eager at heart for a chunk of bone
That its head was in the round teeth of a boar crowned!

499. Brittle Hair (زلف شکننده)

Don't hold any wishes at heart from vanity.
No one has gone from vanity to sanity.
Like a beauty's brittle hair be humble before
A brittle breath exhales you from humanity.

500. Abusive World (دنیای مردم آزار)

In this world, whenever and wherever you could,
Beware not to breathe except for another's good.
Before you and me it's been proven many times
That this world has on nothing but oppression stood.

501. Lancet and Scale (نیشتر و میزان)

Even if one razor is in town on the ground,
It injures the foot of one who's begging around.
Despite the straightness of the beam of the scale,
It tilts in favor of those whose riches abound.

502. Loaned Breath (نفس عاریتی)

Don't ever envy any wealth they have attained!
Did you see one live forever with what he gained?
Even your breaths are body's loans made out to you!
So, they must be treated like how loans are maintained.

503. Left for the Foe (به دشمن ماند)

Neither does a seed outlast the harvest time's end,
Nor will you and I outlast the farmhouse we tend.
The gold and the silver you've earned, a lot or not,
Will be left for foes if not enjoyed with a friend.

504. Before It Gets Cold (زان پیش که گردد سرد)

Beware! Don't inflict on yourself sorrow and pain
To gather white silver or yellow gold in vain.
Before the air of your breaths cools down to a halt,
Enjoy now with friends what your enemy will gain.

هان تا ننهی بر تن خود غصّه و درد
تا جمع کنی سیم سفید و زر زرد
زان پیش که گردد نفس گرم تو سرد
با دوست بخور که دشمنت خواهد خورد

505. Take A Load Off (بردار باری)

Beware! All that you can in your life's winding road,
Take from a friend's or a stranger's shoulder a load.
These days that things go smoothly will never last,
And will slip away from your hands all your abode.

زنهار کنون که میتوانی باری
بردار ز خاطر عزیزی باری
کین مملکت حسن نماند جاوید
از دست تو هم برون رود یکی باری

506. Don't Scatter (پراکنده مشو)

Be wise in life and don't become enslaved to greed.
To avarice don't succumb and never concede.
Be like the bright fire and like a flowing brook,
But don't scatter like dust by wind of any speed.

گر با خردی تو حرص را بنده مشو
در پای طمع خوار و سرافکنده مشو
چون آتش تیز باش چون آب روان
چون خاک به هر باد پراکنده مشو

507. Wish Unfulfilled (به مراد نابوده)

Why travel the world in a worn body, my friend,
Propelled by greed for a long time, until your end?
They left, we'll leave, and all who'll come will also go,
Not fulfilling what we all did at first intend.

چند از پی حرص در تن فرسوده
ای دوست روی گرد جهان بیهوده
رفتند و رویم و دیگر آیند و روند
یک دم به مراد خویشتن نابوده

508. King Between Nothings (شاه میان دو هیچ)

Have you come to this world to be a king someday?
Wake up! Come to yourself! Don't bring on your doomsday!
You were nothing before and will be nothing next.
Does not that make it clear what you must do *today*?

تو آمده ای به پادشاهی کردن
با خویشتن آی زین تباهی کردن
چیزی نبدی دی و نباشی فردا
پیداست که امروز چه خواهی کردن

509. Both Worth the Same (هر دو یک نرخ)

If to two, three, or ten centuries you cling at last,
You'll be taken out of this old dwelling at last.
Whether you are a king or a bazaar beggar,
Under the ground you will be worth nothing at last.

عمر تو چه دو صد چه سیصد چه هزار
زین کهنه سرا برون برندت ناچار
گر پادشهی و گر گدای بازار
این هر دو به یک نرخ بود آخر کار

510. None Escape (هیچکس جان نبرد)

If you have turquoise, or a horse and arms instead,
To the reign of a few days do not proudly wed.
No one has survived the violence of the sphere.
Today to cups and the next to jugs it will spread.

گر اسپ و یراقست و اگر فیروزه
مغرور مشو به دولت دو روزه
از قهر فلک هیچکسی جان نبرد
امروز سبو شکست و فردا کوزه

511. It's Been Around (بودست)

Before you, passing, a thousand eons have been.
Living on the Earth, both poor and rich ones have been.
Whether the earthly mass was fertile or dried out,
Where you step on, many heads, or someone's, have been.

512. World's Kitchen (مطبخ دنیا)

In this worldly kitchen all you eat is the smoke.
How long in "what I have or not" you sadly poke?
World attachments bring spiritual loss, faiths say.
To profit, free your soul from world attachments yoke.

513. Be Content and Free (آسوده باش و آزاده)

When you establish your sustenance justly such
That it's neither too little nor overly much,
You must take comfort in whatever that you have,
And then from whatever you have detach your clutch.

514. Suppose and Go Free (گیر و آزاد شو)

Your wish to be fulfilled, suppose the wheel decreed.
For piling the profits, suppose you quenched your greed.
From all the wealth and jewels of your heart's desires,
From all that you wished to gain, now suppose you're freed!

515. From Skill and Parentage to Gold (از هنر و نسبت به زر)

A man must either his own line of work uphold
Or be trained to do what his father does, I'm told.
Today, when it has come to our turn, well, it seems
That nothing else matters except for having gold.

516. Terkan's Fair Eyes (چشم خوش ترکان)

Alas! Expert jobs are now held by the naive,
And achievement tools held by those who can't achieve.
Seeing Terkan's fair eyes that is pleasing the hearts
Is a favor that only their servants receive.

517. Goodness and Nothingness (نیکی و هیچی)

What can withstand the angel's arrow is nothing.
The worth of richness, gold or silver, is nothing.
The more I think about the world, the more I find
That goodness is its true wealth and the rest nothing.

518. One Night or Two (یکی دو شب)

Not even for one night hurt anybody's heart!
Not even for one night let his 'Oh God, no!' start!
Do not depend on what you own, nor on your looks,
Since they'll be gone one night, or a few nights apart!

آزار دل خلق مجوئیم شبی
تا بر نکشند یا ربی نیم شبی
بر مال و جمال خویشتن تکیه مکن
کانرا به شبی برند و این را به شبی

519. Tomorrow's Wish (هوس فردا)

Today when your joy is a possibility,
Embrace it! The next lacks reliability.
Beware! Things won't stay with you, as they also have
Escaped other folks' inheritability.

امروز که سوی طربت دسترس است
خوش باش که اندیشهٔ فردا هوس است
دریاب که با تو خود نخواهد ماندن
آنها که به جا ماندهٔ بسیار کس است

520. We're All Beggars (گدائیم همه)

Playthings at the mercy of God's powers, we're all.
He is the true Opulent One; beggars, we're all.
Why should we seek more and more of anything when
We will leave from the same door, since lodgers we're all.

بازیچهٔ قدرت خدائیم همه
او راست توانگری گدائیم همه
با یکدگر این زیادتی جست چه
آخر نه ز یک در به سر آئیم همه

521. Royalty in Poverty (شاهی در فقر)

Formal schools tend to do harm in science's guise,
And endowments obscurantism formalize.
In a ruined spot live content with basic means.
Swear to God, from such a state royalties arise.

از مدرسه ها همه تباهی خیزد
وز لقمهٔ وقف دل سیاهی خیزد
در کنج خرابه یی گدا وار بزی
باللّه که از این مرتبه شاهی خیزد

522. Endowment Bite (لقمهٔ وقف)

Whoever takes a bite from endowment riches,
His lion nature to that of a fox switches.
If you're disinterested, you'll agree with me:
Grant breads cause jealousy and miserly glitches.

از لقمهٔ وقف هر که پرورد جسد
روباه شود اگر چه بوده است اسد
گر بیغرضی مرا مصدّق داری
خاصیت نان وقف بخل است و حسد

523. Dust of Attachment (گرد تعلّق)

A must for being human is high endeavor.
But learning from events, too, marks high endeavor.
A human is one who, from Earthly attachments,
No dust settles on his clothes of high endeavor.

مردی باید بلند همّت مردی
زین واقعه دیدهٔ خرد پروردی
کو را ز تعلّق اندرین تودهٔ خاک
بر دامن همّت ننشیند گردی

524. Being Human (انسان بودن)

If you know your fault, *that* is what makes you human.
If you rule your head, *that* is what makes you human.
You won't become human by beating a fallen.
Help a fallen rise! *That* is what makes you human.

گر در نظر خویش حقیری مردی
گر بر سر خویشتن امیری مردی
مردی نبود لگد بر افتاده زدن
گر دست یکی فتاده گیری مردی

525. Keeping Promises (عهد وفا)

Don't judge a man by his many technical skills,
But based on whether his promises he fulfills.
If he succeeds in keeping the word he's given,
He'll succeed in any undertaking he wills.

526. Unending Greed (حرص ناتمام)

O sir, if your efforts proceed not as you've wished,
Nor your sermon was lasting, or judged distinguished,
Be happy and don't grieve, since world affairs will be
Overwhelming if your greed is not extinguished.

527. Rich or Poor Both Pass (سیر و فقیر هر دو گذرند)

The rich man who eats kabab to dine, too, will pass.
The one who from *this* Cup Drinks Pure Wine, too, will pass.
The darvish beggar who in his worn-out bowl dips
His bread to eat his food as a brine, too, will pass.

528. King and Servant Both Die (کشته هم محمود هم ایاز)

This wheel reveals no secrets! Killed thousands, this sphere,
Of Mahmouds and their dear Ayaz servants, you hear?
Taste *this* Sip, "The sphere gives no one a second chance
And lets no one leaving the world return, it's clear."

529. Kārun's Wealth (گنج قارون)

O heart! Until when will you in this life, so brief,
Increase a thousand-fold your suffering and grief?
Don't sink in greed and wishful thoughts. In this Wine, do!
O sir, did his wealth bring Karun lasting relief?

530. Not a Grain Follows (جوی با خود نبری)

As much as you can do not weigh the world's sorrows.
Do not burden your heart with pasts and tomorrows.
Drink *this* Wine *now* and enjoy the days you have left.
Beware! In your grave, not a grain of wealth follows.

531. Times' Good or Bad (نیک و بد زمانه)

Be content! Don't be greedy! Enjoy what's your share!
Don't let your times' good or bad be more weights to bear!
Caress a lover's hair with *this* Wine's Cup in hand,
Since they will pass soon, or when you too won't be there!

532. Share What You Swallow (لقمه ات باز مدار)
Be honorable and God's just mandates follow.
Do not hold from others what you yourself swallow.
Do not talk behind folks, nor hurt anyone's heart.
Fulfill your hereafter *now!* In *this* Wine wallow!

سنّت بکن و فریضهٔ حق را بگزار
وآن لقمه که داری از کسان باز مدار
غیبت مکن و دل کسی را نازار
در عهدهٔ آن جهان منم باده بیار

533. Wish He Did It Now (اکنون کندی)
Oh, I wish so much that God would transform the world,
And does it now, so I see how His acts unfold!
Either He will take my name off its books for good,
Or make me in His hidden Livelihoods enrolled.

یزدان خواهم جهان دگرگون کندی
و اکنون کندی تا نگرم چون کندی
یا نام من از جریده بیرون کندی
یا روزی من ز غیب افزون کندی

534. Freedom From Dependence (آزادی از منّت)
O God! Open a door for my livelihood's sake!
Free me from depending for the breads I can make!
Make me so Intoxicated from *this* Wine's wealth
That my head does not suffer from ignorance ache!

یا رب بگشای بر من از رزق دری
بی منّت مخلوق رسان ماحضری
از باده چنان مست نگه دار مرا
کز بیخبری نباشدم دردسری

535. Ocean, Diver, and Pearl (دریا، غواص، گوهر)
He who has an eye for the way of self-seeing,
Seeing each, rich or poor, as a human being,
Is one who is ocean, diver, and pearl in one.
Dive in and catch the Pearl that's in *these* words fleeing.

آن کس که به چشم خویشتن ره دارد
در چشم شه و گدا گذرگاه دارد
دریا خود و غواص خود و گوهر خود
هان غوری کن که این سخن ته دارد

536. I'm Happy (خوشیم)
My last grain of grief of the times gone, I'm happy!
Having no food but *this* from the dawn, I'm happy!
Being served *this* Cooked Food from His hidden kitchen,
Not begging raw foods from anyone, I'm happy!

یک جو غم ایّام نداریم خوشیم
گر چاشت بود شام نداریم خوشیم
چون پخته به ما میرسد از مطبخ غیب
از کس طمع خام نداریم خوشیم

537. Darvishhood Wealth (توانگری درویشی)
Two loaves of bread and a spot in this world, I chose.
Of greed for wealth and pomp, I did myself dispose.
I sought true darvishhood to guide my soul and heart.
In my darvishhood's riches, I found true repose.

کنجی و دو قرص از جهان بگزیدم
وز دولت و حشمتش طمع ببریدم
درویشی را به جان و دل بخریدم
در درویشی توانگری ها دیدم

538. King's Envy (نه حدّ هر سلطانی)
If you bring together a loaf of bread of wheat,
And lots of *this* Wine beside a leg of lamb's meat,
With a tulip-faced sitting by a garden side,
It would be any king's envy! Oh, what a treat!

گر دست دهد ز مغز گندم نانی
وز می دو منی ز گوسفندی رانی
با لاله رخی نشسته در بستانی
عیشی بود آن نه حدّ هر سلطانی

539. Bravo, Live in Joy! (گو شاد بزی)

To him in this world who earns his own half of bread,
And enjoys a place called home, where his bedding's spread,
To him who'll be no one's slave, nor an enslaver,
Say, "Live in joy! Bravo! *That's* how life should be led."

در دهر به آنکه نیمهٔ نانی دارد
از بهر نشستن آشیانی دارد
نه خادم کس بود نه مخدوم کسی
گو شاد بزی که خوش جهانی دارد

XIV. Today (امروز)

540. What's Left (چه مانده است)

Of my strength, the Wine-Tender is serving what's left,   از من رمقی به سعی ساقی مانده است
While from talking with people, betrayal's what's left.   وز صحبت خلق بی وفایی مانده است
Of yesterday's wine just a cup remained, I know.   از بادهٔ دوشین قدحی بیش نماند
But of my own days of life, I don't know what's left!   از عمر ندانم که چه باقی مانده است

541. What Good Is It? (چه جای طرب است؟)

If I had a ruby-lipped lover by my side,   گر در بر من دلبر یاقوت لب است
If I drank instead of wine from elixir's tide,   ور آب حیات جای آب عنب است
If Venus sang beside me, Jesus keeping friend,   گر زهره بود مطرب و عیسی همدم
What good would they bring if my heart's joy is denied?   چون دل نبود شاد چه جای طرب است

542. What's My Fault? (تقصیر من چیست؟)

Who is Grief who wishes to bleed our eyes to tears,   غم کیست کزو دو دیده خون باید کرد
And to pull down our joy's flag and conquer our spheres?   یا زو علم طرب نگون باید کرد
Before it gains strength to invade seditiously,   زآن پیش که فتنه یی پدید آید از او
It should be repelled away so our heartland clears.   از مملکت دلش برون باید کرد

543. Water and Wind (آب و باد)

These one, two, or three days of life went by too soon.   این یک دو سه روزه نوبت عمر بگشت
They passed like a brook's flow or a breeze over dune.   چون آب به جویبار و چون باد به دشت
But I think no more of the sorrows of two days: دیگر غم دو روز نخواهم خوردن
One that came before and one coming next in tune.   روزی که نیامدست و روزی که گذشت

544. Wine's Shield Boat (سپر کشتی شراب)

I'll Drink from *this* Wine every day and every night.   خود را به شب و روز در شراب اندازم
I'll escape Drunken from the sphere's oppressive might.   وز جور فلک مست و خراب اندازم
Since the boat of the body will sink, I throw now   چون کشتی عمر غرقه خواهد بودن
This Wine's Shield to waters so I can take a flight.   آن به که سپر بروی آب اندازم

545. Consulted You? (تدبیر با تو؟)

Thinking about 'being,' why do you a life spend,   از بودنی ای دوست چه داری تیمار
Wasting time and heart on useless thoughts 'til your end?   وز فکرت بیهوده دل و جان افکار
Live in happiness! Enjoy *now* this passing world!   خرّم بزی و جهان به شادی گذران
Did they consult you to start all of this, my friend?   تدبیر نه با تو کرده اند اوّل کار

546. You're Not Useless (بیهوده نه ای)

O heart! About this world that is worn out, grieve not!
You're not useless; therefore, uselessly worry not!
What was, has passed away; is not yet, what will be.
Enjoy now and let go of "What is left or not"!

ای دل غم این جهان فرسوده مخور
بیهوده نه ای غمان بیهوده مخور
چون بوده گذشت و نیست نابوده پدید
خوش باش غم بوده و نابوده مخور

547. Exhale or Not (بر آرم یا نه)

For how long should I about having or not wail,
Or ask whether joy in life will, or not, prevail?
Fill *this* Cup with Wine now, since I don't even know
If the air I inhale I shall or not exhale!

تا کی غم آن خورم که دارم یا نه
وین عمر به خوشدلی گذارم یا نه
پر کن قدح باده که معلومم نیست
کاین دم که فرو برم بر آرم یا نه

548. Last Act (آخرِ کار)

Since nothing happens beyond what has been constrained,
About fulfillment, one's heart should not be so strained.
Beware not to put on your heart so much weight since
The last act is to leave here and all that you've gained.

چون نیست تو را جز آنکه دادند قرار
چندین ز پی مراد دل رنجه مدار
هان تا ننهی بر دل خود چندین بار
بگذاشتن و گذشتن است آخر کار

549. Who Can Tell? (کس چه داند؟)

One must not wear out a happy heart with more grief,
Nor waste a happy now with tomorrow's relief.
Who can ever foretell what the next day will bring?
Make your Loved One and *this* Wine your goals-in-chief!

نتوان دل شاد را به غم فرسودن
وقت خوش خود به سنگ محنت سودن
کس غیب چه داند که چه خواهد بودن
می باید و معشوق و به کام آسودن

550. Sorrow's Medicine (دوای غم)

Like the spring's coming and the passing of the cold,
The pages of our existence one by one unfold.
Devour Wine, not sadness, since the wise healer said,
"For sorrows' poison, only *this* Wine's drug is sold."

از آمدن بهار و از رفتن دی
اوراق وجود ما همی گردد طی
می خور مخور اندوه که گفتست حکیم
غمهای جهان چو زهر و تریاکش می

551. Don't Waste This Breath (ضایع مکن این دم)

Today is the day to spend, tomorrow's still not!
Illusive are your thoughts on your tomorrow's plot.
Don't ever waste this moment's breath! Are you insane?
The true worth of your time left no one can allot.

امروز تو را دسترس فردا نیست
و اندیشهٔ فردات بجز سودا نیست
ضایع مکن این دم ار دلت شیدا نیست
کاین باقی عمر را بها پیدا نیست

552. Death and Sleep (مرگ و خواب)

A wise old man said to me during Sleep one night,
"From Sleeping, nobody's roses have bloomed delight.
If you are in Bed now, you may as well be dead.
Drink *this* Wine before sleeping in dust, out of sight!"

در خواب بدم مرا خردمندی گفت
کز خواب کسی را گل شادی نشکفت
کاری چه کنی که با اجل باشد جفت
می خور که به زیر خاک می باید خفت

553. Times' Ignoring (کم روزگاری)

It's best to caress the Beloved's Woven Hair,
To Drink from *this* Cup's Wine that has a Wholesome Flair.
Before your times ignore your existence it's best
To ignore your times' ignorance without a care.

554. Wise Are Ruined (فرزانه درو خراب)

The world's not for positions, nor is it a chair.
Its wise are Ruined, its Sobers in Tavern's care.
Pour *this* water of Wine on sorrow's flame before
You go to the dust, with nothing in hand but air.

555. Water in Waist (آب در کمر)

We came from a water that was hidden in waist,
From a passion's fire that was not spent in waste.
Tomorrow is when the wind blows away our dust.
Enjoy these two breaths with *this* Wine, but not in haste!

556. Don't Sadly Seek (غمخوار مپوی)

Friends are rare in this world's magic-house that's so bleak.
Hear my tale; but remember, of it don't yet speak!
Live with life's pains; never expect from it a cure.
Be happy. Don't sit in sadness, nor sadly seek.

557. This Circle (این دایره)

About the times' sorrows, until when will you grieve?
How long will you your tears and gut's blood interweave?
Drink *this* Wine in feasts and remain happy at heart
Before from this circle you permanently leave.

558. Seeking Excess (بیش طلبی)

Ever since the time the human nature was born,
Its happiness was on its full contentment sworn.
Seeking excess is what caused all the infighting.
So, avoid excess, given your lot, or be torn!

559. Wise Attitude (عاقل چو در نگرد)

The wise people, considering how this world goes,
Indulge in feasts, in happiness, and in repose.
Did you know that the wise in these hard times advise,
"For those who're not consumed by grief, life's passing slows"?

560. Saw With Own Eyes (دیدیم به چشم)

If we remember that our lives will someday end,
We'll be ashamed of thinking of a lasting trend.
I saw with my own eyes that the world's just a wind.
Throw dust on the heads of those who on wind depend!

561. Suppose Achieved (ساخته گیر)

O heart, suppose you have everything that you know,
And your house is full of them, adorned for the show.
Be happy now since like their risings and declines,
You'll also be here for two days before you go.

562. Snowflake in Desert (برف در صحرا)

Suppose all the world, as you have wished, will be yours.
Suppose hundreds of jewels and gold coins will be yours.
Suppose you sit on them like snowflakes in desert.
How many of the snowflakes, suppose, will be yours?

563. Donkey-Rider's Legend (افسانهٔ محمر سوار)

Of the place where you're living in, why are you proud?
Can a donkey-rider be legend's fame endowed?
You are sleeping with wind, yet you light a candle?
How can a house built on a flood-path not be plowed?

564. Not a Moment (نه یک ساعت)

O one who from ignorance blew your life, so dear,
And helped the death angel easier to appear!
You've had enough means to think for two hundred years,
Yet don't find a second to ask why you are here.

565. Let Ignorance Go (بنه تو جهل)

O one who've been promoted, you can be depressed,
O one pampered in comfort, you can still be stressed.
So, let your ignorance go as much as you can.
Don't oppress others so that you won't be oppressed.

566. Lustful Self (نفس شهوانی)

Constantly, after vain and lustful selves of yours,
You indignify all the noble selves of yours.
Are you not aware that are like plague for your soul
Those wishes that arise from baser selves of yours?

567. Lust and Base Passions (شهوت و هوا)

I say, if after lust and base passion you go,
It will be after soul's deprivation you go.
See instead who you are and where you have come from.
Know the way and to what destination you go.

568. Detach From Possessing (ترک تعلق)

If you greed after *that* cup's wine and ruby lips,
If you're caught in a drum's, a harp's, or a reed's grips,
God knows, they too are marginal desires since
You're nothing unless from attachments your soul strips.

569. Detachment Skill (مایهٔ تجرید)

A heart that can't free itself from attachments' hold,
The poor thing will be for life in regrets enrolled.
Except for the free-minded who allow for joy,
Much grief from whatever that exist will unfold.

570. Bird and Wild Horse (مرغ و توسن)

Hear this word from me about how your end is set:
Your heart's wish is a bird that is not in your net.
If you have not tamed your young Wild Horse of the sphere,
Don't be depressed that the days don't your ends beget.

571. Next Breath (آن دم)

We fear we don't have enough time left in this world
To meet all our soulmates who're also growing old.
Then, we must be taking note of *these* single breaths,
Since our lives' next breaths may be too late to unfold.

572. Don't Fear (مترس)

From the hazards of time's eroding road, don't fear!
What's not everlasting in this abode, don't fear!
This breath is like cash, so use it for happiness.
What came before now and what is followed, don't fear!

573. Enjoy Now (حالی خوش باش)

Yesterday's grief that passed, you don't need to recall.
About the next's, not yet here, there's no point to howl.
Don't rely on what passed, nor on what has not come.
Don't waste life! Enjoy *now*, even for something small!

574. Life's Chance (فرصت عمر)

Even if a breath's left from your life, waste it not!
Drink *this* Wine mindfully, don't chatter; waste it not!
Don't listen to the mind saying, "Life's good or bad"!
Life's not those; it's a wonderful *chance*! Waste it not!

بر باد دمی ز عمرت ار هست مده
می خواه و جواب عقل سرمست مده
مشنو ز خرد کاین بد و آن نیک بود
عمر این همه نیست فرصت از دست مده

575. Straw and Mountain (کاه و کوه)

O heart! In this passing world, be no longer sad!
O weak straw! To your weight, don't let the mountains add!
This life is much shorter than what you've imagined.
Let go of the lengthy hopes in the life you've had!

ای جان دل ریش بر جهان بیش منه
وی کاه ضعیف کوه بر خویش منه
کوته تر از آن است که پنداری عمر
چندین امل دراز در پیش منه

576. Your Turn (نوبت تو)

Wake up! No more mourn this world's sorrowful passing.
Relax and *invent this* moment's joyful passing!
Had the world been by its nature faithful to you,
Your turn would not have come for a tearful passing.

برخیز و مخور غم جهان گذران
بنشین و دمی به شادمانی گذران
در طبع جهان اگر وفایی بودی
نوبت به تو خود نیامدی از دگران

577. Don't Let Go of Wine (بی باده مباش)

Don't give in to the grief that unjust times unfold.
Don't teach your soul the sadnesses the past enrolled.
Don't fall in Love except with a Sweet-Lipped Divine.
Don't let go of *this* Wine and wastefully grow old.

تن در غم روزگار بیداد مده
جان را ز غم گذشتگان یاد مده
دل جز به شکر لب پریزاد مده
بی باده مباش و عمر بر باد مده

578. Since You Know (چون واقفی)

O friend, since you know that many secrets abound,
Why do you expect in vain that they'll all be found?
If something doesn't go as you wish in this world,
At least enjoy this moment you are still around.

چون واقفی ای دوست که هست اسراری
چندین چه خوری بیهده هر تیماری
چون می نرود به اختیارت کاری
خوش باش در این نفس که هستی باری

579. Time's Sickle (دهرهٔ دهر)

Don't let the bygones of your life turn your face pale.
Fearing what is yet to come is of no avail.
Take your fair share from the betraying wheel before
The lasting time draws out its sickle to assail.

از آمده ها زرد مکن چهرهٔ خویش
وز نامده ها آب مکن زهرهٔ خویش
بستان تو ز چرخ بی وفا بهرهٔ خویش
زان پیش که دهر بر کشد دهرهٔ خویش

580. Untanglings (بندگشایی ها)

Before your name fades away at last from this world,
Fade away grief with *this* Wine whose Cup now you hold.
From hair to hair untangle your Beloved's Hair,
Before you are untangled in a grave gone cold.

زان پیش که نام تو ز عالم برود
می خور که چو می ز دل رسد غم برود
بگشای سر زلف بتی بند ز بند
زان پیش که بند بندت از هم برود

581. Seek Wine Quickly (هین باده)

O heedless! This coy world seeks your complicity.
Don't buy it, since you know of its duplicity.
Don't let your dear life be blown away by such winds.
Seek your Friend through *this* Wine's flood of simplicity.

582. Breath's Taking (دم غنیمت)

Happy is the one who lived in these hard times free,
Finding what God created satisfactory,
Mindfully took every treasured breath of his life,
Thinking freely, Drinking *this* Wine, living simply.

583. World's Prime Wealth (سرمایهٔ جهان)

Every single breath that in your lifetime passes,
Breathe it as if everything its joy surpasses.
Beware that the world's prime wealth is your breath of life.
So, spend its coins such that joyfulness amasses.

584. Freethinker's Way (راه قلندر)

Don't walk except in *this* freethinkers' Drunken way!
From *this* Wine's music and your Beloved don't stray!
With *this* Cup on your palm and Pitcher on shoulder
Drink Wine, O Beauty, to chase mind's chatters away!

585. Path of Blame (کوی ملامت)

This path of blame is for those dying for the truth,
Those who gamble all to clean their slate for the truth.
Humanness needs freethinking and audacity
To search chivalrously and fiercely for the truth.

586. Less or More Chance (قضا کم و بیش)

Why grieve over a task whose time has not yet come?
It's having lengthy hopes that people suffer from.
Enjoy *today*! Don't let the world depress your heart.
From being sad, chances don't more or less become.

587. Not Depending on Others (ز دگر نمی باید خواست)

It's been a hard life, my works have gone on tangent.
Hardships increased; comfort is more or less stringent.
But, I thank God that the basics whose lack brings harm
I don't beg from others, when a need is urgent.

588. My Youth's Turn (نوبت جوانی من)

Today, when it's my season to feel young at heart,
I Drink *this* Wine since from it my joys of life start.
Don't fault Wine for bitterness. It is also sweet.
It's bitter like it is *this*, my life-telling art.

امروز که موسم جوانی من است
می نوشم از آن که شادمانی من است
عیبش مکنید گرچه تلخ است خوش است
تلخ است چرا که زندگانی من است

589. Drum and Falcon (طبل و باز)

Do you know why *this* small instrument drum is played?
So that a lost one returns from where he had strayed.
Or why are a falcon's eyes covered before flight?
So it flies as high as its *own* visions persuade.

دانی به چه می زنند این طبلک ساز
تا گمشده ای ز راه باز آید باز
دانی که چرا دوخته شد دیدهٔ باز
تا باز به قدر خود کند دیده فراز

590. Don't Deny the Sea (منکر بحر مشو)

Be mindful of *now*, not of the future or past.
Self-reflect and yourself in emptiness recast.
If you wish to submerge in His unity's sea,
Don't deny the sea, nor feel like the sea's outcast.

در پس منگر دمی و در پیش مباش
با خویش بباش و خالی از خویش مباش
خواهی که غریق بحر توحید شوی
منکر مشو و نیز بد اندیش مباش

591. Be Civil (آباد زی)

If pained, be content, live a civil, graceful life.
Don't overcomplicate; live free, a playful life.
Overestimating yourself brings only grief.
Caring about lesser ones brings you joyful life.

با درد قناعت کن و آباد بزی
در بند تکلّف مرو آزاد بزی
منگر به فزونی ز خود و غصّه مخور
در کم ز خودی نگه کن و شاد بزی

592. Doesn't Just Threaten (نکند گرای آزار)

In this world, to the extent that you can, beware!
Not a breath without *this* Wine, or its Tender, spare!
Know that, before you and me, so many have learned
That this world does not simply threaten to impair!

گر هست تو را درین جهان دسترسی
هان تا نزنی بی می و ساقی نفسی
پیش از من و تو بیازمودند بسی
دنیا نکند گرای آزار کسی

593. We're All Guests (همه مهمانیم)

The world is a guesthouse; we're its guests, as you know.
Do you suppose you'll still be lodged in tomorrow?
In both worlds, the only One who stays on is God.
All the rest in the world are guests who come and go.

دنیا چو رباط و ما درو مهمانیم
تا ظن نبری که ما درو می مانیم
در هر دو جهان خدای میماند و بس
باقی همه کلّ من علیها فانیم

594. Wine That is This Word (می که همین ست سخن)

For how long should I be grieving to comprehend
Why I arrived at this old lodge, and how I'll end?
O Wine-Tender! Before I close my bag to leave,
Bring me the Wine of *this* Line that is being penned.

تا کی غم آن خورم کزین دیر کهن
احوال مرا نه سر پدیدست و نه بن
زین پیش که رخت ازین سرا بربندم
ساقی بدهم می که همین ست سخن

595. Freed From a Thousand Tasks (رستی ز هزار پیشه)

Why do you give in to the mind's worries, O heart,
And fear being cut like trees from your root apart?
Do you fear being taken elsewhere from this world?
Be glad that a thousand hardships you won't restart.

596. Five-Fingers (پنجه)

What is old will not again grow young in this world,
Nor will our wish-fulfilments certainly unfold.
Tender! The five fingers holding *this*, your Wine's Cup,
Will soon rest on someone's grave while prayers are told.

597. Not Quit Kissing (لب بر نگرفت)

Tender! Bring a Cup! My heart's candle is not lit.
This Wine's flames can a new light in my life emit.
Ah, what a pure Ruby Wine you pour in *this* Cup.
One who pressed lips on it could not the kissing quit.

598. Life-Giving Dawn (صبوح جان بخش)

My heart that was not able to tell joy from grief,
Beside *this* Cup's Wine found no other world relief.
Tender, pour *this* Wine, since none appreciated like
Jesus his last breath at dawn, of a life so brief!

599. Two Types of People (دو نوع مردم)

The turnings of this endless circle that unfold
Benefit two types of people, it has been told:
Either those who've Awakened from its "good or bad,"
Or those who're still Asleep to themselves and the world.

600. Self-Cultivators (مجرّدان)

The joys and comforts He created from Himself
Were meant for the world's cultivators of oneself.
Those who fell Asleep under the inverted bowl
Lost comfort by placing it on 'forgottens' shelf.

601. Not A Drop (نه یك قطره)

You cannot change what the pen has already writ.
You cannot, from grieving, your gut's bleeding omit.
Even if all your life you shed tears mixed with blood,
They won't go away but will return, bit by bit.

602. Sweet and Sour (شیرین و شور)

On the supper table of times sweet with sour blends.
The joy of knowing Him exile's bitterness ends.
Although this lasting world is not always joyful,
At least it's enough to match the grief it amends.

603. Beloved's Loving (دوست داشتنِ دوست)

Whatever comes along, look well, see its good sides,
Since it's made by Him and in it His Will resides.
Don't be too concerned with my destitute life's tale.
This may be how my Friend His Love for me provides!

604. Know Yourself (در خود نگر)

Don't become possessive toward God's creations.
Don't see the faults of just others in relations.
God already knows all the secrets in our hearts.
Know yourself! Don't give in to prying temptations.

605. If You Lost Your Way (اگر جدا افتادی)

If you left the path and lost the way of your soul,
Then examine *yourself* wherein you lost control.
It was not 'there' but in 'here' that you lost your God.
So, 'here' is where you will find why you missed your goal.

606. Door Opening (در گشودن)

Not having acted as told, in one breath or more
You wish to be like all those who heavens explore!
It is you who have not tried to walk the way; when
Did knocks not lead to the opening of His door?

607. No Name and Sign (نی نام و نشان)

Neither will last the flowers that have bloomed on grass,
Nor will the worth of Aden's pearls their doom surpass.
Be glad, since in the cycles of this finite world,
Your name and signs, like those of mine, will come to pass.

608. Stolen Slowly (خوش خوش ببرد)

The ruined lives' dust was washed away by a flood,
And the cup of life began floating on a flood.
Beware, O heart, that the porter of times may take
Your garments of life slowly, and not in a flood!

609. Advice for the Youthful (پند برای تازه جوان)

O youthful! Hear an advice from this ancient man! ای تازه جوان شنو ازین پیر کهن
A two-fold point summarizes a good life's plan: یك نكته كه هست مایهٔ مغز سخن
Don't befriend anyone who lacks *understanding*. یاری که درو معرفتی نیست مگیر
Don't do what does not benefit your *whole* lifespan. کاریکه درو منفعتی نیست مکن

610. Sixty or More (بیش از شصت)

Don't suppose that you'll live through your sixties or more. اندیشهٔ عمر بیش از شصت منه
Be Drunken wherever you take steps on the floor. هر جا که قدم نهی بجز مست منه
Don't lay *this* Jug and Cup down from shoulder and hand زان پیش که کاسهٔ سرت کوزه کنند
Before from your head they'll make jugs or cups galore. تو کوزه ز دوش و کاسه از دست منه

XV. Pottery (کوزه گری)

611. My Own Cup of Gold (جام زرینم بود)

I once purchased a jug that a jug-maker sold.
It whispered many secrets and once I was told,
"Don't think that I'm now just a plain wine-seller's jug.
I was once a king, toasting my own cup of gold!"

612. Hand and Head (دسته و سر)

I passed by a jug-maker's shop some time ago,
And found him there standing by his wheel set below,
Putting on the jugs and the pitchers heads and hands
That with the kings' and beggars' bodies used to go.

613. Jug's Cry (خروش کوزه)

I went to a jug-maker's workshop yesterday.
I saw two thousand jugs, mute or chatting away.
All of a sudden a jug cried aloud asking,
"Which of you made, which bought, and which sells us away?"

614. Glazed Pitcher (سبوی کاشی)

I broke last night a glazed blue jug without a par.
I was Drunk, so my Rowdiness had gone too far.
The jug cried in my heart's tongue, "You'll be broken too,
Just as I was whole yesterday, like now you are."

615. Go Easy Please (نیکو دار)

A jug-maker in the bazaar, a day before,
Was kicking hard a patch of clay, more, more, and more.
"I was like you, O potter," was pleading the clay,
"Can you treat me better, now that I'm on the floor?"

616. Stop! (ساکن)

On a building site, I saw a lone man one day
Kicking and humiliating a heap of clay.
The clay was crying, "Oh please, stop for your own sake!
Otherwise, *you'll* be kicked for what you do today."

617. Don't You Know? (چه می پنداری؟)

O jug-maker! Get up, if you're now more Awake,
And demean no more the people's clay you remake!
These are Kaykhosrow's hands and Fereydoun's fingers
You're turning on the wheel! Don't you know what's at stake?

618. Forefathers' Clay (خاک پدران)

All these jug-makers who have their hands on their clay
Must think well and wisely now about what I say.
How long will they hit the clay with fists, kicks, and slaps?
Don't they know it's their fathers who've long passed away?

619. Father in Palm (پدر در کف)

I passed by a potter, a day or two before.
He was artfully shaping some clay on the floor.
As I watched, I saw something odd the heedless missed.
My father's clay passed through potters' palms ever more!

620. Be Patient Now! (دمی با من ساز)

Out of greed, I pressed my two Lips on a Jug's Lips,
Eager to seek a long life from my hurried Sips.
The Jug kissed back and whispered, "Oh, be patient now!
I used to do the same with you in prior trips!"

621. Lips on Lips (لب بر لب)

"Why do our lips kiss each other?" I asked the jug.
"That's because each *is* the other," answered the jug.
"As ruled by God, our existence won't stay the same.
Our lips become one another," whispered the jug.

622. Poor Lover (عاشق زار)

This jug used to be, like me, a poor lover once,
Captive to the lock of hair of his lover once.
This handle you see on its shoulder was her hand
Resting over the shoulder of her lover once.

623. Don't Step On (قدم ننهی)

This cup that was made so beautifully, they've said,
Is today broken and thrown by the road instead.
Beware not to step on and belittle the cup,
Since it was long ago the Cup of someone's head!

624. Harmless Wine (می بی ضرر)

From *this* Jug that is brimful of *this* harmless Wine,
Fill your Cup and Drink, and once again pour me mine
Before it's too late, O love, when in an alley
You and I will be poured as jug dust, sifted fine.

زان کوزهٔ می که نیست در وی ضرری
پر کن قدحی بخور به من ده دگری
زان پیشتر ای صنم که در رهگذری
خاك من و تو کوزه کند کوزه گری

625. Jug and Pitcher (کوزه و سبو)

The worn-out clothing of our lives will not renew,
Nor will your expectations for the world come true.
Instead of grief, Drink Wine from *this* Pitcher and Jug!
After breaking, they will to each other debut!

نی جامهٔ عمر کهنه نو خواهد شد
نی نیز جهان به کام تو خواهد شد
می خور به سبو کوزهٔ اندوه مخور
کین کوزه چو بشکند سبو خواهد شد

626. Spirit's Song (نعرهٔ روح)

Be happy! This world will go on and on for long,
And the spirit will howl to the body this song:
"These bowls of heads that you will for a short while see
Will soon break down under the steps of potters' throng."

خوش باش که عالم گذران خواهد بود
روح از پی تن نعره زنان خواهد بود
این کاسهٔ سرها که تو بینی یکچند
زیر قدم کوزه گران خواهد بود

627. Chatter's Slavery (اسیر عقل)

Why be enslaved to our minds' chatter every day,
About living one day or a hundred years, say?
Bring me *now* a Cup, brimful of *this* Wine, before
These potters make me a jug from my Potters' clay.

تا چند اسیر عقل هر روزه شویم
در دهر چه صد ساله چه یك روزه شویم
در ده قدح باده از آن پیش که ما
در کارگه کوزه گران کوزه شویم

XVI. Cemetery (گورستان)

628. Eye Pupil (مردمك چشم)

Before you and me, there've been many days and nights.
The spheres have been at work too in heavenly flights.
Beware to walk gently on the ground since there are
Pebbles that were once the pupils of lovers' sights.

پیش از من و تو لیل و نهاری بودست
گردنده فلک نیز به کاری بودست
زینهار قدم به خاک آهسته نهی
کآن مردمک چشم نگاری بودست

629. Human Horizons (آفاق انسان)

Many men and women have come and gone 'til now,
Adorning all horizons on and on 'til now.
Wake up now, since your body will soon be the earth
That has embodied thousands each eon 'til now.

پیش از تو بسی مرد و بسی زن بودست
کافاق ز جمله شان مزیّن بودست
زود آ که تن تو خاک گردد زیرا
خاک ره تو دگر هزار تن بودست

630. Grave's Tile (خشت گور)

When the pure spirits leave the bodies, mine and yours,
They put a few tiles on the bodies, mine and yours.
Then, for a tile or two on the graves, hers and his,
They mold a few tiles from the bodies, mine and yours.

از تن چو برفت جان پاک من و تو
خشتی دو نهند بر مغاک من و تو
وآنگاه ز برای خشت گور دگران
در کالبدی کشند خاک من و تو

631. Selfless Dusts (غبارهای بی خود)

The dusts from all these grave-dwellers have blown away
Such that they are now mixed and with each other stay.
Ah, what's this courthouse that, in their day of judgment,
They've become so selfless and have nothing to say?

این اهل قبور خاک گشتند و غبار
هر ذرّه ز هر ذرّه گرفتند کنار
آه این چه سرائیست که در روز شمار
بی خود شده و بیخبرند از همه کار

632. Heart's Howls (نعره های دل)

Wants to own the world's everything, the howling heart!
Wants to become everlasting, the howling heart!
About how the death angel hunts it day and night,
Does not have a clue, the poor thing, the howling heart!

دل نعره زنان ملک جهان می طلبد
پیوسته وجود جاودان می طلبد
مسکین خبرش نیست که صیّاد اجل
پی در پی او نهاده جان می طلبد

633. Flowing Down Water (آب فرو رو)

How long will you be tied to things' color and smell,
Or let greed for good or bad things your life propel?
Even if you're Mecca's or elixir waters,
Won't you at the end sink down to where the dead dwell?

تا چند اسیر رنگ و بو خواهی شد
تا کی پی هر زشت و نکو خواهی شد
گر چشمۀ زمزمی و گر آب حیات
آخر به دل خاک فرو خواهی شد

634. Tulip's Secret (راز لاله)

Drink *this* Wine, since for long you'll sleep beneath the clay,
With no intimates, friends, pals, or loved ones to stay.
And beware! To no one tell this hidden secret:
No more blossoms the tulip that withers away!

635. When You're Gone, You're Gone (چو رفتی رفتی)

O you, from the four natures and seven-fold sky,
Who heatedly about fours and sevens ask 'why?'
Drink *this* Wine! For more than a thousand times I've said,
"You won't be back! When you're gone, you're gone! You will *die*!"

636. Don't Leave Something (چیزی نگذاری)

Of those who've walked along this long road of travail,
Who has returned to lift for us its secret's veil?
Don't leave something on this crossroad from need or greed,
Thinking that you'll come back to fetch it off the trail.

637. One Way Street (راه بی بازگشت)

I crossed many plains and meadows under my feet.
I searched across lands where many horizons meet.
Yet I heard no one say he returned on this road.
They all walked away, but none came back on this street.

638. Grave's End (آخر گور)

If you're the Aristotle of Republic's land,
Or as the ruler of Rome or of China stand,
Sip *this* Wine from Jamsheed's Cup: "As Bahrām was kicked
By the wild ass, you'll too be kicked into the sand."

639. Seen A Hundred Thousand (دیده صد هزار)

This church has seen a hundred thousand Jesus-likes.
This mount has seen a hundred thousand Moses-likes.
In this palace stayed a hundred thousand Caesars.
This arch has seen a hundred thousand Khosrow-likes.

640. No News Came (خبر نیامد)

I asked an old man whom in *this* Tavern I saw,
"Don't you have some news about all those gone, somehow?"
He said, "Drink *this* Wine, and think how many like us
Left but no news from them has come back until now."

641. Seven-Thousand-Year Olds (هفت هزار سالگان)

O friend! Let's not worry about another day!
Let's enjoy *today*, this moment's bountiful pay!
Tomorrow, when we'll leave this ancient two-doored lodge,
With seven-thousand-year-olds we will have to stay!

642. Grave Tiles (خشتهای گور)

Be happy *today* since sorrows will be unbound.
The stars will again conjunct as they whirl around.
The bricks people will make from your body today
Will tomorrow surround others under the ground.

643. Drink Wine, Not Sorrow (باده خور، غم مخور)

Enjoy *now*, since tomorrow grief will rule the day.
The bodies of all you know will hide in the clay.
Drink *this* Wine to lighten the sorrows of the world
Since, on the hearts of those who stay, sorrows will weigh.

644. Drink or Not (خوری یا نخوری)

Ask yourself whether you have been Asleep or not,
What you brought to life and what you will take or not.
You say, "I don't Drink *this* Wine since death is the end."
You'll die anyway, whether you Drink *this* or not.

645. No One Came Back (یکی باز نامد)

Go and throw dust on all the world's heavenly spheres.
Drink *this* Wine instead and make friends with lovely dears.
Why blame the spheres, or plead for something you have now?
No one's coming back from the next world, it appears!

XVII. Paradise and Hell (بهشت و جهنم)

646. O Baffled One (ای حیران شده)

O you who have come from the world of spirit hot,
And four, five, six, and seven baffle you a lot!
Drink *this* Wine, if you don't know where you have come from!
Be happy *now*, since where you're going you know not!

647. Rumors (آوازه)

In this lasting world when the spring brings fresh flowers,
Say, "O idol, pour enough in *this* Cup of ours!"
Hell's deprivations or beauties of paradise
Are just rumors; the real news comes from *these* hours.

648. Dog's Better Bark (سگ بهتر)

If, in the spring, an idol of houri-souled line
Brings me by the garden a Cup full of *this* Wine,
It may sound crude, but if I talked of *that* heaven
A dog's bark would sound better than such talk of mine.

649. Things Will Be Like This (چنین عاقبت کار)

Paradise and fine beauties, they say there will be!
Wine and milk and honey, everywhere you will see!
Then, why fear choosing my Wine and Beloved *now*?
Is not *this* how things will be there supposedly?

650. Cash Better Than Credit (نقد خوشتر از نسیه)

They say that paradise has houris by its streams
Of wine, milk, honey, syrup, and all such supremes.
Fill *this* Cup of Wine and lay it in my hand, since
This cash fulfills *now* a thousand such promised dreams!

651. Drumbeat from Afar (آواز دهل از دور)

They say that heaven's houris will bring you delight.
I say *this* Wine delights *now*, a Grape Juice gone bright!
Take *this* cash and let go of that promised reward!
Drumbeats from distance delight; from nearby, not quite!

652. Sufi's Illusion (پنداشت صوفی)

Drink *this* Wine to be judged less hard *this* judgment day,
Since you'll be happier with *this* Wine, Drunk *today*!
Our Sufi does not drink wine, hoping for heaven,
As if folks there will their thirst with dry dates allay!

می خور که حساب کمترک خواهد بود
عیش تو به باده خوشترک خواهد بود
صوفی به امید خلد می می نخورد
پنداشت که آن جای خرک خواهد بود

653. Paradise Like Empty Hand (بهشت چون کف دست)

Lovers and Drunkards, I am told, are bound for hell.
It's a claim the heart can reasonably dispel.
Were they hell-bound, you'd then have to find tomorrow
Heaven to be, like a hand's palm, empty to dwell!

گویند که دوزخی بود عاشق و مست
قولی است خلاف و دل درو نتوان بست
گر عاشق و مست دوزخی خواهد بود
فردا بینی بهشت همچون کف دست

654. Sustaining the Situation (باشد که چنان انگیزند)

They tell me that he who persistently abstains,
As he dies in this world, in the next he obtains.
Then I take *this* Wine and my Loved One in arms *now*
So that, on that day, the situation sustains!

گویند هر آن کسان که با پرهیزند
زانسان که بمیرند چنان برخیزند
ما با می و معشوق از آنیم مدام
تا بو که به حشرمان چنان انگیزند

655. Worth Both Worlds (دو عالم ارزد)

"Avoid wine," they say, "or you'll suffer in this world,
And on judgement day, be in hell's fires enrolled!"
But it's better than both worlds to enjoy *this* now:
A moment's joy of *this* Wine from the Cup I hold!

گویند مخور می که بلاکش باشی
در روز مکافات در آتش باشی
این است ولی ز هر دو عالم خوشتر
این یک دم که از شراب سرخوش باشی

656. Had They Been Doomed to Hell (گر دوزخی خواهد بود)

Drinking *this* Wine around Beauties is more preferred
To faking a hermit's life, with their joys deferred.
Had all the Lovers and Drunkards been doomed to hell,
Of *that* paradise no one would have even heard.

می خوردن و گرد نیکوان گردیدن
به زانکه ز زرق زاهدی ورزیدن
گر عاشق و مست دوزخی خواهد بود
پس روی بهشت را که خواهد دیدن

657. Written From the Start (از ازل نوشته)

They say that they have set up a hell in that world,
And pull your sin records before you are enrolled.
Who was it that witnessed such records? Is he back
To tell me where or why such tales he had been told?

ما را گویند دوزخ افراشته اند
وانگه ز گناه تو بر انباشته اند
که رفت به دوزخ که گناه من دید
ور نه چه به هرزه خود بر این داشته اند

658. What's My Fault? (تقصیر من چیست؟)

Say, you live in shrines, I, with the Loved One and Wine.
Say, I'm bound for hell, but you'll in paradise dine.
What is my fault, then, if for an eternity
The Painter so drew on the fate's tablet my sign?

ما با می و معشوق و شما دیر و کنشت
ما اهل جهیمیم و شما اهل بهشت
تقصیر من از روز ازل چیست بگوی
نقاش چنین به لوح تقدیر نبشت

659. Sit in This Heaven (بنشین به بهشت)

As I look at this vast Earth that stretches around,
I see lovely brooks in gardens, everywhere found.
Then, talk less of the heavenly rivers, for *this*
Is heaven! So, with heavenlies sit on *this* ground!

660. Anyone With More Guts? (که را بود زهرۀ این)

I saw a Rogue man meditating on the ground,
From this or that world, blind faiths or unfaiths, unbound,
Free of presumptive truths, certitudes, rights, or wrongs.
In both worlds could one with more guts be ever found?

661. Lucky He Is (به اقبال نشست)

Caressing *this* Ruby Wine and a lover's hair,
He is lucky who sits by the grass with his pair,
Drinking *this* Wine, not thinking of the spheres, until
He's Drunken from the joy in *this* Sphere in his care.

662. Run Away from It (از آنجا بگریز)

From where there is no Rosy Wine like *this* to try,
Nor a tulip-faced, nor a lover, cypress-high,
Run away even if they say it's paradise.
This is all I say, since fighting's not worth a sigh.

663. Be Free of That Hell and Paradise (فارغ از آن دوزخ و بهشت)

Drink *this* Wine *today*, since you'll soon be a dust crowd,
Molded in cups or barrels, if time is allowed.
Become free from *that* hell, and from *that* heaven too!
If the wise know *this*, why would they be vainly proud?

664. Perhaps They'll Forget (شاید فراموش کنند)

Pour *this* Wine so I Drink a Cup of it, or two,
And hear *its* rhymed Sips with the reed that's played anew.
There's still some time left before our judgment day comes.
Perhaps they'll forgive our sins in this world's review!

665. Go Wherever You (هر کجا خواهی رو)

I'm a buyer of all kinds of Wine, old or new.
I sell that 'heaven' for this world's barley of two.
You ask me, "Where do we go to after we die?"
"Bring me *this* Wine," I daresay, "go wherever you!"

666. Don't Listen to Times' Rulers (مشنو سخن زمانه ساز آمدگان)

Do not listen to those who conform to the times,
But seek *these* nice and well-balanced Pure Wine sublimes.
One by one, all the risers collapsed in their graves,
And no one sees a sign of any graveyard climbs.

667. God Does Not Need (خدا مستغنی است)

Take your share from what the changing time is dealing.
Sit on *this* joy's Throne and let *this* Cup bring healing.
God is free of any needs, worships done or not.
Be self-fulfilled *today* under this sky's ceiling.

668. They'll Regret It (پشیمان گردند)

Those who are aware that to the dust they'll return,
From any blind faith and unfaith free their concern.
Those who do not enjoy this world, will certainly
Regret it in their supposed next-worldly sojourn.

669. They Both Sigh (هر دو در حسرتند)

For this world's pleasures some ignore the holy 'why.'
For the pleasures of the next, some without end cry.
I have *this* Wine, Beauty, and heavenly garden.
It is no wonder, then, that they both often sigh!

670. Our Garden Temple (مزرعۀ کنشت ما)

This flower garden is a temple, yours and mine.
It can be a heaven or a hell, yours and mine.
This jug that today you are drinking water from
Will soon become the tiles of the graves, yours and mine.

671. No Heaven But This (جز این نیست بهشت)

If there's music, a beautiful soul, and *this* Wine,
Joining me by the crop or a river to dine,
Ask for nothing better, uselessly causing hell.
This is truly the heaven, if there's one, of mine.

672. Who Said There's A Hell (که گفت دوزخی خواهد بود)

For how long should I lay bricks on the seas in vain?
Those who idolize their faiths, their creeds I disdain.
Those who said that Khayyam goes to hell, which of them
Went to hell or can come from heaven to explain?

673. Whoever Knows the Secrets (آن کس که اسرار دانست)

In the temple or synagogue, school or convent,
They seek *that* paradise and fear *that* hell's torment.
But those who are aware of their Divine meanings,
Cultivating such seedlings in their hearts resent.

674. One Sip Bests Both Worlds (یک جرعه به است از دو جهان)

This Wine makes me healthier by feeding my soul.
It lets me unwind the world's deepest secrets' scroll.
Why should I be concerned with the hereafter when
This Sip lets the truth of the "two worlds" to unroll?

675. Here is There (اینجاست آنجا)

Tender! The yearning for heaven, what is it for?
It has Wine and its Tender; does it something more?
There, they have Wine and its Tender; I do here too!
Is there something better in the two worlds in store?

676. Wine, the Teacher (رهبری می)

O Tender, in this life there is no better guide
Than the old wisdoms that in *this* Wine's Cup reside.
This Wine is my true confidant because its warmth
One can't find in heaven's brooks or elixir's tide.

677. Don't Rough and Tumble (درشتی نکنی)

Do not rough-and-tumble the Drunkards, O behold!
Don't treat good folks hideously, nor be a scold.
Drink *this* Wine, since it is not because of the wine
That you will be from paradise to hell enrolled.

678. Why Am I Not There (چونست که ره نیست مرا)

O one for whose love God, since the eternal past,
This world's plays of heaven's joys and hell's torments cast!
There *may* be a feast in heaven; I have *this* Wine.
Why am I not already there, O the outcast!

679. Paradise's Address (نشان بهشت)

To harness true wisdom, turn to *this* Glass instead.
Pass hell, reach heaven, and by *this* Wine river tread.
Trade in your turban for *this* Wine. Drink, don't fear!
Hide its fresh Pearls somewhere wrapped all around your head.

680. Repenting from Repentance (توبه از توبه)

O God! Given *this* Wine and *this* songful meeting,
How can one like me miss the roses, so fleeting?
Better than *that* heaven and its brooks and beauties,
Is *this* garden, *this* Wine brook, and *this* harp's beating.

681. Drunken and Loving Author (نگارنده در مستی و عشق)

Tender! Pour a Cup! He who brew *this* Earthly Blend
Also our lives, for Love and Drunkenness, He penned.
Why not enjoy *this* Wine and *this* world's Beauties *now*?
Did He not promise *this* Beauty and River's bend?

682. Paradise Now (بهشت اکنون)

To make *this* Earth a heavenly paradise *now*,
A time for *this* Wine with friends by the brook allow.
Tomorrow, when the world's writing of joy is done,
Could we ever write back the day that passed, somehow?

683. Next's Uncertain Goal (کی دانم آن جهانم باشد)

I Drink *this* Wine to cultivate my lasting soul,
So that from the world's false riches I disenroll.
O soul of the world, let me live in joy *today*.
Why waste it now for a next world's uncertain goal?

684. Longing for Rose and Wine (میل به گل و می)

I wish so much to be *now* by roses embraced,
While my hands are with *this* Wine's Cup and Jug enlaced.
I want to take my share of joy from each part *now*,
Before the parts are gone and in the whole defaced.

685. I'm Taking the Three in Cash (این هر سه مرا نقد)

I don't know whether the One who created me
Meant to bring me heaven's joy or hell's misery.
This Wine, *this* Beauty, and *this* lute played by the crop
Are cash! You hope for heaven! I'm taking the three!

The Robaiyat of Omar Khayyam:
Part 3 of 3: Songs of Joy Addressing
the Question "Why Can Happiness
Exist?"

رباعیات عمر خیام: بخش سوم از سه بخش: آوازهای شادی
در پاسخ به سؤال «چرا سعادت می تواند موجود باشد؟»

XVIII. Garden (باغ)

686. Garden Time (فصل گل)

It's the garden, riverbank, and crops strolling time,
With dear friends and a lover, angel-souled, sublime!
Bring your Cup since those who Drink from *this* Wine at dawn
Are comforted and freed in any faith, as I'm.

687. Neither Hot, Nor Cold (نه گرم است و نه سرد)

Ah, what a nice day! It is neither hot, nor cold!
The cloud is washing garden roses' dust, behold!
In old heroic Persian tongue nightingale sings,
"O yellow rose, you must Drink *this* red Wine! Be bold!"

688. Why Did He Paint Me? (بهر چه آراست مرا؟)

Although my colors and scents are works of beauty,
My face like a tulip, and height, a cypress tree,
In this jolly garden of Earth I wonder why
Has the Artist of eternity painted me?

689. Rose's Tale (حکایت گل)

One morning, a rose was agitated and shed
Dew tears, telling the eastern wind her tale. She said,
"See how the lasting time betrays; in just ten days
I bud, blossom, bloom, grow, wither, and then I'm dead."

690. Perfumer's Oppression (ستم گلابگر)

The rose said, "There is nothing nicer than my dress.
Why does the perfumer tear me up to impress?"
The Drunken nightingale said, "Who has laughed a day
Without shedding a year's tears in unhappiness?"

691. Torn Dress of Rose (دامن گل چاك شدست)

Look! The eastern wind's tearing the dress of the rose,
Even as her pose enchants the nightingale's blows!
Sit in the rose's shade *soon*, since it has for long
Weathered to and from the earth many comes and goes.

692. Next Week (هفتهٔ دگر)

Notice How festive are these grasses and roses!
Beware, though, they'll just be dust when the week closes!
Pour *this* Wine! Let's clip a rose before it's too late,
When the rose goes dust, and the grass decomposes.

بنگر گل و سبزه بس طربناک شدست
دریاب که هفتهٔ دگر خاک شدست
می نوش و گلی بچین که تا در نگری
گل خاک شدست و سبزه خاشاک شدست

693. Drunken Nightingale's Message (پیام بلبل مست)

When the Drunken nightingale flew the garden's way,
And found the rose and *this* Wine Cup joyful that day,
It whispered these words in the heart's tongue in my ear,
"All the years that went by won't be coming back, hey!"

چون بلبل مست راه در بستان یافت
روی گل و جام باده را خندان یافت
آمد به زبان حال در گوشم گفت
دریاب که عمر رفته را نتوان یافت

694. Cloud's Crying (گریهٔ ابر)

Here comes a cloud! It's again on the green crying.
Without *these* Rosy Wine drops, I'd too be dying.
Watching the green landscape today, I still wonder,
Who'll be watching tomorrow my earth's green, sighing?

ابر آمد و باز بر سر سبزه گریست
بی بادهٔ گلرنگ نمی باید زیست
این سبزه که امروز تماشاگه ماست
تا سبزهٔ خاک ما تماشاگه کیست

695. Blood Rain (خون باران)

The sphere does not raise any flower from the clay
Unless it returns it to clay to fade away.
Were the clouds able to lift its dust to the sky,
Lovers' blood would be raining 'til their judgment day.

گردون ز زمین هیچ گلی برنارد
کش نشکند و باز به گل نسپارد
گر ابر چو آب خاک را بردارد
تا حشر همه خون عزیزان بارد

696. Watched Green (سبزهٔ تماشاگه)

When the cloud in Nowrooz washes the tulip's face,
Wake up and seek after *this* Cup of Wine with grace,
Since all the green that you enjoy watching today
Will be growing tomorrow from your resting place.

چون ابر به نوروز رخ لاله بشست
برخیز و به جام باده کن عزم درست
کاین سبزه که امروز تماشاگه تست
فردا همه از خاک تو برخواهد رست

697. Nowrooz's Tulip (لالهٔ نوروز)

In Nowrooz raise *this* Wine Cup like how tulips grow,
With a tulip-faced lover, if chances allow.
Drink *this* Wine *now* happily since this ancient wheel
Will suddenly flatten you like the earth below.

چون لاله به نوروز قدح گیر بدست
با لاله رخی اگر تو را فرصت هست
می نوش به خرّمی که این چرخ کهن
ناگاه تو را چو خاک گرداند پست

698. When Today Nicely Goes (امروز خوش است)

On the rose, the breeze of Nowrooz so nicely blows!
On the grass, her heartwarming face so nicely glows!
What you say of yesterday cannot be as nice
As enjoying *now*, when the day so nicely goes!

بر چهرهٔ گل نسیم نوروز خوش است
در صحن چمن روی دل افروز خوش است
از دی که گذشت هر چه گویی خوش نیست
خوش باش و ز دی مگو که امروز خوش است

699. Blood and Bounties (خون و مال)

As the fields of grass are swept by the northern breeze,
With *this* Wine and *this* Rose, your today's troubles cease.
Drink *this* Wine, since the wise say that today it's fair
To shed *this* Vine's Blood, and *these* Rose bounties to seize.

700. Narcissus Rain (ریزش نسترن)

The sphere's thundercloud pours down narcissus-like flakes,
As if white blossoms pour down on grass without breaks.
I pour *this* red Wine in lily's Cup like the sight
The violet-like cloud pouring jasmine-likes makes.

701. Worth the Wait (انتظاری ارزد)

A rose's scent is worth being by its thorns bruised.
This Wine is worth being of Hangover accused.
Be fair to the Friend who revives a thousand lives!
Can't this long exile's wait for Him not be excused?

702. So and So's Cup (پیالهٔ فلانی)

Like how the nightingale sits for its singing pose,
I hold like a tulip *this* Wine Cup in repose.
I do this before people say, from ignorance,
"There he goes again toasting in *these* Cups his prose!"

703. Tulip and Violet (لاله و بنفشه)

In a place where you find roses or tulips spread,
The red patches are marking where a king had bled.
Every violet that is sprouting from the ground
Was a lovely mole adorning a beauty's head.

704. Green Makeup (خطّ سبزه)

Don't suppose that removing from the Loved One's face
The nature's green makeup diminishes His grace.
His face's garden, a scenery for the soul,
Had its roses and the green just enhanced the place.

705. Who's Awakened? (هشیار کیست؟)

When the violet's dress is in its colors blown,
It becomes to the blow of the eastern wind prone.
Awakened is he who Drinks, with a graceful friend,
This Wine and breaks its repentance Cup on the stone.

706. Bud's Own Robe (دامن غنچه)

Each morning when dew appears on the tulip's face
The violet bows to the green for an embrace.
In fairness, though, I delight in that tiny bud
Who meditates in the robe of its own space.

707. Cypress and Lily (سرو و سوسن)

Have you ever thought why for being free are famed
The two plants that have been 'cypress' and 'lily' named?
One stands tall with two hundred hands, yet never begs.
The other, with ten tongues, is for silence acclaimed.

708. Garden's Joseph (یوسف چمن)

"I'm the garden's Egyptian Joseph," the Rose said,
"A Red Ruby with a mouth from which gold is spread."
I said, "If you are Joseph, then show me a sign!"
It said, "See here, my torn red shirt shows that I bled."

709. Riverbank Green (سبزهٔ کنار جوی)

Any green that is on a riverbank growing
Is like the beard that's by an angel's lip showing.
Don't step on the green meanly, since it also grew
From a tulip-faced lover's dust that's still blowing.

710. May Suddenly Depart (ناگه برود)

When the times bring to you lots of sorrows, O heart,
Beware that your pure soul may suddenly depart!
Rest on the green and enjoy your days that are left,
Before the resting of the green on your soil start.

711. Shirts and Petals (پیراهن و گلبرگ)

With a cypress-high lover, fresh in roses' bed,
Don't let go of *this* Wine Cup and *its* Rose in red.
Enjoy this moment before the whirlwind of death
Tears our clothes like how the rose's petals are shed.

712. Sphere's Intention (قصد فلک)

This wheel's intending to set the goals, yours and mine,
Of destroying all the pure souls, yours and mine.
Sit on the green and Drink from *this* pure Wine before
The green grows again from the head Bowls, yours and mine.

713. Happiness Farming (برزگری شادی)

We're the peasants of this old renewable field.
From planting joyfulness, we can reap a new yield.
Yet, like the short-lived tulip in a transient land,
Before we've blossomed, by the wind we're blown afield.

ما برزگران این کهن دشت نویم
از کشتهٔ شادی همه نو می درویم
چون لاله کم عمر درین دشت فنا
سر برزده از خاک به بادی گرویم

714. Where's Someone (کو آنکس)

Where is someone who does not let the sphere again
Sadden him or be seduced by his grim time's gain,
One who can cherish life down to a single breath
That blooms at dawn like a rose to the secrets' plane.

کو آنکه غم گردش گردون نخورد
وین عشوهٔ روزگار واژون نخرد
تا ساعتی از عمر غنیمت شمرد
هنگام سحر که پرده بر گل بدرد

715. You're Not a Leek (ترّه نه ای)

For the good of humankind, *this* mind is inclined
To advise a hundred times daily to remind
You to take heed of this moment's breath, since you're not
The reaped-often leek that grows once again in kind.

این عقلی که در ره سعادت پوید
روزی صد بار در خود تو را می گوید
دریاب تو این یك دم وقتت که نه ای
آن ترّه که بدروند و دیگر روید

716. Grab a Cup (برگیر پیاله)

Grab *this* Cup and Jug, O dear pure soul seeking friend.
Slowly walk in the garden, by the river's bend.
There've been so many dear loved ones that this cruel wheel
A hundred times to cups and to decanters turned.

بردار پیاله و سبو ای دلجوی
خوش خوش بخرام گرد باغ و لب جوی
بس شخص عزیز را که چرخ بدخوی
صد بار پیاله کرد و صد بار سبوی

717. Don't Brag, Sir! (خواجه، مناز)

In the roses' season, their wealth in hand must be.
Repeated Sips from *this* Wine Cup in hand must be.
O sir! Don't brag about your perfect intellect!
All that's nothing since *this* Vine's pen in hand must be.

در موسم گل به کف درم میباید
جام می ناب دم به دم میباید
از عقل و کمال دانش ای خواجه مناز
کاینها همه هیچ ست کرم میباید

718. Don't Let (مگذار)

Don't let yourself be overwhelmed by daily woes,
Letting futile sorrows waste how your lifetime goes.
Be surrounded by *this* book, a friend, and the crops,
Before the earth surrounds you in your final pose.

مگذار که غصّه در کنارت گیرد
واندوه محال روزگارت گیرد
مگذار کتاب و لب یار و لب کشت
زان پیش که خاک در حصارت گیرد

719. You're the Cure (به تو گشت درست)

The meadow's face is rain-washed by Nowrooz's cloud.
For this heartbroken age, you are the cure endowed.
Enjoy with your youthful on the Earth's green *this* Wine,
Because, O fool, your earth will soon be a green crowd.

صحرا رخ خود به ابر نوروز بشست
این دهر شکسته دل به تو گشت درست
با سبزه خطی به سبزه زاری می خور
ای بیخبرا که سبزه از خاک تو رست

720. Will Become For Long (بسی خواهد شد)

Sip *this* Wine. Flowers that face the blue come and go.
Enjoy life. Trees that face the stars, too, come and go.
Rest on the grass to live your life in full because
You, facing the grass, and the grass, you, come and go.

721. Pregnant (آبستن)

See how *this* Cup's belly is with *this* life pregnant.
It is as if jasmine is with redbuds pregnant.
Well, no, I was wrong, since *this* Wine is so Loving
That it's as if water is with soul's fire pregnant.

722. Before I Disappear (زان پیش که ناپدید گردم)

O love! Bring me *this* Wine! I have a heart that's sad,
Since *this* Wine clears me from the griefs this world has had.
The green's sprouting from the dust, behold! Bring *this* Wine,
Before my body disappears in dust, unclad.

723. Rose's Secret (سرّ گل)

The rose said, "*These* gold Pollens in my hands, I hold.
Laughing, laughing, I bloomed their secrets to the world.
I Unknotted the string of their Sack when I left.
All the Cash I had I gave up, for nothing sold!"

724. Oud Twins (دو عود)

Fill *this* Cup, since today came with the flakes of snow!
Teach them to be red like *this* Ruby Wine below!
Take the two ouds in your hands; organize a feast.
Burn the oud of incense and let oud's music flow.

725. Don't Sleep (خواب مرو)

The cloud is masking the rose with its lifeline, still!
In my nature and heart, I long for *this* Wine, still.
Don't fall Asleep! Can't you see it's not Sleeping time?
O my dear, Drink *this* Wine, since there is Sunshine, still!

726. Bubble's Joy (خرّمی حباب)

When the blossom blooms its Decanter for *this* Wine,
The narcissus makes in joy its Cup for *this* Wine.
But, happy at heart is he whose house is Ruined
Amid the high-riding Bubbles burst for *this* Wine.

727. Balanced Candle (شمع طراز)

By the green and the stream, O balanced candle light,
End repentance, bring *this* Wine, and the harp excite!
Be happy! The roaring stream is howling aloud,
"Farewell! I won't be back from where to I take flight."

728. Divining Choice (اختیاری بکنم)

It's the tulips season, so I'll divine and choose
To do what goes counter to faith's prevailing views.
For many days, the tulip-faced youthful, I will
With Tuliplands of *these* Cups on the green amuse.

729. Repenting Now? (اکنون توبه؟)

If you have it with you, don't repent of *this* Wine.
A hundred penitents are already in line.
Roses are still undressing, nightingales singing,
"Why are you wasting your time in repentance whine?"

730. World-Play (ایهام)

This Wine, the red rose, the green, and the springtime's scent
Are here, but You, O Beauty, seem to be absent!
Where You seem to be absent, wordplay would not help,
And it's of no use when You seem to be present.

731. Repenting of Repentance (توبه ز توبه)

Every day I tell myself I'll repent tonight,
I'll repent of *this* Jug and Cup full of delight!
But the rose's season has now arrived! O God,
Can I now repent of *this* Wine-repenting plight?

XIX. Wine (شراب)

732. Molten Ruby (لعل مذاب)

This Wine is a molten Ruby in *this* Jug's mine.
This Cup is a body, its soul being *this* Wine.
This Glass Cup that is from *this* Wine laughing in joy
Is a tear that hides in it a heart's bleeding whine.

می لعل مذابست و صراحی کان است
جسم است پیاله و شرابش جان است
آن جام بلورین که ز می خندان است
اشکی است که خون دل درو پنهان است

733. Wine Ink (جوهر شراب)

In *this* Cup's body, *this* Wine that is Divine flows.
In its congealed spirit, *this* life of Wine flows.
What flows in the iced water is a liquid fire
That on blank paper like *this* Ruby of Mine flows.

در جسم پیاله می چو جانست روان
در روح مجسّم آن روانست روان
در آب فسرده آتشی سیالست
در درج بلور لعل کانست روان

734. Don't Dilute (آبش مرسان)

This Wine that's a soul for which humankind's a Bowl,
Over dry thinking has a masterful control.
Don't dilute *this* with water; it's sinful to do.
This Vine's Juice is complete to cultivate the soul.

آن باده که جان به جای جام است او را
عقل از سر خواجگی غلام است او را
آبش مرسان کآب حرام است او را
آبی که به رز خورد تمام است او را

735. Moon Veiling Sun (مهتاب حجاب آفتاب)

Is not *this* Cup's Wine a Rosewater of delight?
Is not in *this* Glass a Ruby that's pure and bright?
Is not a molten Ruby flowing from *this* Cup?
Is not its Moonlight's beauty veiling the Sunlight?

می سرخ گل و قدح گلابست مگر
در درج بلور لعل نابست مگر
یاقوت گداخته در آبست مگر
مهتاب حجاب آفتابست مگر

736. Three Conditions (سه شرط)

This Wine is barred, but it depends on who Drinks it,
How much of it and also with whom, one Drinks it.
When these three conditions are met, tell me the truth,
If the wise do not Drink it, then who else Drinks it?

می گر چه حرامست ولی تا که خورد
وآنگاه چه مقدار و دگر با که خورد
هرگاه که این سه شرط شد راست بگو
پس می نخورد مردم دانا که خورد

737. Don't Listen (مشنو)

O heart! Don't listen to the fraud of those who say
That *this* Pure Wine taints the faith or intellect's way.
For the body's comfort and as food for spirit,
Sip *this* Wine in the garden as its Rose songs play.

ای دل مشنو نصیحت اهل حیل
کز بادۀ ناب عقل و دین راست خلل
گر راحت جان و قوت روحت باید
می نوش به بوستان به گلبانگ غزل

738. Sweet Bitterness (تلخى شيرين)

A Cup of *this* Wine bests a hundred human creeds.
The worth of each of *its* Sips, China's worth exceeds.
On this Earth there is nothing like *this* Ruby Wine
Whose bitterness bests a thousand lives rolled in sweets.

يك جام شراب صد دل و دين ارزد
يك جرعه مى مملكت چين ارزد
جز باده لعل نيست در روى زمين
تلخى كه هزار جان شيرين ارزد

739. Rogue's Sigh (آه رند)

A sip of *this* Wine bests all the lands of Kāvoos.
It bests the throne of Qobād and the town of Ṭoos.
A sigh of a Rogue Drunkard from the heart at dawn
Bests the worships of a duplicitous recluse.

يك جرعه مى ز ملك كاووس به است
وز تخت قباد و ملكت طوس به است
آهى كه سحرگاه كشد رندى مست
از طاعت زاهدان سالوس به است

740. Morning Sigh (آه سحرى)

Than Jamsheed's lands, *this* Wine Barrel's Cap brings more joy.
Than Mary's food, *this* Cup's Wine fragrance brings more joy.
Than all the cries of Abu Sa'id and Adham,
A morning sigh from a Drunken heart brings more joy.

خشت سر خم ز ملكت جم خوشتر
بوى قدح از غذاى مريم خوشتر
آه سحرى ز سينهٔ خمّارى
از نالهٔ بوسعيد و ادهم خوشتر

741. Grand-Tent Idols' Wine (مى بتان خرگاهى)

To abstain from everything but *this* Wine, it's best.
Served by the Grand-Tent idols, I opine, it's best.
The best is a rogue freethinker's lost wandering.
From the Moon to Earth, sipping this Wine's Shine, it's best!

جز مى ز هر آنچه هست كوتاهى به
وآن مى ز كف بتان خرگاهى به
رندى و قلندرى و گمراهى به
يك جرعهٔ مى ز ماه تا ماهى به

742. One Sip of Old Wine (يك جرعه مى كهنه)

To a new land, a Sip from *this* Old Wine prefer.
To stay away from paths without *this* Wine, prefer.
A Cup of *this* bests a hundred Fereydoun thrones.
To Kaykhosrow's crown, *this* Barrel Cap of Wine prefer.

يك جرعه مى كهنه ز ملكى نو به
از هر چه نه مى طريق بيرون شو به
جاميش به از تخت فريدون صد بار
خشت سر خم ز تاج كيخسرو به

743. Higher Ruin (خراب اوليتر)

Than your youthful times, *this* Wine will make you higher.
With a beauty, *this* Pure Wine will make you higher.
This passing world is broken down, just a ruin.
Being Ruined by *this* Wine will make you higher.

ايام جوانيست شراب اوليتر
با روى نكو بادهٔ ناب اوليتر
اين عالم فانى چو خرابست و يباب
از باده درو مست و خراب اوليتر

744. Arrogance Remover (تكبّرزدا)

From *this* Wine, our heads become empty of false pride.
From *this* Wine, head, heart, and faith become one inside.
If Satan had Sipped *this* Wine, he would have for sure
With two thousand prostrations to Adam complied.

از باده شود تكبّر از سرها كم
وز باده شود عقل و دل و دين محكم
ابليس اگر ز باده خوردى يك دم
كردى دو هزار سجده پيش آدم

745. Why Repent? (چرا توبه؟)

If you serve mountains *this* Wine, they will start to dance.
Those who fault it are faulting themselves in their stance.
Why do you ask me to repent of *this* Wine when
It's a spirit that gives learning of joy a chance.

گر باده به کوه بدهی رقص کند
ناقص بود آنکه باده را نقص کند
از باده مرا توبه چه میفرمایی
روحیست که او تربیت شخص کند

746. Bring Wine (باده بیار)

The Ruby that's flowing in *this* Simple Cup, bring!
This confidant of free souls that won't break up, bring!
Since you know that Earthly life passes like a breeze,
Pass a breeze from *this* Cup of Wine! Hurry up, bring!

آن لعل در آبگینهٔ ساده بیار
وآن محرم و مونس هر آزاده بیار
چون می دانی که مدّت عالم خاک
بادیست که زود بگذرد باده بیار

747. I Can't Endure (نتوانم)

Living without *this* pure Wine, I cannot endure!
Wineless uprighting my spine, I cannot endure!
I live for the moment the Tender asks, "One more?"
And, still Drinking it, I whine, "I cannot endure!"

من بی می ناب زیستن نتوانم
بی باده کشیده بار تن نتوانم
من بندهٔ آن دمم که ساقی گوید
یک جام دگر بگیر و من نتوانم

748. My Excuse (عذرم)

They tell me, "Old man, Drink less, from Drinking resign!
For what reason do you not quit Drinking *this* Wine?"
My excuse is Drinking *this* with my Friend at dawn!
Be fair! What else could be brighter than such a Line?

گویند مرا که می خور کمتر از این
آخر به چه عذر بر نداری سر از این
عذرم رخ یار و بادهٔ صبحدم است
انصاف بده چه عذر روشنتر از این

749. Even He Drank (میسره گفت)

In the feast of wisdom, the mind said something bright,
Yet, Arabs and Romans still fight it, left and right.
If someone untrustworthy says, "*This* Wine's not pure!"
Why listen? God also poured His Pure Book's delight!

در بزم خرد عقل دلیلی سره گفت
در روم و عرب میمنه و میسره گفت
گر نا اهلی گفت که می ناسره است
من کی شنوم چونکه خدا میسره گفت

750. Gourd-Maker (کدوساز)

The Everlasting who makes the face and the head
Is the Might that brings justice to the foes we dread.
They say that the jug-maker can't be a Muslim.
Well, how about the One making the gourd instead?

حیّی که به قدرت سر و رو می سازد
همواره همو کار عدو می سازد
گویند قرابه گر مسلمان نبود
او را تو چه گویی که کدو می سازد

751. Evolving Grape (تکامل انگور)

From tasting so Sour on the early winter Vine,
Why did the Grape go Sweet, then Bitter in *this* Wine?
For the same reason a hatchet carves such a lute,
Or the woods that grow a reed sounding so divine.

در باغ چو بد غوره ترش اوّل دی
شیرین ز چه گشت و تلخ چون آمد می
از چوب به تیشه گر کسی کرد رباب
وز بیشه چه گوئی تو که همی روید نی

752. Enemy's Blood (خون عدو)

I Drink *this* Wine and the foes say, from left and right,
"It is faith's enemy! Drinking wine is not right!"
Now that I know it's their faith's enemy, I swear,
I'll Drink *this* since Drinking the foe's Blood is a right!

753. Inner Companion (دوست اندرون)

Pour in *this* Tulip's Cup, *this* Ruby Wine that's clear.
Draw from *this* Glass Jug's throat *this* Bloody Line that's clear.
That's because today is never outside *this* Cup
The soul of the dear Companion of mine that's clear.

754. Best Confidant (بهترین همدم)

Wine in *this* Cup, to be frank, is a gentle soul.
In the body's Glass Jug, there is a gentle soul.
No friend deserves to be my confidant except
For what's in *this* Wine Glass that is a gentle soul.

755. Drink or Not (خورم یا نه)

I said, "I will never again drink the red wine!
I will not drink it again, the blood of *that* vine!"
"Are you sure?" asked my old wise self. So, I replied,
"Well, it'd be wrong not to Drink the Wine of *this* Line!"

756. Wine Scent Bests Vanity (بوی می به ز غرور)

Even for a good name, fame just leads one to shame.
Pity him who from the wheel's cruelty ill became.
Drunkenness from the Scent of *this* Juice of the Grape
Bests the vanity feeding an ascetic's fame.

757. Special Month (ماه خاص)

They say it's not right to drink wine in Sha'bān days,
Nor in Rajab that's a month just for God always.
If Rajab's for God and Sha'bān for the prophet,
Drinking *this* Wine in our Ramadan will amaze!

758. Drunken Until the Feast (مست تا عید)

They say that as soon as the fasting month revives,
One should be abstaining from one's Wine-Drinking strives.
Then, I Drink *this* so much at the prior month's end
That I'd be Drunk when fasting end gala arrives.

759. Bags of Wine (خیکهای می)

The month of fasting has ended, the next has come.
The time of singing, joy, feasts, and the rest has come.
The time has come for them to say, "Bags of *this* Wine
On haulers' backs, back-to-back, for the fest has come."

760. Revelation Night Too (شب قدر هم)

I have never been Sober in life from *this* Wine!
On the Revelation Night, too, I Drink *this* Wine!
Lips on *this* Cup's Lips and Breast on *this* Barrel's Breast,
Hand on *this* Decanter's Neck, I devour *this* Wine.

761. Sorrow's Antidote (تریاك غم)

The day the Juice of *this* Vine I cannot procure
Will be one that even the lasting time can't cure.
The world's poison is sorrow, its cure is *this* Wine.
With *this* cure you can yourself from all griefs secure.

762. Stay Away! (دور از بر)

O feastful Cup! *Here's* your Rose-colored guest, enjoy!
Serving *it* with the oud and harp's music, Deploy!
O ascetic with no inkling of *this* Wine's worth,
I'll be thrilled if you're miles away from *this* Convoy!

763. Wine Mantra (ورد می)

In life, my mantra has been that of *this* Wine's praise.
Around me have been all its Wine-related clays.
O ascetic! If your master is dry thinking,
Be glad, since your master's been my pupil always!

764. Grief's Snake (افعی غم)

With heart-stealing Beauties who're quick-witted you must
Drink *this* Wine! It bites back your grief's serpent. O, trust
Me since I Drink *this* Wine for my heart's happiness!
Why should I care that you don't? Go and bite the dust!

765. World Is Wind (عالم باد است)

Exited the Pub, Ruined, Drunken, an old man
With a prayer rug and Cup, when our talk began.
"What is wrong?" I asked. He replied, "Oh, all is wind!
So Drink *this* Wine's second wind, whenever you can!"

766. Torn Tent (پردۀ دریده)

Without *this* Wine, one can't in *this* Tavern ablute.
Name can't be cleared once it's no longer in repute.
Be happy, since *this* tent we've used to veil ourselves
Was torn so unmendably that we can't restitute.

در میکده جز به می وضو نتوان کرد
وان نام که زشت شد نکو نتوان کرد
خوش باش که این پردۀ مستوری ما
بدریده چنان شد که رفو نتوان کرد

767. Why In-"toxic"-ating? (چرا شرآب؟)

From *this* Spirit called "Pure Wine" that's Pouring always,
One that heals the ill whose hearts are breaking always,
Swiftly bring two or three Jugful. I wonder why
They call *this* Fine Juice in-"toxic"-ating always!

زان روح که راح ناب میخوانندش
تیمار دل خراب میخوانندش
جام دو سه سنگین به من آرید سبک
خیر آب چرا شرآب میخوانندش

768. If not now, when? (اکنون نه، کی)

I leave grief for tomorrow. I'm now choosing rest!
My stars are aligned *now* for *this* Wine Drinking quest!
My Beloved agrees and the day's going well.
If not *now*, when else can I enjoy living best?

فردا الم فراق طی خواهم کرد
با طالع سعد قصد می خواهم کرد
معشوقه موافق است و ایام به کام
اکنون نکنم نشاط کی خواهم کرد

769. Noah's Ark (کشتی نوح)

Drink *this* Cup's Wine since it comforts your soul always.
It heals the many heart-wounds of your soul always.
If sudden storms of past or future griefs arise,
It will be the Noah's Ark of your soul always.

می خور که مدام راحت روح تو اوست
آسایش جان و دل مجروح تو اوست
طوفان غم ار در آید از پیش و پست
در باده گریز کشتی نوح تو اوست

770. Wine's Miracles (معجزات شراب)

When I place on my palm a Cup full of *this* Wine,
Being Ruined joyfully, Drunken in *this* Mine,
I find a hundred miracles on each topic
When my soul's flame and words' water meet in *this* Line.

روزی که به دست بر نهم جام شراب
وز غایت خرّمی شوم مست و خراب
صد معجزه پیدا کنم اندر هر باب
زین طبع چو آتش و سخنهای چو آب

771. I'm Not Hopeless (نومید نیم)

Though I'm called a sinner, living an awful state,
Unlike idolators I don't hopelessly wait!
When I rise Hungover at dawn, I seek *this* Wine
And my Beloved, hell or heaven be my fate!

هر چند که از گناه بدبختم و زشت
نومید نیم چو بت پرستان کنشت
خیزم چو گه سحر ز مخموری باز
می خواهم و معشوقه چه دوزخ چه بهشت

772. Freethinkers' Feast (بزم قلندران)

O heart! Don't be obsessed with mundane daily tasks.
Detach from them like how a Rogue in Rogueness basks.
Enjoy sitting with your freethinking friends in feasts.
Seek freedom, joy, and the Wine pouring from *these* flasks.

بگذار دلا وسوسۀ عقل معاش
از هستی خویشتن ببر چون اوباش
در بزم قلندران معنی بنشین
آزاده شو و شراب نوش و خوش باش

773. Mind Writing in Heart (نگاشت عقل در دل)

Whoever wrote a page of wisdom in his heart,
He did not waste a single moment from the start.
While he sought after pleasing his God in his life,
He tried meditating with *this* Cup of Wine art.

هر كو ورقى ز عقل در دل بنگاشت
يك لحظه ز عمر خويش ضايع نگذاشت
يا در طلب رضاى يزدان كوشيد
يا راحت خود گزيد و ساغر برداشت

774. In-Between State (حال ميان)

So long as I'm just thinking, joys escape from me.
When I'm joyful and Drunken, thoughts escape from me.
Between thinking and joyful Drunkenness there is
A state of life I wish would not escape from me.

تا هشيارم در طربم نقصان است
چون مست شوم بر خردم تاوان است
حاليست ميان مستى و هشيارى
من بندهٔ آن كه زندگانى آن است

775. My Wine Drinking (مى خوردن من)

It's not for the fun of it that I Drink *this* Wine,
Nor is *it* of rudeness or faith-bashing a sign.
I Drink *this* to become free from my lower selves.
That is why toward *this* Wine-Drinking I incline.

مى خوردن من نه از براى طرب است
نز بهر خلاف شرع و ترك ادب است
خواهم كه ز خويشتن دمى باز رهم
مى خوردن و مست بودنم زين سبب است

776. Why I Drink Wine (علت مى خورى)

I Drink *this* Wine; but 'drunken,' no, I'll never be!
I won't encroach except upon *this* Cup's Ruby!
Do you know why I am so much praising *this* Wine?
So that I don't worship like you my lower 'me.'

من باده خورم وليك مستى نكنم
الّا به قدح دراز دستى نكنم
دانى غرضم ز مى پرستى چه بود
تا من چو تو خويشتن پرستى نكنم

777. Four Silk Strings (چار ابريشم)

When my observing self in my inner world climbs,
It returns my spirit to the source of its chimes.
This existence harp plays its four natures' silk strings
When it goes mute to being picked on by the times.

چون شاهد روح خانه پرداز شود
هر جنس به اصل خويشتن باز شود
اين ساز وجود چار ابريشم طبع
از زخمهٔ روزگار بى ساز شود

778. Throat Bleeding (خونريزى گردن)

Ruined souls are rebuilt from *this* Wine-Drinking, ours.
Repented two thousand times *this* throat-bleeding, ours.
If I do not sin, what would be His mercy for?
Has not mercy come to clear all *this* sinning, ours?

آباد خرابات ز مى خوردن ماست
خون دو هزار توبه در گردن ماست
گر من نكنم گناه رحمت كه كند
رحمت همه موقوف گنه كردن ماست

779. Why I Don't Repent (چراست توبه ناكردن من)

Do you know why I do not repent? It's because
Drinking *this* Wine's not a sin. But those who applause
For *that* mundane wine will surely be barred from *this*
Wine from my throat that is secretive for its cause.

دانى كه چراست توبه ناكردن من
زيرا كه حرام نيست مى خوردن من
بر اهل مجازست به تحقيق حرام
مى خوردن اهل راز در گردن من

780. Freeing Myself from Myself (خودرهایی)

If you are wise, you'll know that you'll surely demise.
So, Drink *this* Wine since no harms from it will arise.
Even supposing there's no other use for *this*,
Does it not at least free you from your lower I's?

781. Second Spirit (روح ثانی)

Wine has been called the 'second spirit' by the wise.
Why, then, would a wise man rejecting it advise?
Even if there's no good coming from *this*, at least
Does it not briefly free you from your lower I's?

782. Splashing Wine (مشتی می زنم)

Let me stand up and seek after *this* Wine that's pure!
Let me dye my face with *this* Redness that's a cure!
Let me splash now on my prying mind's Sleepy face
From *this* Wine that surely does one's Waking assure!

783. Restless Mercury (سیماب گریزپا)

Lay *this* Wine on my palm, since my heart is restless.
Like the mercury, my fleeting life is restless.
Beware that my youth's flame is flowing in *this* Juice.
Be warned that false wealth brings a Sleep that is restless.

784. How to Drink (طریق می خوری)

When you Drink *this* Wine, you should Drink it with the wise,
Or with a tulip-faced lover with smiley eyes!
Avoid excess, don't parrot, keep it to yourself!
Sip it, bit by bit, on occasions, in disguise!

785. Avoid the Lowbred (مخور با سفله)

With mindless villains, snappy, with no dignity,
Beware, don't Drink *this*, since it'll cause malignity!
On Drinking night: wildness, raciness, hollering!
At dawn: headaches, regrets, and fake benignity!

786. When to Drink (کی خور)

Do you know, O one, higher than all be your might,
When it's most soul-raising, *this* Wine that is so bright?
Every Sunday, Monday, Tuesday, and on Wednesday,
Thursday, Friday, and Saturday, all day and night.

787. Friday and Saturday (آدینه و شنبه)

Even if you're Drinking *this* Wine during weekdays,
Beware not to lose Friday's chance among the days.
In our faith, Fridays and Saturdays are the same.
Seek freedom from habits, and not just those of days.

788. Drink Twice on Friday (آدینه دو خور)

Today that's been for a while as 'Friday' recalled,
From big Bowls not of Cups made of clays be enthralled.
If you Drank a Cup of *this* Wine during weekdays,
Drink two today, since 'the master of days' it's called.

789. Bubbling Wine (قلقل می)

In *this* Jug by my side, *this* Bubbling Wine is nice.
The music for dancing from the reed's whine is nice.
With a heart-stealing idol, mindful of *this* Wine,
Being freed from the times' sorrows of mine is nice.

790. Simple Event (واقعهٔ سهل)

Whether *this* Wine is pure or with some dregs obscured,
Whether our dress is woolen or with silk secured,
The main point must be clear to the wise and that is
knowing the simple truth that one's death is assured!

791. What I Sell (چه فروشیم)

I sell the nobles' hats, the crown of Kaykhosrow,
And turbans and silk robes, for the reed's single blow!
The rosary of an army of hypocrites
I trade for the improvised Sips of *this* Wine's flow!

792. I'm the Ring-Leader (سرحلقه منم)

Drunkards' ringleader of Ruins-clinging, I am.
From worship duty to *this* 'sin' swinging, I am.
I'm someone who spends a long night with *this* pure Wine.
Its prayers, from a bleeding gut, singing, I am.

793. We're the Rogue (همه رندیم)

Lovers and Rogue Drunkards and Wine-praisers, we are!
On Ruined roads, *this* mindful Cup raisers we are!
We are freed from the 'good or bad' myths! Ask not of
Thoughts, since of *this* Drunkenness trailblazers we are!

794. Wine Mix (ترکیب می)

I don't ever Drink *this* pure Wine just from gladness,
Without also Drinking it from grief and sadness.
I don't sprinkle on bread the salt of another,
Without eating it too with my guts in madness.

795. Permissible Wine (می حلال)

Don't let go of reasoning when you Drink *this* Wine.
Don't be dazed, nor yourself to ignorance confine.
To make *this* Ruby Wine permissible for you,
Don't go mad in life and with oppressors align.

796. Wine's Residue (خاک می)

Pour *this* Wine, since it's a balm for my broken heart!
It soothes the sorrows of all Lovers kept apart.
For my heart, just the residue in its Sip bests
The wheel that has turned this world around from its start.

797. Where Are You From? (از کجا می آیی؟)

O beloved, I am in love with you, O Wine!
I am not ashamed of devouring you, O Wine!
I Drink you such that when people see me, they ask,
"Where is *your* Barrel from? From where *are you*, O Wine?"

798. Lips Rag (کهنۀ لب)

This Sip of Wine bests the world they wish to acquire.
This Wine Barrel's Cap meets a thousand souls' desire.
The rag that they use to wipe *this* Wine from their lips
Is worth more than a thousand justices' attire.

799. Meaning of Humankind (مقصود ز آدمی)

Tender, my nobleness is in *this* Wine's wisdom.
It rebels against all the folks without wisdom.
Without wisdom, what for would be the humankind?
Does not being humankind mean having wisdom?

800. Feast Wine (می عید)

It's a festive day, let's Drink *this* Rose-colored Wine.
Let's Drink *this* Wine while the harp shares with oud their whine.
Let's sit together with a pure-spirited friend.
Let's Drink a few Cups of *this* dignified Divine.

801. What a Pity! (حیف است)

This Wine offers an effective cure for the wise.
Is it not a pity in *this* Clay jail it lies?
Be fair! Isn't it a pity that a happy soul
Like *this* mingles for too long with Repressed allies!

802. Wine Thrill (ذوق باده)

The worth of *this* Wine and roses, Wine praisers know;
The hard-hearted and the miserly would not know.
The ignorant are excused for their ignorance.
There's a thrill in *this* Wine that only Drunkards know.

803. Problem-Solver Wine (می مشکل کشا)

How long tell the tales of eternity or past?
Trying to know them, my ability surpassed.
But there's nothing like *this* Wine, wrapped in its music.
Any problem can be solved by *this* Wine at last.

804. Drink While There's A Bowl (نوش چو کاسه است بجا)

Today, when the head's Bowl is attached to its base,
Drink *this* Wine in your Bowl, in a wise friend's embrace,
Since a hundred bowls and heads of beggars and kings
Won't be worth a Jug of *this* in Wine-sellers' place.

805. An Hour (یک ساعت)

Hey! Don't let *this* Cup slip from your hand for an hour!
When you throw feasts, *this* Raw Wine brew and devour!
Since you have no permanent station in this world,
Take your life's share *now*, with all that's in your power!

806. Peasant's Wine (می دهقان)

Of *this* old Persian brewed rustic clay-covered Wine,
Bring to me since for it wishes this heart of mine.
Take the clay lid off your wishes *now*, since the world
Has buried in the clay many wishers, supine.

807. Wine to Wine (می به می)

I became in essence a Ruby like *this* Wine.
So, began wailing in complaint, my Glass of Wine,
Saying, "I Drank *this* so much, Wine on top of Wine,
That Wine went to my head as to your head my Wine."

808. Disgrace Until When (تا کی ننگ)

For how long should I be disgraced by their cruel deeds,
Or be deceived by the nobodies our time breeds?
Be happy that the fasting month's prayers are done.
It's the feasting time to make *these* Rosy Wine pleads.

809. Wine's Knot (بند می)

O tasty Wine in *this* Cup! Do your good and Rise!
What a knot you're tying on the feet of the wise,
Giving no respite to the one who dares a Sip
Until you hand him Pearls of what's behind his guise!

810. Repent? Not! (توبه؟ نی)

I repent of anything, but of *this* Wine? Not!
I depart from anything, but from *this* Wine? Not!
Can I be a Muslim and remain a faithful,
And let go of the Magian Drink, *this* Wine? Not!

811. Drink for Fulfillment (می برای کام)

Do not let the heart's tree take root in your grief's mire.
You must Drink *this* Wine and seek after heart's desire.
Always read *this* from the leaves of *this* Pure Wine's book:
"It *will* happen! Your leaving this world *will* transpire!"

812. Drunken Particle (ذرّهٔ مست)

Until the Rose Wine is left in *this* Wine-Cellar,
Try hard to Drink *it*, O dear wise Earthly dweller,
So that if a dust from your grave's blown by the wind,
It goes, still Drunken, back to its Tavern Seller.

813. Purest Pearl (درّ خوشاب)

I said a hundred times, O Pearl of *this* pure kind,
Let my self-understanding be in you refined.
The rolling of days will be like rolling of nights,
With not even a dream of events left behind.

814. Emerald in Box (زمرّد در حقّه)

Drinking *this* Wine makes people from their wealth denude.
A world of passions will be from their cries imbued.
I pour Emeralds in *this* Ruby box, because
I wish to blindsight the snake of my saddened mood.

815. What Will Be, Will Be (هر چه بادا باد)

May the lover, year-long, Drunken and Lovelorn be!
May he mad, ecstatic, defamed, not forlorn, be!
When sober, we grieve for anything, but Drunken
We say, "Whatever will be, will be! Don't mourn, be!"

عاشق همه ساله مست و شیدا بادا
دیوانه و شوریده و رسوا بادا
در هشیاری غصّهٔ هر چیز خوریم
ور مست شویم هر چه بادا بادا

816. Be Ruined (خراب باش)

Each day a few times Drink *this* Wine that is so pure,
Since, O beware, for a life that passed there's no cure.
Since you know the world is heading for the ruin,
With *this* Wine you must your Ruin, before, assure.

روزی که دو مهلتست می خور می ناب
کین عمر گذشته در نیابی دریاب
دانی که جهان رو به خرابی دارد
تو نیز شب و روز به می باش خراب

817. Coffin in Noah's Ark (تابوت در کشتی نوح)

The Tender whose lips pour *this* joyful Ruby Wine,
The one who serves Wine to sad hearts and souls to Dine,
Is one that one should die to in a storm of grief.
If not, in Noah's Ark one joins the coffined line.

ساقی که لبش مفرّح یاقوت ست
دل را غم او قوّت و جان را قوت ست
هر کس که نشد کشته به طوفان غمش
در کشتی نوح زنده در تابوت ست

818. Ways of Seeing (منگر، آن بین)

The Wine that makes life's moments suddenly go bright
Always begins from *this* Cup in my hand its flight.
You should not see what it is I have on my hand.
See instead what a hand *this* Wine has on my plight.

آن باده که روی عیش روشن دارد
همواره به دست من نشیمن دارد
منگر تو بدان که من چه دارم در دست
آن بین تو که او چه دست بر من دارد

819. All Left for Wine (هر آنچه هست برای می)

On this Earth, whatever Cash is left that I own
Is for buying *this* Wine, though it's disrepute prone.
They ask me what's left to pay for tomorrow's Wine.
My robe and turban, I say, ones by Mary sewn.

در روی زمین اگر مرا یک خشتست
آن وجه می ست گر چه نامی زشتست
گویند تو را وجه می فردا نیست
درّاعه و دستار که مریم رشتست

820. When to Drink (وقت نوشیدن)

This Wine gives the melancholic two wings to fly.
This Wine's Lines and Dots the wisdom's face glorify.
We did not Drink in the fasting month that just passed.
It's the night before the next, so it's fair to try.

سودا زده را باده پر و بال بود
می بر رخ خاتون خرد خال بود
ماه رمضان باده نخوردیم و برفت
باری شب عید از مه شوّال بود

821. Boiling Pot (دیگ اندر جوش)

While my pot of survival's *here*, boiling inside,
I will Drink *this* Wine of joy that's *here* purified.
O jug-maker! When you will make a jug from me,
Will you make sure it's to *this* Wine's sellers supplied?

تا دیگ بقای من بود اندر جوش
در کاسهٔ خوشدلی کنم از وی نوش
هان کوزه گرا گر گِلَم کوزه کنی
آن کوزه بجز به می فروشان مفروش

822. Shedding Which Blood? (ریختنِ کدام خون؟)

A drop that's wasted on earth of *this* Tender's Wine
Brings, to the hearts' fire of those who care, their whine.
Praise to God! How sad it is that you think is air
This water that cures hundreds of pains, yours and mine.

823. Dust on Whose Head? (خاک بسر که؟)

The grief of having or not, the wise consume not.
Other than all *these* brimful Cups, they consume not.
Grief is in the heart, and *this* Wine in Decanter.
Go to dust those who drink grief, and *this* consume not.

824. Eternally Embraced (در ابد هم آغوشان)

Those who amid Drunkenness became excited
And while singing about *this* Wine were delighted,
Drank from *this* Cup and became bewildered before
In the eternity's dusts with All united.

825. Wine-Drop Cure (دوای قطرهٔ می)

They say that opium serves to heal depressions,
That it's better than *these* harp-tuned Wine confessions.
But according to the faith of the perfect wise
This Wine cures a hundred opium obsessions.

826. Wine for the King, Wise, and Rogue (می شاه و حکیم و رند)

If I don't drink wine, they say that I am naive.
When I Drink Wine, it's infamy that I achieve.
This Wine is what the King, the wise, and the Rogue Drink.
If you're neither, don't Drink *this* Friend in the foe's sleeve.

827. Hurry Up, Tend the Cup! (بشتاب، بر نه قدح)

From *this* Wine that a different kind of life breeds
Fill a Cup, no matter how long trouble proceeds.
Place it on my palm, since the world affairs are tales.
Hurry up! Since my life only for a while breathes.

828. What Wine Does (باده چه کند)

Drinking *this* Wine, a beggar will become a king,
And a fox's courage to a lion's will swing.
The old who Drink it, will begin once again young.
To him who is young, it will the old's wisdom bring.

829. Beloved's Lips (لب یار)

O Wine! Kiss the ruby lips of lovers. Beware
That of such a wondrous job you need to take care.
The reason *this* Cup deserved such a Ruby Wine
Is that it conquered the Beloved Lips with dare!

ای می لب لعل یار میدار به دست
ز آنرو که شگرف داری این کار به دست
زان شد ز می لعل قدح برخوردار
کاورد به خون دل لب یار به دست

830. Noah-Old Advice (قصۀ نوح)

These morning Sips are telling of His Love, Tender.
They're not what I can firmly repent of, Tender.
Until when will you give your Noah-old advice?
Pour down your Comfort Drink from the above, Tender.

ما و می و معشوق و صبوح ای ساقی
از ما نبود توبه نصوح ای ساقی
تا کی خوانی قصۀ نوح ای ساقی
پیش آر سبک راحت روح ای ساقی

831. Confession (اعتراف)

They say that I'm too much praising *this* Wine; I am!
They say that I'm from the mystic Drunks' line; I am!
Don't pay too much attention to my outer side.
It's my words' inner meanings that define "I am"!

گویند مرا که می پرستم هستم
گویند مرا عارف و مستم هستم
در ظاهر من نگاه بسیار مکن
کاندر باطن هستم چنانکه هستم

832. Nothing But Wine (نیست بجز باده)

Here I am, persistently Drunken from *this* Wine.
In meetings nothing is to be served but *this* Wine.
O raw ascetic, let go of your advice, please!
With lips on my Lover's Lips, I devour *this* Wine.

مائیم که سرمست شرابیم مدام
در مجلس ما نیست بجز باده و جام
بگذار نصیحت من ای زاهد خام
ما باده پرستیم و لب یار به کام

XX. Love (عشق)

833. Pearl-Pouring Pen (کلک گهربار)

Whoever writes his lines from a Pearl-pouring pen
Starts with 'A' for the 'Almighty' Loved One, as when
God wrote once for His creation 'a' for 'angel.'
The angel wrote 'a' hundred times, time and again.

834. Intuitive Knowing (علم لدنی)

The heart said, "I seek the mystic intuitive way.
Teach me its alphabet, if you can, right away."
I said, "First comes A …" The heart said, "Please say no more.
When there's someone home, a knock's all you need to say."

835. Beloved Was With Us (معشوقه با ما بود)

My Beloved was here; it was I who knew not!
He was present to me; it was I who knew not!
I said perhaps I'll reach Him by worshiping more.
I was split and that's why it was I who knew not!

836. First Lesson (درس اوّل)

When the Eternal Grace wrote my life and was done,
His Love was the first book whose lessons had begun,
Turning *this* small scrap of the notebook of my heart
Into a key to *these* Pearl meanings of the One.

837. Free From Being and Non-Being (رستن از بود و نبود)

O heart! When you attend the feast of His Being,
Detaching from low selves to meet His Self's Being,
When you Drink a Sip of such annihilation,
You'll be freed at last from 'being and non-being.'

838. Heart Without Fire (دل بی سوز)

Oh, I pity the heart that is devoid of fire
And is not all-consumed by the Sweetheart's desire.
The day you do not feel his Love's presence at heart
Is a low day of which all others are higher.

839. Love Today (عشق امروز)

On His Love's path, puritans must still clear their dross.
In seeking Him, their positions great men must toss.
And begin *today* since 'tomorrow' may not come.
Those who seek 'tomorrow,' will die grieving its loss.

840. Freedom from Duality (آزادی از دویی)

Seekers don't care if the truth is pleasant or not.
Mystics don't care if hell or heaven is their lot.
The clothes of the lost-hearted may be rich or poor.
Lovers don't care if bed or grave is their tryst spot.

841. I Know He Knows (من دانم او داند)

I closed my wish-fulfillment's door to who I am,
Freed myself from indebtedness for who I am.
Since no one gives me a hand except for the Friend,
Only He knows, and I know, why I'm who I am.

842. Three Happinesses (سه چیز باید خوش)

Where's the musician and Wine so I sing at dawn?
Happy is the heart that recalls that time at dawn.
In this world I need three things to remain happy:
Drunkenness, Loving Him, and singing *this* at dawn.

843. The Origin of Heart (منشا دل)

It was from His Love's dew that Adam's clay was made,
But to lots of seditions did the world degrade.
For his healing, they Love-lanced the spirit's blood vein.
A drop of blood named "the heart" trickled down and stayed.

844. Threshold of Creation (درگاه الست)

I am in Love, excited, and Drunken today,
On the Magis' road reached *this* Wine's heaven today.
Liberated from what I was, I am joining
The threshold of Adam's recreation today.

845. Sorrow to Love and Drunkenness (غم به عشق و مستی)

For any heart that's trampled under sorrow's feet,
Nothing is better than Love through *this* Wine's repeat.
Since there is no more wine at hand, then send me more
Of *this* Wine whose Cup finds my writing hand its seat.

846. Light of Kindness (نور محبّت)

When His bright light of kindness is shed on the heart,
Whether shining through this or that faith gone apart,
For one whose name is written in *this* book of Love,
Freedom from *that* hell and *that* paradise will start.

847. Freed From the Times' Suffering (از محنت ایّام برستیم)

In the meeting of Lovers, elated we are.
From the times' sufferings, liberated we are.
We Drank *this* Cup of Wine of ecstasy for Him.
Free and tranquil and Intoxicated, we are.

848. Disobey the Wheel (مپذیر چرخ را)

Even if the wheel serves you fortune more and more,
Don't accept it since it'll debase you more and more.
But let the world put your arms in embrace around
The Beloved who's Imbibing you more and more.

849. Tavern of Love (میکدۀ عشق)

In the Tavern of Love, we too have a desire,
And by His face's candle a feverish fire.
We ablute with *this* Wine of Love and are praying
To our Idol who is of everything higher.

850. All Is the Friend (همگی دوست)

Love came and like blood spread through all my skin and veins,
Emptied 'me' such that His Love filled all my domains.
All parts of my existence were filled by the Friend.
Except for Him and my name, nothing else remains.

851. What's Heart For? (به چه کار آید دل؟)

The burden of Love's sorrow will lift from the heart,
Once its horse reins are taken wisely by the heart.
Except in the heartland, where else could Love reside?
Were it not for Love, why would there exist the heart?

852. Head and Love (سر و عشق)

Unless head's chatter is cut by the sword of Love,
One's mind is not cleared to earn the Beloved's Love.
You may seek after Love and head separately.
Yes, you can try, but that will not earn you His Love.

853. Go to Its End (قدم زنی محکم زن)

In His Love's path, you must firmly walk to its end,
And from both eyes to the world a flood of tears send.
When you arrive where you meet the Beloved, sigh,
And from the worlds' twoness to His Oneness ascend.

در عشق اگر قدم زنی محکم زن
وز آب دو دیده موج بر عالَم زن
آنجا که نظاره گاه مقصود رسی
آهی بزن و هر دو جهان بر هم زن

854. Happy in Sadness (خوشی در محنت)

Any heart that's in His longing sad, is happy.
Any head that's gone in His way mad, is happy.
Don't fault Him for the coming arrow of sadness.
He who knows it comes from the Comrade is happy.

هر دل که اسیر محنت اوست خوشست
هر سر که غبار سر آن کوست خوشست
از دوست به ناوک غم آزرده مشو
خوش باش که هر چه آید از دوست خوشست

855. Compass of Head and Soul (پرگار سر و جان)

O soul, you and I are like compass two-headed.
Though we have two ends, in body we are wedded.
I, the mind, and you circle one another's points,
But we'll be at last in each other embedded.

جانا من و تو نمونهٔ پرگاریم
سر گرچه دو کرده ایم یک تن داریم
بر نقطه روانیم کنون دایره وار
تا آخر کار سر به هم باز آریم

856. God's Favor (عنایت الهی)

In His mercy's path, a mount's offered for a grass,
A hundred sins forgiven for a deep 'alas!'
Where the favor of God intervenes, just a glance
Pardons a hundred remorseful sinners en masse.

در راه کرم کوه به کاهی بخشند
صد گونه گناه را به آهی بخشند
آنجا که عنایت الهی باشد
صد مجرم را به یک نگاهی بخشند

857. What to Ask For (چه طلب)

I've no faith but in God's Love, if faith's another.
I'm the feeble ant, and Solomon's another.
All I have is an old face, wrapped in *this* old Robe.
The silk-sellers' shop in the bazaar's another.

ما کافر عشقیم مسلمان دگرست
ما مور ضعیفیم سلیمان دگرست
از ما رخ زرد و جامهٔ کهنه طلب
بازارچهٔ قصب فروشان دگرست

858. Moth Knows (پروانه داند)

Heart is a light whose source is the Beloved's face.
It goes on when it dies in longing for His Grace.
The candle's trait can be best known to moth-like hearts.
Only the Love-burned know why a moth does its chase.

دل چراغیست که نور از رخ دلبر گیرد
ور بمیرد ز غمش زندگی از سر گیرد
صفت شمع به پروانه دلی باید گفت
کین حدیث است که با سوختگان در گیرد

859. Dying in Joy (مرگ خندان)

If you Love God, be consumed in His exile's fire.
Amid pains await the cure in His Love's desire.
Gut-wrenched, be focused like a bud onto your heart.
When dying, smile as if blooming to a higher.

گر عاشقی اندر تب هجران می باش
با درد در انتظار درمان می باش
خون میخور و همچو غنچه در دل بنگر
جان می ده و همچو گل خندان می باش

860. Immortal Sun (خورشید لایزال)

It's the Sun of eternal heavens that is Love.
It's *this* bird of benefic gardens that sings Love.
Love is not that when, like a nightingale, you sing.
If you die and still you go on singing, that's Love.

خورشید سپهر بی زوالی عشق است
مرغ چمن خجسته فالی عشق است
عشق آن نبود که همچو بلبل نالی
هر که که بمیری و بنالی عشق است

861. Lovers' Door (در عاشقان)

Wake up! Lovers do nothing but caress at night,
When for their Friend through their rooftop's door take a flight.
At night, where there is a door it is closed except
For Lovers, one that opens when goes out the light.

برخیز که عاشقان به شب ناز کنند
گرد در و بام دوست پرواز کنند
هر جا که دری بود به شب در بندند
الّا در عاشقان که شب باز کنند

XXI. Night (شب)

862. Your Presence (تو در کنار)

O Tender, when you're present, soul-raising tonight,
Unlike that of my foes, my luck wins in its fight.
Tell the candle to die out, and the Moon to set,
Since the night you're in my presence is always bright.

امشب که حضور یار جان افروزست
بختم به خلاف دشمنان فیروزست
گو شمع بمیر و مه فرو شو که مرا
آن شب که تو در کنار باشی روزست

863. Venus and the Moon (زهره و ماه)

Until Venus joined the Moon in the sky at night,
Nothing better than *this* Pure Wine had come in sight.
So, I've been puzzled about those who sell *this* Wine!
What else can they buy instead that's even more bright?

تا زهره و مه در آسمان گشت پدید
بهتر ز می ناب کسی هیچ ندید
من در عجبم ز می فروشان کایشان
به زان که فروشند چه خواهند خرید

864. Angel's Thunder and Lightning (رعد و برق اجل)

Tender! What a festive night! The Moon is lighted!
Pour *this* Wine! To say this the sphere is excited:
You know how like a lightning-rod the angel strikes;
Our crop's long burned by when its rumor is cited!

ساقی شب عیش ست و مه افروخته است
می ده که فلک نکته ای آموخته است
دانی که اجل چه برق خرمن سوزیست
تا درنگری خرمن ما سوخته است

865. Appeal to Wine-Tender (تمنا از ساقی)

With a candle, the Moonlight, and *this* Wine, Tender,
And a watchful self, Drunken from *this* Wine, Tender,
Raise from the depth of the earth, *this* flame of my heart!
Don't let it waste in the wind; bring *this* Wine, Tender!

شمع ست و شراب و ماهتاب ای ساقی
شاهد ز شراب هم خراب ای ساقی
از خاک بر آر این دل پر آتش را
بر باد مده بیار آب ای ساقی

866. Waste Not A Drop (یک قطره رها مکن)

Day and night Drink *this*, my forbidden Wine, always.
Drink, day and night with harp, *this* rhyming Line always.
If you're offered a Cup full of *this* Ruby Wine,
Drink it all, don't waste a Drop, I'd opine always.

می گرچه حرامست مدامش مینوش
با نغمه و چنگ صبح و شامش مینوش
جامی ز می لعل گرت دست دهد
یک قطره رها مکن تمامش مینوش

867. Night-Day Scissors (تراش شب و روز)

Since night and day shred away bit by bit your life,
Don't be so buried by the shreds from their twin-knife.
Enjoy your days and nights since for a long time, still,
The scissors of night and day will cut all in strife.

از عمر تو چونکه می تراشد شب و روز
مگذار که خاک بر تو پاشد شب و روز
روز و شب خویشتن به شادی گذران
ای بس که نباشی تو و باشد شب و روز

868. This is the Blessing (کرم از خداست)

Last night, Drunken, I arrived at *this* Tavern's door.
An old Drunk had a Jug on his shoulder to pour.
I said, "Old man, you too are not ashamed of God?"
He said, "*This is* God's blessing! Be quiet! Drink more!"

869. Tight-Lipped Mouth (دهان تنگ)

Wake up and pour *this* Wine; let's futile chatters quit,
Since tonight your Tight-Lipped Mouth's feeding me a wit.
Serve me *this* Wine that's Rose-colored like your face, since
My repentance, like your Hair, won't Straightness admit.

870. Shine But Not Find (بتابد و نیابد)

Since no one can foretell what will come tomorrow,
Now bring joy to lighten this lovelorn heart's sorrow.
Drink *this* Wine in Moonlight, O my moon, since the Moon
Will shine for long but no longer find our shadow.

871. Book Divination (فال دفتر)

From *this* book of life I divined a page just now.
From the depth of my heart it told me *this* somehow:
"Happy is he who can, by his side, a Beauty
Like the Moon of one night for a whole year allow!"

872. Dew's Meditation (نشست شبنم)

O heart! Take what's in the world for granted today,
And go to a joyful garden and therein stay.
For a whole night sit on the green, like a dew drop,
And meditate 'til dawn and then just walk away.

873. Moonlight's Routine (مهتاب بسی خواهد تافت)

The Moonlight has just pierced through the veil of the night!
Drink *this* Wine, it's the best time to taste its delight.
Be happy and think how often the Moon will shine
Night after night on your gravestone to make it bright.

874. Balkh or Baghdad (چه بغداد چه بلخ)

When life ends, it matters not in Balkh or Baghdad.
Sweet or bitter may have been what the Cup has had.
Drink *this* Wine! After you and me, the Moon will move
From the month's first to its last skies like a nomad.

875. Nightly Raid (شبیخون)

Before they strike you to death in a nightly raid,
Tell them to bring *this* Cup that's Rosy Wine inlaid,
Since you're not made of gold, O you negligent fool,
Whom they bury and then again dig up to trade!

زان پیش که بر سرت شبیخون آرند
فرمای که تا بادهٔ گلگون آرند
تو زر نه ای ای غافل نادان که تو را
در خاک کنند و باز بیرون آرند

XXII. Death and Survival (مرگ و بقا)

876. Oh, I Wish! (ای کاش)

Oh! I wish this world was a place for lasting rest,
Or that I could reach that goal by doing my best,
Or that I could rise, in a hundred thousand years,
From the earth's heart, just like a green, again with zest!

877. Death's Knot (بند اجل)

From the black clay mass of the Earth to Saturn's height,
I solved all the universal problems in sight.
I untied all their problems' knots in crafty ways,
Except for the knot of death that is still closed tight.

878. Secrets of Death (اسرار اجل)

No one has unriddled the secrets of dying.
Outside this circle no one has stepped when trying.
As I see it, everyone, novice or teacher,
Has remained as baffled as a newborn crying.

879. Home in Another Substance (مسکن در جنس دگر)

When your lucid substance leaves your body, I'd say,
It can find a home in other substance to stay.
But many have come and gone, none having yet learned
What happens to your body, buried under clay.

880. Time of Death (وقت هلاک)

On the days when the last breaths, yours and mine, will flow,
Our pure souls from the bodies, yours and mine, will go.
Absent us, from the gray skies, the Moon and the Sun
Their lights on the buried grounds, yours and mine, will throw.

881. Surrendering Day (وقت تسلیم)

I'm not one who is afraid of passing away.
I'll leave for that half, when in this half I can't stay.
Life is a loan that's been offered to me by God.
I'll surrender it, come my surrendering day.

882. My Fear (ترس من)

Don't think that my fear is about worldly events,
Or about death, or the pains the death pang presents.
Dying is certain. I do not fear it. My fear
Is about not fulfilling what life represents.

883. Body and Pure Soul (تن و روان پاک)

From fire, air, water, and earth, coming we're all.
In this, our worldly existence, passing we're all.
To the extent that we're bodies, we will be doomed.
But, beside bodies, in spirit living we're all.

884. What You Plant Can Still Grow (ز فنا شاخ بقا خواهد رست)

Death fears and thoughts awaken your being to know
That despite the body's death your spirit can grow.
I, too, can resurrect from breaths, like Jesus did.
When my time comes, I'd then survive the angel's blow.

885. Pity the Earth (بیچاره زمین)

Although my secret is no more to you unknown,
I won't regret having let *these* seeds to be sown.
Know this, sir, as I do, that for *these* words and deeds,
The earth will be pitied for hosting me alone.

886. Suppose You're In Dust (انگار در خاکی)

Remain calm since under a reckless sphere you are.
Drink *this* Wine, if in plagued lands, far or near, you are.
Since you come from and go to the dust, think you are
In the dust now to enjoy while still here you are.

887. Branch of Hope (شاخ امید)

If on a branch of hope I cultivate *this* fruit,
I could also branch from my human tree a shoot.
Until when should I feel I'm bound in being's jail,
Wishing that I must find to my dying a route?

888. Rooster's Saw (ارّهٔ خروس)

Ascetics who on duplicity base their art,
Come and think that *this* Wine is not from me a part.
Then, I'll hold on my head *this* Wine's Jug, so they won't,
Like the comb of a rooster, saw my head apart!

889. Wine-Tender Love (مهر ساقی)

Wine-Tender! My heart, planting *these* Seeds of your love,
Will in secret eternally embrace your love.
Even if all your seekers do not touch your Robe,
I will never let go of the Robe of your love.

890. Death Angel in Stone (اجل در سنگ)

O Wine-Tender! Even if one hides in the stone,
From death's fire, it will still be to melting prone.
The world is just some dust, sing *these* songs, O player!
Breath's a wind! Bring Wine, Tender! Let it blow its tone.

891. Intimate Friends (یاران موافق)

My intimate friends are gone. They one by one died.
By falling to the angel's feet, they did abide.
They were easy Wine Drunkards in life's gathering.
Rounds before others, *this*, our Wine's Drunkenness, tried.

892. My Wine Mindfulness (هوشم به شراب)

My mindfulness has come from *this* Pure Wine always.
My ears are lent to *its* reed and lute whine always.
If you make a Wine Jug from my earth tomorrow,
I'd like it to be full of *this* divine always.

893. Jug Made of My Dust (کوزه از خاک من)

When they vacate my body from its soul inside,
And lay it down in a dark ditch, rolled to its side,
When recalling your lips, will be filled with *this* Wine
The Jug made from *these* Dusts that in my grave reside.

894. Tavern Wall Gaps (رخنه دیوار خرابات)

If you are my friends, then let useless mourning go.
Clear your griefs for me with *this* Wine, flow after flow.
When I die, mix my Dust, that's *this* Wine, with your clay
And use it to fill *this* Tavern's gaps, high and low.

895. Defeathered Bird (مرغ پر کنده)

When I, before the angel's feet, crestfallen die,
And like a bird by the angel defeathered lie,
Beware, mold my clay into nothing but *this* Jug,
So I may live again from its Fragrant Supply.

896. Plain Weave (نخ ساده)

When my time arrives and you begin to prepare
My grave, spread *this* plain Wine on its bedding of lair.
And when you lay bricks of Clay around its Corners,
Be sure the Clay is mixed with *this* Wine everywhere.

در وقت اجل چو کارم آماده کنید
در بستر خاکم ز می ساده کنید
در خاک لحد چو خشت خواهید نهاد
زنهار که آب و گلش از باده کنید

897. Wine's Fragrance (بوی شراب)

I will Drink so much from *this* Wine that from its smell
You can always my grave from those of others tell.
When a Drunkard passes by my tomb, he would be
Even more Drunken mad from *this*, my Fragrant Spell.

چندان بخورم شراب کاین بوی شراب
آید ز تراب چون روم زیر تراب
تا گر سر خاک من رسد مخموری
از بوی شراب من شود مست و خراب

898. Wine! Push the Capstone (باده! سر بردار)

Before my grave is filled with my earthly remains,
And I disintegrate to the earth's subterrains,
O Wine, flood the Decanter's capstone off my grave
So that my heart starts to beat again on the plains.

زان پیش که گوری ز من آکنده شود
و اجزای مرکّبم پراکنده شود
ای باده سر از گور صراحی بردار
باشد که دل مردۀ من زنده شود

899. Pure Wine Prayer (تلقین ز شراب ناب)

When I pass away, wash my body with *this* Wine.
Pray in my ear *these* Wine Sips of the purest Line.
If on my judgment day you look around for me,
Search for my body's dusts in *this* Tavern's confine.

چون درگذرم به باده شویید مرا
تلقین ز شراب ناب گویید مرا
خواهید به روز حشر یابید مرا
از خاک در میکده جویید مرا

900. Lose My Dusts (خاک مرا گم سازید)

When I die, let *these*, my life's Dusts, be lost away,
To teach lessons through their verses of my life's play.
Mix *these* Dusts of my body with your Wine and then
Make a Wine Barrel's Cap from *this*, my body's Clay.

چون مرده شوم خاک مرا گم سازید
احوال مرا عبرت مردم سازید
خاک تن من ز باده آغشته کنید
وز کالبدم خشت سر خم سازید

901. Leaves Falling (برگ ریزان)

Before the death angel's wings usher up my flight,
And like a leaf's journey begins my falling rite,
I'll sift my heart's joyfulness from the world's sorrows,
Before I am screened by the dust-sifters outright.

آن لحظه که از اجل گریزان گردم
چون برگ ز شاخ عمر ریزان گردم
عالم ز نشاط دل به غربال کنم
زان پیش که خاک خاکبیزان گردم

902. Tree of Life (نهال عمر)

When the tree of my life is uprooted, and when
All the stars have scattered and slowed down from their spin,
If you mold my body of clay into your Jug
And fill it up with *this* Wine, I will live again.

آنگه که نهال عمر من کنده شود
و اجرام ز یکدگر پراکنده شود
گر زانکه صراحیی کنند ز گل من
حالی که پر از می اش کنی زنده شود

903. Vine Coffin (تابوت رز)

O soulmates! Drink *this* Wine, my life's tale, with your bread!
Turn *this*, my amber face, into your Ruby red!
Wash my body with *this* Wine when I'm gone, and then
Build my coffin from *its* wood stock of Vine instead!

ای همنفسان مرا ز می قوت کنید
وین چهرۀ کهربا چو یاقوت کنید
چون درگذرم به می بشویید مرا
وز چوب رزم تختۀ تابوت کنید

904. When You Tryst (چو میعاد کنید)

O dear pals! When you're meeting around *this* diwan,
Enjoying your gathering as much as you can,
When the Wine-Tender serves you *this* Magian Wine,
Cheer a prayer or two for me, this cheerless man!

یاران چو به اتّفاق میعاد کنید
خود را به جمال یکدگر شاد کنید
ساقی چو می مغانه بر کف گیرد
بیچاره مرا هم به دعا یاد کنید

905. Flip the Cup (نگونسار کنید)

My dear friends! When in companionship you intend
To gather, you must many times recall your friend!
After you Drink *this* Wholesome Wine, Cup after Cup,
Flip mine so that I can Drink *this* Wine to its end!

یاران به موافقت چو دیدار کنید
باید که ز دوست یاد بسیار کنید
چون بادۀ خوشگوار نوشید به هم
نوبت چو به ما رسد نگونسار کنید

XXIII. Liberation (رهایی)

906. Swiftly Fasten Belt (میان بند چست)

If in my coming to this life I had no say,
Should my leaving unfulfilled be part of the play?
Get up, O Wine-Tender! Swiftly fasten your belt,
Since I now aim to Drink this world's sorrows away!

چون آمدنم به من نبد روز نخست
وین رفتن بی مراد عزمی ست درست
برخیز و میان ببند ای ساقی چست
کاندوه جهان به می فرو خواهم شست

907. Grieve No More (دیگر غم نخوریم)

No, I'll no longer bemoan this world's whirling chart!
I'll enjoy nothing but *this* Pure Wine Drinking art!
This Wine is the world's Blood, so I'll Bloody the world.
Why not Drink *this*, the Blood of my own healing heart?

دیگر غم این گردش گردون نخوریم
جز بادهٔ ناب صاف گلگون نخوریم
می خون جهانست و جهان خونی ما
ما خون دل خونی خود چون نخوریم

908. War Now (جنگ اینک)

If the sphere brings no peace, then, let my war begin!
If it does not clear my name, let it my shame spin!
Here! I hurl an arms-load of *this* Red Ruby Wine!
He who Drinks *this* not, let dusts catapult his chin!

گر صلح نیابم ز فلک جنگ اینک
ور نام نکو نباشدم ننگ اینک
جام می لعل ارغوان رنگ اینک
آن کس که نمیخورد سر و سنگ اینک

909. Triple Divorce (سه طلاق)

I'll finish the whole of *this* Barrel's Wine tonight.
I'll enrich myself from *this* Ruby Mine tonight.
I'll divorce intellect and faith with triple seals.
I'll then wed myself *this* Daughter of Vine, tonight.

امشب می جام یک منی خواهم کرد
خود را به دو رطل می غنی خواهم کرد
اوّل سه طلاق عقل و دین خواهم گفت
پس دختر رز را به زنی خواهم کرد

910. Khezr's Wine (می خضر)

The Wine the majestic Khezr is guarding is *this*
Elixir and I'm his Elijah! Drink *this* bliss!
I call *this* food for the heart and the spirit's strength,
One that God said its benefits folks can't dismiss.

می را که خضر خجسته دارد پاسش
او آب حیاتست و منم الیاسش
من قوت دل و قوّت روحش خوانم
چون گفت خدا منافع للناسش

911. Wine's My Lot (می قسم من است)

'Wine' is the forty chant of *this* Tavern of mine.
To praise *this* Wine as a Rogue, *is* the lot of mine.
In *this* house of Magis, I'm the life of the world.
This whole universe is in *this* body of mine.

در میکده ذکر باده چل اسم منست
رندی و پرستیدن می قسم منست
من جان جهانم اندرین دیر مغان
این صورت کون جملگی جسم منست

912. I Don't Repent (من توبه نکنم)

Since life is fleeting, I fleet to *this* work of art,
To *this* Bright Wine that joy is its goal from the start.
They tell me, "May God help you to repent of it."
He won't. If He does, I won't from my art depart.

913. My Pledge (قول من)

With a beauty, by the rose, on a river side,
I will be with Drinking *this* Wine preoccupied.
As long as I have lived, am living, and will live,
With the vow of Drinking *this* Wine I will abide.

914. I Am Who I Am (چنان که هستم هستم)

Am I high from *this* Magian Wine? Yes, I am.
Am I a Rogue Lover of *this* Wine? Yes, I am.
Every crowd has its own supposition of me.
I am my own. I'm the way I am. Yes, I am!

915. Fiery Water (آب آتش افروز)

Before sorrow's fire scorches my hopes, a few,
And gather around my gravestone, gut-wrenched, a few,
Before the angel flaps the last breath of my life,
I will spread *these*, my fiery water drops, a few.

916. It's All About Happiness (حاصل همه عشرت است)

Without *this* Wine and *its* Tender, this world's in vain.
Without the Iraqi Reed hums, this world's in vain.
The more I think about the world, the more I find
That it's for joy and the rest of this world's in vain.

917. The Right Point of View (رای درست)

From the beginning, I searched by way of the sky
To find where the tablet, pen, heaven, or hell lie.
Then the teacher told me, "From the right point of view,
The pen of fate, paradise, or hell, is your 'I.'"

918. If I Had a Hand (گر دست بدی)

If I, like God, had a hand on my sphere at will,
I would unravel this sphere entirely until
I rebuilt another sphere anew so the free
Could, without an ordeal, their goals in life fulfill.

919. Heaven's Brink (به چرخ افراشتمی)

If I had a hand on luck's tablet, pen, and ink,
I would rewrite it and do what I like and think.
I'd cross out the world's sorrows at once and for all,
And from such happiness fly to the heaven's brink!

920. Depends On You (با تست)

O the mixture of the four elements! Yes, you!
Hear these words that came from the Divine world to you:
You can be a devil, beast, angel, or human.
Who you are, and who you can be, depends *on you*!

921. Don't Be Lost (گم نکنی)

Beware not to lose your grip on the wisdom's thread.
Don't let yourself be to the times' good or bad wed.
You're the traveler, the road, and the journey's end.
Beware not to be lost but to your true self led.

922. Is Is Not, Is Not Is (هست نیست، نیست هست)

Since from all that exists, all that is left is air,
Since what exists, past what does not, is failure,
Then imagine what there is in the world, is not.
Think as if what is not in the world, is now here.

923. Your job, Soul's Wine Brewing (کار تو می جان پروردن)

If you wish the wheel to be aligned with your goal,
Your job here being to self-cultivate your soul,
Like me, be convinced of proceeding as follows:
Drink *this* Wine! In the world's joys, not its griefs, enroll!

924. Will Pass As You Pass It (هر گونه که گذرانی گذرد)

Both the good and the bad of this changing world pass.
All its sorrows and joys also arise and pass.
But know this! Thanks to the blessing of God, this world
Can, as you and I and all like to make it, pass!

925. Hands Together, Dance In Joy (دست اتفاق، پای نشاط)

Unless we *ourselves altogether* clap our hands,
We will not kick away grief with joy and in dance.
Let's Wake up and breathe before the breathing of dawn,
Since many dawns will breathe after we've had our chance.

926. Sixties' Joy (ذوق شصتی)

Stand up *now*, let's dance and clap hands, and splash quickly
This Wine to Awaken our Drunken self's beauty.
Drinking *that* wine in our twenties was not as nice
As the odd joy *this* Wine brings us past our sixty.

927. Passing World (دنیای گذران)

The world passes and its secrets you do not know,
Of how it ends or began a long time ago.
So, when a new day comes, play the tune of that day,
Not the tunes of yesterday, nor of tomorrow.

928. True Dawn's Shell (صدف صبح صادق)

With a graceful friend by the brook, the day before,
I sat with *this* Cup of Rosy Wine on the floor.
The Wine glass was a Seashell from whose inner Pearl
The drummer of the true dawn sprang up to the fore.

929. Last Wine (بادهٔ قیام)

If there is more of *this* Wine in your Cup, raise it!
Prying in other people's lives, give up! End it!
And do so before they say in your life's meeting,
"Tender! It's time for his last Sip! Cheer up, bring it!"

930. Stop Old Tales (چه جای حدیث)

It is morning now! Singing aloud, O Tender,
We are with *this* Wine in the street of its Vendor!
This is not the time to be falsely puritan.
Quit ascetic tales and let us Drink *this* Splendor!

931. Dying to Exist (پستی تا هستی)

Unless I know that I'll die, landing below lands,
I won't appreciate that a standing world stands.
Is it not better that I Drink *this* to be Drunk,
Dancing at times, in others clapping hands on hands?

932. Drink Slowly (نرمك نرمك خور)

O hesitating beloved! It's dawn, Arise!
Sip by Sip Drink *this* Wine as the harp gently cries!
These who still remain will not be here for too long,
And will not come back again those who'll soon demise!

933. O Still-Young (ای طرفه پسر)

O the still young! Wake up and hear *this* morning Chime!
Fill your Glass with *this* Ruby Wine that's always prime!
Drink, because you will not find, if you seek again,
This borrowed passing moment in the march of time.

934. It's Morning (صبح است)

Here comes the morning! Let us breathe *this* Rosy Wine!
Let us shatter the glass of our fame and shame's twine!
Let us withdraw from our lengthy hopes, and caress
The dress and the long hair of *this* Harp that's divine!

935. O Unfailing Idol (ای صنم فرخ پی)

Morning is here, my love, O unfailing divine!
Come and compose a new song and bring us *this* Wine,
Since the passing of this month and that of the next
Will thousands of Jams and Kays to their graves assign.

936. Wake Up to Drink (برخیز تا بخوریم)

Wake up from your Sleep so that we may Drink *this* Wine!
Let's Drink *this* before time twists in the grave our spine!
Let's Drink before the combative wheel suddenly
Won't let us sip even some water drops to dine!

937. Teaching Drunkards Music (طرب آموزی مستان)

Wake up! Let us sing from our happy hearts today.
Let's teach morning Drunkards our music arts today.
Let's shed our dress like the rose as nightingales sing.
Let's blow away our youth like blossom starts today.

938. Depression Drug (دوای دلتنگی)

Wake up and bring *this* Wine's drug for the depressed heart,
And let the healing by *this* Red Musk-Scented start!
If you are asking what turns sorrow into joy,
It is *this* Ruby Wine wrapped in harp's silk-lined art!

939. Morning Mourning? (غمناک صبح؟)

The dark night's robe has torn, the dawn is aborning.
Wake up! Why are you sad, not Drinking this morning?
Drink *this* Wine, O heart, for many mornings will come
Looking for us while they look down in our mourning.

940. Nightingale's Thousand Tunes (داستان هزاردستان)

When the nightingale sings a Thousand tunes, so fine,
Take from Drunkards' hands nothing but *this* Ruby Wine.
Wake up and come, since the rose has blossomed in joy.
Clip a few you deserve from *this* Garden of mine.

اکنون که زند هزاردستان دستان
جز بادۀ لعل از کف مستان مستان
برخیز و بیا که گل به شادی بشکفت
روزی دو سه خود ز بستان بستان

941. Wine Cup As Prayer Rug (سجّادۀ پیاله)

Come, let us grab the harp *now* and play it! Arise!
Let's Drink *this* Wine and ignore their name-shaming tries.
Let's sell *mindless* prayer rugs for *this* Cup of Wine,
And breaking the Glass of fame-and-shame exercise.

برخیز و بیا که چنگ بر چنگ زنیم
می نوش کنیم و نام بر ننگ زنیم
سجّاده به یک پیاله می بفروشیم
وین شیشۀ نام و ننگ بر سنگ زنیم

942. Moses Hands, Jesus Breaths (موسی دستان و عیسی نفسان)

It's time for *this* eastern wind to fashion the world,
So that new views through *its* thundercloud eyes unfold.
Let Moses hands grow from the branches of *its* trees.
Let Jesus breaths resurrect from *its* dusts, behold!

وقتست که از صبا جهان آرایند
وز چشم سحاب چشمها بگشایند
موسیٰ دستان ز شاخ کف بنمایند
عیسی نفسان ز خاک بیرون آیند

943. Muhammad's Wine, Ali's Pool (شراب احمد، حوض مرتضی)

O Heart! With *this* Wine, the Beloved, and flowers,
Let deceit and duplicity go in these hours.
If you follow Muhammad, Drink his Cup of Wine
From the pool Ali tends, one the soul empowers.

ای دل می و معشوق بکن در باغی
سالوس رها کن و مکن زراقی
گر پیرو احمدی خوری جام شراب
زان حوض که مرتضاش باشد ساقی

944. Where Is It? (کو؟)

The Ruby Lip that's Badakhshānī, where is it?
The Wine of the Line that's Reyhānī, where is it?
They say it became prohibited for Muslims.
The Wine of wisdom that's Islāmī, where is it?

یاقوت لب لعل بدخشانی کو
وان راحت روح و راح ریحانی کو
گویند حرام در مسلمانی شد
تو می خور و غم مخور مسلمانی کو

945. Faith Wine (بادۀ دین)

What a faithful beloved has been *this* old Wine!
My code is not to feast without *this* Bride of Vine!
O Wine-Tender! They say the Drunkard has no faith.
I Drink since *this* Wine is *itself* the faith of mine!

ساقی می کهنه یار دیرین منست
بی دختر رز عیش نه آئین منست
گویند که باده خوار را دینی نیست
من باده خورم که باده خود دین منست

946. Your Emanation (چشمۀ فیض تو)

Tender! My Wine's distilled from the sweat of your face.
Not in any eyeshot, you are what our eyes chase.
Your emanation is sourced from your Ruby lips.
Hundreds of Khezr and Jesus souls to your Wine trace.

ساقی می ما ز عارض پر خوی تست
چشمت نرسد که چشمها در پی تست
سرچشمۀ فیض جز لب لعل تو نیست
صد خضر و مسیح جرعه نوش می توست

947. Friends' Hearts (دل دوستان)

Since we don't know at night if we'll live the next day,
We must plant the seeds of what is good from *today*.
Since no one will remain in this world lastingly
At least we can make to the hearts of friends a way.

چون نیست امید عمر از شام به چاشت
باری همه تخم نیکوئی باید کاشت
چون عالم را به کس نخواهند گذاشت
باری دل دوستان نگه باید داشت

948. Secret to Joy (راز خوشدلی)

When grief becomes suddenly coupled with your heart,
Or some new troubles in your life suddenly start,
Then ask someone how he or she has been doing.
You'll see how suddenly all your sorrows depart.

هرگاه که غمی ملازم دل شودت
یا قصهٔ کار خویش مشکل شودت
حال دل دیگری بباید پرسید
تا خوشدلی تمام حاصل شودت

949. Medicine Will Come (دوایی یابی)

Live with your pain so that the medicine you'll find.
Don't bemoan suffering so the healing you'll find.
In poverty, thank for the wealth of life you've had,
So that in the end what is true richness you'll find.

با درد بساز تا دوائی یابی
وز رنج منال تا شفائی یابی
میباش به وقت بینوائی شاکر
تا عاقبت الامر نوائی یابی

950. Futile Threat (بیهده تهدیدستی)

If they let me change this world's habitual play,
I will treat each day as if it's a new year's day.
Each can then clap his hands as he reached fulfillment,
Saying the threat was a myth to be cast away.

این کار جهان اگر به تقلیدستی
هر روز به جای خویشتن عیدستی
هر کس به مراد خویش دستی بزدی
گر زانکه نه این بیهده تهدیدستی

951. Few Gut-Wrenched (جگرسوزی چند)

In the street of Ruins, a few gut-wrenched dwellers
Sought solace from a few happy-heart revellers,
With a musician playing, Wine-Tender serving,
"These sad moments will pass, too, O sadness quellers!"

در کوی خرابات جگرسوزی چند
بنشسته بدند با دل افروزی چند
ساقی قدحی بر کف و مطرب میگفت
هم بگذرد و نماند این روزی چند

952. Wet Fire (آتش تر)

Drink *this* Wine so that sorrows depart from your hearts.
You'll care no more about a world split in two parts.
Drink *this* Wet Fire *now* so you won't blow away
This elixir's chance before your last breath departs.

می نوش که تا غم از نهادت برود
شغل دو جهان جمله ز یادت برود
رو آتش تر گزین که این آب حیات
آنگه که شوی خاک ز بادت برود

953. Tomorrow Disobeys (فردا عاقی)

How joyous and cheerful this morning is, Tender!
From last night's Wine *this* Glass's fills increase, Tender!
Let's Drink *this* Wine *today* and renew our joy since
Tomorrow won't obey and will displease, Tender!

صبحی خوش و خرّمست خیز ای ساقی
در شیشه کن از آن شراب از شب باقی
تا باز خوریم و عیش را تازه کنیم
این یک دم عمر را که فرداست عاقی

954. Break Up World's Grief (غم جهان در شکنم)

How long should I tear life's pages in grief apart?
I'd rather pour *this* Wine's joy from *this* Pitcher's heart.
Wake up *now* and fill your Laughing Cup with *this* Wine,
So that I can clear this world's sorrows through *this* art.

955. Many Lives to Sleep Across (عمرهات میباید خفت)

A counterfeit coin cannot be coupled with us.
This sweeping of our joy's house has left nothing dross.
A wise elder emerged from *this* Tavern and said,
"Drink *this* Wine, or many lives you will Sleep across."

956. Sweeping Tavern's Door (در میخانه رفته)

Having safely Swept with Lip's Hair *this* Tavern's Door,
From now the good and bad of both worlds I'll ignore!
Even if the "two-world" worries roll over me,
I'll be Drunk, barley-food poor, asleep on the floor.

957. Cooked Soulmate, Raw Wine (همدم پخته، می خام)

Now that from joy just its name's dot and line remained,
And no refined soulmate but *this* Raw Wine remained,
Then do not let your hand slide from *this* Jug of Wine,
Now that nothing but *this* Wine's Jug of mine remained.

958. Dress Will Tear (جامه چاک شود)

O friend, to rest in hard times, I give in a gist
An advice, "Succumbing to useless griefs, resist!"
When your life's clothing eventually tears, it tears,
No matter what you've done and said, or what you've missed.

959. Here It Is (این است)

To seek happiness in a Rogue way you must try
To be mindful even when you are sad and cry.
In joyful times anyone can remain joyful.
Joy is itself a way to lift the low times high.

960. That's Its Elegance (نغز آن است)

In a world where the feet of our survival slip,
And lasting persistence is a brainless mind's trip,
There is no doubt that its sweet feasts will also pass.
"It's bitter but passes" *is* its elegant Sip!

961. My Way (آیین من)

My way is to Drink *this* Wine and to be happy.
My faith is to be of faith-unfaith twoness free.
I asked what the universe wants to be my bride.
"My bride-price is your heart's happiness," answered she.

962. Twisted Eye, Twisted Building (دیدهٔ کج، نمای بد)

They say that this ruined world is bad and unfair.
The world is good, what's been bad is our own affair.
From a twisted eye the building will grow twisted.
The world will be just when it's in our wisdom's care.

963. O Gist of the World (ای خلاصهٔ جهان)

O humankind! You are the gist of space and time!
Let go of obsessions with profit's loss or climb!
Drink a Cup of *this* Wine, from its lasting Tender,
To become free of the "two worlds" sorrowful rhyme.

964. One Soul At A Time (یک خاطر، یک بنده)

If improving the whole Earth is your lifetime's goal,
It's better to bring joy *now* to *one* grieving soul.
If you freely earn the respect of someone *now*,
It's better than 'hoping' to free thousands on roll.

965. I Give You An Advice (پندی دهمت)

I give you an advice, if you lend me your ear:
For God's sake, don't wear duplicitous clothes. You hear?
The times you live in the world last just a second.
Don't sell human survival for a pause you're here.

966. Gain Stock Here (سرمایه بدست آر اینجا)

Before being from the angel's cup hungover,
Or before being in accidents stepped over,
Achieve your spiritual stock here; otherwise,
There, it will not help to become poor all over.

967. Die Before Death (بمیر پیش از مرگ)

Since death is ultimately a one-time matter,
Why not die *now* to your low selves, a willed matter?
Neither blood, nor filth, nor grabs of some veins and skins,
Would be involved in it; what's with you the matter?

968. Rebirth of Attributes (حشر صفات)

If some day they judge your attributes of some kind,
Your worth will be based on your self-knowledge defined.
Therefore, do your best to cultivate your soul since
Your chance of rebirth will be to your traits confined.

969. Your Seat Is By the Divine (عرش است نشیمن تو)

O heart! If you're purified now from body's reign,
As spirit, the highest of the spheres you will gain.
Your seat is by the Divine's Throne; it'd be a shame
If you're preoccupied with just this Earth's domain.

970. Your Mustache, My Beard (سبلت تو، ریش من)

O friend! Listen well to this truthful line I say:
With a lovely friend Drink *this* Ruby Wine *today*.
He who Created this world does not care about
A mustache such as yours, or a beard like mine, gray.

971. Hot-Tempered Dear (عزیز تندخو)

They say there will be lots of chatter on that day,
And our Dear will then have it the hot-tempered way.
From Absolute Goodness only goodness can come.
Rest assured that the end will be fine, I daresay.

972. No One Has Seen (کس ندیدست)

No one's seen *that* hell or *that* paradise, O heart!
Has someone returned to share their advice, O heart?
Then, our hopes and fears are made dependent on what,
Beside just the names, says nothing precise, O heart!

973. Hell and Heaven Now (دوزخ و بهشت اکنون)

The sphere is a belt around the worn gait of ours.
The Oxus is a flow of tears, of late, of ours.
Hell is just a spark of our futile toil and stress.
Heaven is just a breath in a calm state of ours.

974. Caravan of Life (قافلۀ عمر)

This caravan of life is so strangely passing!
Cherish, then, a breath that is joyfully passing!
Tender! Why grieve now for when your Wine pals will pass?
Pass *this* Wine Cup *now*, since the night's swiftly passing!

975. Wine and Divan (می و دیوان)

With *this* Ruby Wine in Jug, a book to inspire,
Half a loaf of bread, and some strength left to retire
To a nice garden with you sitting by my side,
I'd be happier than the king of an empire!

تنگی می لعل خواهم و دیوانی
سدّ رمقی باید و نصف نانی
وانگه من و تو نشسته در ویرانی
خوشتر بود از مملکت سلطانی

976. Here I Am, Free (ماییم آزاد)

Here I am, in *this* Wine's tomb, singing *this* knowledge,
With my life, soul, Cup, and shroud in *this* Wine's mortgage,
Free of hope for mercy or fear of hell's torments,
Free of dust, wind, fire, and water's spoilage.

ماییم و می و مطرب و این کنج خراب
جان و دل و جام و جامه در رهن شراب
فارغ ز امید رحمت و بیم عذاب
آزاد ز خاک و باد و از آتش و آب

977. Elixir of Life (آب زندگانی)

From *this* Wine that has an everlasting life, Drink!
From *this* lasting source of joyfulness in life, Drink!
It burns you like fire but dissolves all your sorrow!
From *this* that heals like the elixir of life, Drink!

زان می که حیات جاودانیست بخور
سرمایهٔ لذّت جوانیست بخور
سوزنده چو آتش است لیکن غم را
سازنده چو آب زندگانیست بخور

978. Wine, Life's Delight (می، لذّت عمر)

If you want your foundation of life to be tight,
And taste for a while griefless, this-worldly delight,
Don't let a moment go free of Drinking *this* Wine
So that you can bring joy to your life, day and night.

خواهی که اساس عمر محکم یابی
یکچند به عالم دل بی غم یابی
غافل منشین ز خوردن بادهٔ دمی
تا لذّت عمر خود مدام یابی

979. Moon's Suffering (رنج ماه)

Cheer up! The festive Moon will once again arrive!
Conditions for happiness will once again thrive!
The Moon has thinned, paled, and bent from weakness, but still
Its torment will end to be once again alive!

خوش باش که ماه عید نو خواهد شد
و اسباب طرب همه نکو خواهد شد
مه لاغر و زرد و خم شدست از سستی
ناچار از این رنج فرو خواهد شد

980. One More Week (یک هفتهٔ دیگر)

On the grass, some picturesque tents suppose are set,
And the attracted lovers' lips suppose are met.
Since from the life that has passed not one breath returns,
For one more week such kissful breaths suppose are let.

بر طرف چمن خیمه منقّش زده گیر
لب بر لب لعبتان دلکش زده گیر
از عمر گذشته چون دمی نتوان زد
یک هفتهٔ دیگر این دم خوش زده گیر

981. Be Happy at Heart (خوشدل باش)

These one or two breaths you live, be happy at heart!
With a cypress-high or Moon-faced a friendship start!
Since you'll die at last, then try to be perfectly
Self-fulfilled, since you are of the Perfect a part!

این یک دو سه دم که زنده ای خوشدل باش
به سرو قدی یا به ماه رخی مایل باش
چون عاقبت الامر نخواهی ماندن
یا کامل باش یا بر کامل باش

982. Suppose You're Not, to Be (انگار نیستی تا باشی)

Let futile sadnesses go; walk the joyful path.
Amid injustice be just; *that's* the rightful path.
Since the end of the world is nothingness, assume
Nothing constrains you. Freely walk the mindful path.

چندین غم بیهوده مخور شاد بزی
و اندر ره بیداد تو با داد بزی
چون آخر کار این جهان نیستی است
انگار که نیستی و آزاد بزی

983. Wine Better Than "Two Worlds" (می خوشتر از دو جهان)

Drink *this* Wine, since nothing else is more delighting.
Nothing is better than *its* Beloved sighting.
Where there is *this* Wine, the singer, and the Loved One,
Is the best place in both worlds for joys uniting.

می خور که بجز می طرب افزایی نیست
خوشتر ز معاشری تماشایی نیست
آنجا که می و مطرب و معشوق بود
اندر دو جهان خوشتر از آن جایی نیست

XXIV. Return (بازگشت)

984. You'd Be Blind If (کوری اگر)

O one seeking after God every night and day! ای آنکه شب و روز خدا می طلبی
You'd be blind to think that He's from you far away! کوری اگر از خویش جدا می طلبی
He tells you plainly with each breath, "Where do you seek? حق با تو به هر زمان عیان میگوید
I'm right here! Comes from Me, all your head-to-toe's clay!" سر تا قدمت منم که را می طلبی

985. Each Particle a Universal Cup (هر ذره جامی جهان نما)

Searching for Jamsheed's Cup, rather short-sightedly در جستن جام جم ز کوته نظری
You suppose each time that mere words bring you its key. هر لحظه گمانی نه به تحقیق بری
Seek inner insight to learn that each of your cells رو دیده به دست آر که هر ذرّهٔ جان
Is a Cup that serves you a universe to see! جامیست جهان نمای تا در نگری

986. Your Building Blocks (مایهٔ تو)

I said, "The universe and the Earth are Your stocks, گفتم که جهان و ملک سرمایهٔ تست
The Sun and the spheres, of Your presence, shadow rocks." خورشید فلک چو ذرّه در سایهٔ تست
He said, "No, you're wrong! Of Me, you can't find a sign. گفتا غلطی ز ما نشان نتوان داد
All that you see from Me are your own building blocks." از ما تو هر آنچه دیده ای مایهٔ تست

987. Eternal Love (عشق بی زوال)

I'm in Love, one that's purer than the purest tears. عشقی دارم پاکتر از آب زلال
About its betrayal I will never have fears. وین باختن عشق مرا هست محال
Other kinds of loving go through their ups and downs. عشق دگران بگرود از حال به حال
In my Beloved's Love no corruption appears. عشق من و معشوق مرا نیست زوال

988. Who Saw? (که دید؟)

Such a Perfect Love's from You, O Lover Divine! عشقی به کمال و دلربایی به جمال
My heart can say a lot, my tongue no more a Line. دل پر سخن و زبان ز گفتن شده لال
Has one seen a rarer state in the world, O God? زین نادره تر که دید یا رب به جهان
Thirsty, I've always had in *this* Cup Your Pure Wine. من تشنه و پیش من روان آب زلال

989. Nothingness In You Is Better (نیستی در هستی تو خوشتر)

If idol is Your Face, Your worship is better! گر بت رخ تست بت پرستی خوشتر
With Wine from Your Cup, being Drunken is better! ور باده به جام تست مستی خوشتر
From Your Love's Being I became just a nothing. از هستی عشق تو از آن نیست شدم
Such nothingness from any thingness is better. کان نیستی از هزار هستی خوشتر

990. Your Fragrance (بوی تو)

When from the eastern wind my heart took on Your scent
It left 'me' behind, and searching for 'You' it went.
Now it recalls not even who it was before,
Since Your fragrance has spread now to all its content.

991. Invitation to Garden Feast (دعوت به بزم باغ)

At dawn, in the garden, praisers of *this* Wine here,
With a singing beauty, skilled, Drunkenly sincere,
Roses fragrant, birds chirping, friends mindful with Wine,
Come, since I wish to be in Your presence, my Dear!

992. O Everything (ای همه)

O the Source of my life's body and strength, that's You!
O my soul's heart, O the world's Heart and Soul, that's You!
You caused my existence. You made all that I am.
I became nothing in the Everything that's You!

993. You and My Impermanence (تو و زوال من)

Since from Your being came to being my being,
Without Your being where else could be my being?
You are, You have been, and You will forever be.
How can impermanence be without my being?

994. Not Ashamed of Blame (از ملامتم ننگی نیست)

Amid loving You, I am not ashamed of blame.
On this matter, it is not worth fighting the lame.
This Love Potion is a healing Drug for the brave.
Its Wine's red content turns colorless for the tame.

995. You and I (تو و من)

My sad heart became happy from seeing Your face.
I will not choose any face other than Your face.
I see in You my own face when I look at You.
When I look at myself, all I see is Your face.

996. Faith is Love (مقصود عشق)

Seventy-two sects exist in faith, more or less.
But to one way, to Your Love, I hereby confess.
Whether pagan, Muslim, obeying, or sinful,
O faiths, let substitutes go! *Love* is faithfulness!

997. I Will Find Rebirth (برخیزم من)

On the day the pure souls of those buried in earth,
Riding new bodies from their dusts again unearth,
Like tulips rising from *this* Shroud with blood-tear dews,
In Your alley of the Earth, I will find rebirth.

روزی که مقدّسان خاکی مسکن
گردند سوار باز بر مرکب تن
چون لاله به خون مژه آغشته کفن
از خاک سر کوی تو برخیزم من

998. News of an Event (خبر واقعه)

I will announce an event's news the day I'll die,
And to condense it now to just two lines, I'll try:
"I go now to *these* Dusts while Loving You, O God,
And with Your Love, from *them* rising again, I'll fly."

از واقعه ای تو را خبر خواهم کرد
وآنرا به دو حرف مختصر خواهم کرد
با عشق تو در خاک فرو خواهم شد
با مهر تو سر ز خاک بر خواهم کرد

999. A Hundred I Became (صد ساله شدم)

I'm he who from Your power to existence came,
And from Your blessings a hundred-year-old became.
For a hundred more, test my sins to see what's more:
These "misdeeds" or Your mercy forgiving the same.

آنم که پدید گشتم از قدرت تو
صد ساله شدم به ناز در نعمت تو
صد سال به امتحان گنه خواهم کرد
یا جرم من است بیش یا رحمت تو

1000. Mid-Gemini Dot (نقطهٔ میان جوزا)

On that day when they fastened this blue dome above,
Then fastened *this dot* to mid-Gemini thereof,
Like a candle's flame burning for eternity,
They fastened me with *these* thousand threads to Your Love.

آن روز که این گنبد مینا بستند
وین نقطه چو بر میان جوزا بستند
تا روز ازل بسان آتش بر شمع
عشقت به هزار رشته بر ما بستند

Note: The page numbers given in the following index may be different from the actual page numbers of the links in the ebook edition of this book, also depending on the readers' ebook view customizations. However, the live links in the ebook editions correctly resolve to the proper passages with which the indexed items are associated. The index only offers links to the Robaiyat as shared in this volume, based on the titles given to each quatrain.

Robaiyat Index

The Robaiyat of Omar Khayyam: Part 1 of 3: Songs of Doubt Addressing the Question "Does Happiness Exist?" p. 21

I. Secret Book of Life (راز دفتر عمر) p. 23
1. When It Unveils (چون پرده بر افتد) p. 23
2. Can't Be Told (گفتن نتوان) p. 23
3. No Eye, Tongue, or Ear (بی چشم و زبان و گوش) p. 23
4. Sunset in Clay (غروب در گل) p. 23
5. Falcon from the Secret World (باز از عالم راز) p. 23
6. Indescribable State (حال شرح ناپذیر) p. 23
7. Telling Like Nightingales (بیان چو بلبلان) p. 24
8. What's This Symbolic Portrait? (چیست این نقش مجاز؟) p. 24
9. Perfected Pearl (درّ تمام) p. 24
10. More Hidden than the Phoenix (نهفته تر ز عنقا) p. 24
11. Diving Technique (هنر غواصی) p. 24
12. Book of Love (دفتر عشق) p. 24
13. Hundred-Toothed Comb (شانه صد شاخ) p. 24
14. Droplet's Efforts (رنج قطره) p. 25
15. Knowing-Not to Not-Knowing (از بیخبری تا بیخبری) p. 25
16. Guideless Love (عشق بی سالار) p. 25
17. Head to Heart (قال به حال) p. 25
18. Juiceless Love (عشق بی آب) p. 25
19. Freethinking Way (راه قلندری) p. 25
20. My Jamsheed Cup (جام جم من) p. 25
21. Dust to Dust (خاک به خاک) p. 26
22. That Day (آن روز) p. 26
23. Wine on the Greens Paradise (بهشت می بر سبزه) p. 26
24. 'Two-Worlds' Secret (سرّ دو جهان) p. 26
25. Fire in Harp-Tuned Water (آتش در آب چنگ) p. 26
26. Erased from the Book of Life (پاک شدن از دفتر عمر) p. 26
27. Nightingale Singing (غلغل بلبل) p. 26
28. Nightingale and Dove (بلبل و قمری) p. 27
29. Wine Alchemy (کیمیای می) p. 27
30. Return! Return! (باز آ باز آ) p. 27

II. Alas! (افسوس) p. 28
31. Youth Letter (نامۀ جوانی) p. 28
32. Slipped from Hand (ز کف بیرون) p. 28
33. Sky's Sickle and Mill (داس و آسیای سپهر) p. 28
34. Empty Mesh (غربیل خالی) p. 28
35. Remained Untold (ناگفته ماند) p. 28
36. Nothing, Nothing (هیچ هیچ) p. 28
37. Sewed Tents of Wisdom (خیمه های حکمت می دوخت) p. 29
38. Don't Go! (نرو) p. 29
39. Arrow to Bow (تیر به کمان) p. 29
40. Nearing Destruction (رو به خرابی) p. 29
41. Flimsy Tent (خیمه سست) p. 29
42. Wheel's Benefit? (سود گردون؟) p. 29
43. Was for What? (چه بود مقصود؟) p. 29
44. Fire to Water, Wind to Dust (آتش به آب، باد به خاک) p. 30
45. None Inherit (به کس نماند) p. 30
46. How Is He Doing? (احوالپرسی او) p. 30
47. Childhood Teacher (به کودی به استاد) p. 30
48. So What? (آخر چه؟) p. 30
49. Heart Unfulfilled (دل ناکام) p. 30
50. Which Plot? (چه جای؟) p. 30
51. Night Reached (به شب رسیده) p. 31
52. World of Rest? (عالم آسایش؟) p. 31
53. If I Had a Say (گر به من بدی) p. 31
54. Sphere's Music (آواز فلک) p. 31
55. 'Death-Spared' Illusion (وهم از مرگ رستگی) p. 31

56. Latecoming Soon-Departed (دیرآمدگان زودرفته) p. 31
57. A Dream Seen (خوابی دیده) p. 31
58. Soul's Job? (کار جان؟) p. 32
59. Who Told You? (که گفتت؟) p. 32
60. Needless to Needless (بی نیازی به بی نیازی) p. 32
61. They Thought Too (آنها نیز پنداشته اند) p. 32
62. Known Way (راه مشهور) p. 32
63. Up and Down (فراز و نشیب) p. 32
64. Life Wasted Away (عمر بیهوده) p. 32
65. Endless Lore (افسانۀ بی پایان) p. 33
66. Gut's Wine (می جگر) p. 33
67. Wine-Server's Deceit (حیلۀ ساقی) p. 33
68. Walking A Dead-End Way (طمع محال پیمودن) p. 33
69. Being's Disgrace (ننگ وجود) p. 33
70. Jail Break? (شکست قفس؟) p. 33
71. No Soulmate But This (نه همدمی جز این) p. 33
72. Trapped Birds (مرغان دام) p. 34
73. Solitude's Friendship (یاری عزلت) p. 34

III. Times (زمانه) p. 35
74. Humankind's Secret (راز آدم) p. 35
75. What I See (چه می بینم) p. 35
76. Almond Cake (لوزینه) p. 35
77. Agile Hands (دستان چابک) p. 35
78. Sour Sand (شورستان) p. 35
79. Misery's Weight (بار عنا) p. 35
80. Free-Riders (رایگان خوران) p. 36
81. Anonymous Living (زندگی گمنام) p. 36
82. Perfect Yet Lacking (کامل و کم) p. 36
83. Times' Plight (بلای زمانه) p. 36
84. Get Up, Let's Go! (برخیز و بیا) p. 36
85. Sit and Watch (بنشین به تماشا) p. 36
86. O Eye, See! (ای دیده، ببین) p. 36
87. Don't Seek the Crown (شاهی مطلب) p. 37
88. Old Caravansary (کهنه رباط) p. 37
89. Bahrām's Game (گور بهرام) p. 37
90. Animal's Footprint (جاپای حیوان) p. 37
91. Bokhari's Dust (خاک بخاری) p. 37
92. Face's Dust (گرد رخ) p. 37
93. Veiled Lip (لب مستور) p. 37
94. Bird's "Alas!" (افسوس مرغ) p. 38
95. Who, Who? (کو؟ کو؟) p. 38
96. Sift Gently! (نرمک می بیز) p. 38

IV. Spheres (افلاک) p. 39
97. Counts for Nothing (هیچ است) p. 39
98. Nothingness Horizons (آفاق هیچ) p. 39
99. Let the Myth Go (بگذر از این خیال) p. 39
100. Real Dolls (لعبتکان حقیقی) p. 39
101. Tricks Box (حقۀ شعبده) p. 39
102. World Without Us (جهان بی ما) p. 39
103. Sphere's Game (بازی فلک) p. 40
104. Whose Spheres? (فلک کهٔ) p. 40
105. Lasting Regret (دهر حسرت) p. 40
106. Where's the Weft? (پودی کو؟) p. 40
107. Lips and Hairs (لبها و زلفها) p. 40
108. Not Eaten You? (نخورده است تو را؟) p. 40
109. Cat's Parenting (بچه داری گربه) p. 40
110. So Hungry Are They (بس گرسنه اند) p. 41
111. Raw Overflowing (خام لبریز) p. 41
112. Blood-Run Mill (آسیاب خونرو) p. 41
113. Mill's Immeasurable Appetite (اشتهای بی اندازۀ آسیاب) p. 41
114. Torch-Bearing Thief (دزد شعله دار) p. 41
115. Buds too (غنچه هم) p. 41
116. Torn New Shirt (چاک نوپیراهن) p. 41
117. If They Know (گر بدانند) p. 42
118. Heart's Sear (داغ دل) p. 42
119. Your Old Art (شیوۀ دیرینۀ تو) p. 42
120. Are You Blind? (کوری؟) p. 42
121. Lowbred Raiser (ناکس پرور) p. 42
122. O Wheel, Tell the Truth! (ای چرخ، راست بگوی) p. 42
123. Peace Missions Rejected (ردّ صلح جویی) p. 42
124. Time Gone Senile (دهر خرف) p. 43
125. Wrong Impelling? (چرخ اشتباهی؟) p. 43
126. Miser Wheel (چرخ خسیس) p. 43
127. O Wimp-Grower! (ای مخنّث پرور) p. 43
128. Salt on Wound (نمک بر زخم) p. 43
129. Better Weaving Wheel (چرخ زنی به) p. 43
130. Wind to Fire, Water to Dust (باد به آتش، آب به خاک) p. 43
131. Not Getting It (پند ناپذیر) p. 44
132. Wasted Wheel (چرخ بد مست) p. 44
133. It'd Be Odd (عجب است) p. 44
134. Lowbred Raiser Times (زمانۀ دون پرور) p. 44
135. Eyelash Storm (سیل مژه) p. 44
136. Miser Raiser (خس پرور) p. 44
137. Even Supposing (حتی گیرم) p. 44
138. Creativity's Dust (گرد حدوث) p. 45
139. Here Comes the Moon (ماه می آید) p. 45
140. Grand Tent's Sigh (آه خرگاه) p. 45
141. Time to Avenge (فرصت تلافی) p. 45
142. Expectations from the Times (انتظار از زمانه) p. 45

143. Fed Up Latecomers (دیرآمدگان سیر) p. 45
144. What's the Point? (چه فایده؟) p. 45
145. Hands Tied (دست بسته) p. 46
146. Cup of Sediments (قدح دُرد) p. 46
147. Betraying Jolly House (خوش سرای بی وفا) p. 46
148. Breathing World (دنیای نفس کش) p. 46
149. Fate's Sheriff (شحنهٔ تقدیر) p. 46
150. What Would You Do? (چه کنی؟) p. 46

V. Chance and Fate (قضا و قدر) p. 47

151. Middle of Nothings (میان دو هیچ) p. 47
152. Deal Without You (قرارداد بی تو) p. 47
153. Bring One, Take One (بیار و ببر) p. 47
154. Familiar Stranger (غریب آشنا) p. 47
155. Glad for Sadness (شاد غم) p. 47
156. You Make, Then Break? (سازی و شکنی؟) p. 47
157. Luck's Spin (دوران قضا) p. 48
158. Written Tablet (لوح نوشته) p. 48
159. Untrappable Chance (قضای تله ناپذیر) p. 48
160. Saddled Horse (اسب زین شده) p. 48
161. Hunter's Blame (بهانهٔ صیّاد) p. 48
162. Regressive Blame (تسلسل تقصیر) p. 48
163. Fate of Earth and Sky (تقدیر زمین و آسمان) p. 48
164. Did They Consult? (مشورت کردند؟) p. 49
165. Judgment Day? (روز حساب؟) p. 49

VI. Puzzle (معمّا) p. 50

166. I've Not Mastered (استاد نیم) p. 50
167. Nobody Knows (هیچکس آگاه نشد) p. 50
168. I Know I Don't Know (می دانم نمی دانم) p. 50
169. I Don't Know (هیچ معلومم نیست) p. 50
170. By and Large Slow (غم خوش غم خوش) p. 50
171. Miser Self (خست خود) p. 50
172. Cup Full of Illusions (کاسهٔ پرسودا) p. 51
173. Who Knows? (واقف کیست؟) p. 51
174. Happy Lies (دروغهای خوش) p. 51
175. Magic Lantern (فانوس خیال) p. 51
176. Not Sure They Knew (آگاه نیم که آگه بودند) p. 51
177. Ocean of Being (بحر وجود) p. 51
178. Ant and Cow (مور و گاو) p. 51
179. Secrets' Tent (پردهٔ اسرار) p. 52
180. Circle of Coming and Going (دایرهٔ آمد و رفت) p. 52
181. Bedtime Story (فسانهٔ خواب) p. 52
182. Chin Movers (زنخ زن ها) p. 52
183. Hundred Kisses (صد بوسه) p. 52
184. Whose Love, Whose Hate (مهر که؟ کین که؟) p. 52
185. Whose Fault? (عیب کراست؟) p. 52
186. Before-the-Judge-Throwing (به داور خواندن) p. 53
187. Impossible to Decline (پرهیز محال) p. 53
188. Knew From the Start (از ازل می دانست) p. 53
189. When Forbidden? (حرام کی؟) p. 53
190. Why the Burning? (سوختن برای چه؟) p. 53
191. Whose Want? (خواست چه کسی؟) p. 53
192. Prohibition Enough (منع بس) p. 53
193. Problem Unsolved (مشکل حل نشده) p. 54
194. Polo Ball (گوی چوگان) p. 54

VII. O God! (خدایا) p. 55

195. O Book of Secrets' Opening! (ای سردفتر اسرار) p. 55
196. O Absolute Survivor! (ای باقی محض) p. 55
197. O Hidden Apparent! (ای پنهان آشکار) p. 55
198. Ant's Eyes, Fly's Legs! (دیدهٔ مور, پای پشه) p. 55
199. O Sun's King! (ای شاه خورشید) p. 55
200. O Author! (ای نگارنده) p. 55
201. O Candle of Delight! (ای شمع طرب) p. 56
202. O Beauty! (ای زیبا) p. 56
203. O Unfathomable! (ای شناخت ناپذیر) p. 56
204. O Just! (ای عادل) p. 56
205. O Sought After (ای مطلوب) p. 56
206. O Most Precious! (ای پربهاترین) p. 56
207. O Outside Both Worlds! (ای برون از هر دو جهان) p. 56
208. O Beloved! (ای معشوق) p. 57
209. Hills and Clouds the Same (یکسان کُه و مِه) p. 57
210. O Owner! (ای مالک) p. 57
211. Seventy-Two Sects (هفتاد و دو فرقه) p. 57
212. Futile Chase (جستجوی بی حاصل) p. 57
213. Wandering Horse (براق سرگردان) p. 57
214. O All Knower! (ای دانای همه چیز) p. 57
215. O Refuge (ای پناهگاه) p. 58
216. O Matchless! (ای بی مانند) p. 58
217. Eyes and Intellect From You! (چشم و عقل از تو) p. 58
218. Wondering Design (نقش حیران) p. 58
219. Why the Wondering? (چرا سرگشتگی؟) p. 58
220. Why the Exile? (چرا هجر؟) p. 58
221. Futile Effort (کوشش بی سود) p. 58
222. Not Reaching You (بوصالت نرسیدن) p. 59
223. Don't Look? (منگر؟) p. 59
224. Arise! Excite! (خیز, شور انگیز) p. 59
225. Why Hell-Bound? (چرا دوزخی؟) p. 59
226. Love's Trap (دام عشق) p. 59
227. Creation and Sin (آفرینش و گناه) p. 59

228. What Sin? (چه گناه) p. 59
229. Rebel? (عاصی) p. 60
230. This Is A Payment (این مزد بود) p. 60
231. Forgiving Heals (کرمی مرمست) p. 60
232. What's the Difference? (فرق چیست؟) p. 60
233. Broke My Decanter (ابریق مرا شکست) p. 60
234. Questioning Back (پرسش متقابل) p. 60
235. Which Name? (کدام نام؟) p. 60
236. Hope for Mercy (امید رحمت) p. 61
237. I'm Excused (معذورم) p. 61
238. You Decide (چسان دار) p. 61
239. Worse Than Us (بتر از ما) p. 61
240. Unveiling (پرده دری) p. 61
241. What Can I Do? (من چه کنم؟) p. 61
242. Forgive the Parts (رحمت بر اعضاء) p. 61
243. No Road But Yours (فقط درگه تو) p. 62
244. O Needless! (ای مستغنی) p. 62
245. Torment? Where? (عذاب؟ کجا؟) p. 62
246. Tavern's Altar (محراب غاز) p. 62
247. O Repentance-Accepter! (ای عذرپذیر) p. 62
248. Breeze of Mercy (نسیم بخشش) p. 62
249. Tell Him Who Does Not Know (به کسی که نشناسد) p. 62
250. Far Far Far (دور دور دور) p. 63
251. Dark Listing (سیه نامه) p. 63
252. Accept Me (بپذیرم) p. 63
253. Essence Knows Essence (ذات دانندۀ ذات) p. 63
254. Wisdom Chain (زنجیر خرد) p. 63
255. Hearer of the Mute (شنوای لالان) p. 63
256. What About the Shame? (با شرم چه کنم؟) p. 63
257. One, Not Two (یک، نه دو) p. 64
258. Open the Door (باز کن در) p. 64
259. Offer a Hand (دست گیر) p. 64
260. Hope for Forgiveness (امید عفو) p. 64
261. Each Dawn (هر پگاه) p. 64
262. I Seek Your Door (نیاز به درگه تو) p. 64
263. Take Back Your Gift (گوهرت نثارت) p. 64
264. I Am at Wit's End (سر آمده ام) p. 65

VIII. Tavern Voice (ندا از میخانه) p. 66

265. Tavern Voice (ندا از میخانه) p. 66
266. Wine Lasso (کمند شراب) p. 66
267. Why Grieving? (ماتم چیست؟) p. 66
268. Rooster's Crow (نوحۀ خروس) p. 66
269. Just a Fly? (مگسی بود؟) p. 66
270. Drop and Sea (قطره و بحر) p. 66

271. Lantern, Reed, Jug (صراحی، نی، فانوس) p. 67
272. Primordial Intellect (عقل قدیم) p. 67
273. All the Same Substance (سرتاسر از یک گل) p. 67
274. Ring Crown (نگین انگشتر) p. 67
275. See the Friend (دوست بین) p. 67
276. Not Within, Then Where? (با خود نه، کجا؟) p. 67
277. Ten to One (ده تا یک) p. 67
278. Adam's Part (جزو آدم) p. 68
279. You Are It! (تو آنی) p. 68
280. All Is Humankind (همه انسان است) p. 68
281. Wine's Evolution (تکامل شراب) p. 68
282. Oneness (توحید) p. 68
283. This and That (این و آن) p. 68
284. Separation Illusion (این اصلی فصل) p. 68
285. You Make You (هر چه خواهی تویی) p. 69
286. Guest (مهمان) p. 69
287. Between Two Nothings (بین العدمین) p. 69
288. Tent Furnisher (فراش خیمه) p. 69
289. Drink and Enjoy to Know (نوش و خوش باش تا بدانی) p. 69
290. Wine's Benefit (سود می) p. 69
291. Wine Meditation (باده نشینی) p. 69
292. Times' Treachery (زمانۀ غدار) p. 70
293. Wine's Bitterness (تلخی می) p. 70
294. Cup's Verse (آیۀ پیاله) p. 70
295. Don't Sit Depressed (ننشین دلتنگ) p. 70
296. Wine Prayer (دعای می) p. 70
297. Decline's Reason (دلیل کم و کاست) p. 70
298. Why Depressed? (چرا دلتنگ؟) p. 70
299. Myths Choice (انتخاب افسانه) p. 71
300. From Dead Bone (از استخوان رمیم) p. 71
301. Wheel's Grand Tent (خرگاه چرخ) p. 71
302. Tent of Needlessness (خیمۀ بی نیازی) p. 71
303. Who'll Bear the Fruit? (که را بار دهد؟) p. 71
304. Imagine Not to Be to Be (انگار نباش تا باشی) p. 71
305. Everlasting Life Is This (عمرجاودانی این است) p. 71

IX. O Wine-Tender (ای ساقی) p. 72

306. Wine for that Heart (می برای آن دل) p. 72
307. Where Were You? (از کجا برخاسته ای؟) p. 72
308. Who Can Help? (که فریاد؟) p. 72
309. More Worn Out Than the Dead (ز مرده فرسوده تر) p. 72
310. Can I Be So Lucky? (هرگز بود این بخت؟) p. 72
311. Winter's Greeting (بهار زمستان) p. 72
312. See I'm Happy (ببین خوشم) p. 73
313. Your Mindful Heart (دل آگاه تو) p. 73

314. Your Face Bests Jamsheed's Cup (رخت ز جام جمشید بهتر) p. 73
315. Our Soul (جان ما) p. 73
316. Rooster's Wine (بادهٔ خروس) p. 73
317. Past Wine Drinking (می خوری در گذشته) p. 73
318. New Food (قوت نو) p. 73
319. Devoted I Stand (سر بفرمان) p. 74
320. New Praying (دعای نو) p. 74
321. Won't Leave (سفر نخواهیم گرفت) p. 74
322. Fill Up (پر کن) p. 74
323. Hit the Veins (رگ بزن) p. 74
324. Brazenness (گستاخی) p. 74
325. Absent Wine (می غایب) p. 74
326. Healer of Pain (طبیب درد) p. 75
327. For God's Sake (بهر خدا) p. 75
328. Heart's Cure (مرهم دل) p. 75
329. Letting Chatters Go (رها از گفتگو) p. 75
330. Wine's Chain (زنجیر می) p. 75
331. Moment's Detachment (دمی رهایی) p. 75
332. Arise (برجه) p. 75
333. Bragging (لاف زن) p. 76
334. Tend the Wine (در ده شراب) p. 76
335. Stealing A Breath (ربودن دمی) p. 76
336. Hurry (بشتاب) p. 76
337. Pure Wine (می ناب) p. 76
338. Rise O Idol! (برخیز بتا) p. 76

The Robaiyat of Omar Khayyam: Part 2 of 3: Songs of Hope Addressing the Question "What Is Happiness?" p. 77

X. Drunken Way (راه مستی) p. 79

339. There's Nothing But God (جز هست خدا نیست) p. 79
340. Shows His Grace Day and Night (جمال می نماید شب و روز) p. 79
341. Where's That Heart? (آن دل کجاست؟) p. 79
342. Raw to Cooked (خام به پخته) p. 79
343. Head Praying? (نماز سر؟) p. 79
344. Prayer Game? (بازیچهٔ نماز؟) p. 79
345. Self-Critique (نقد خود) p. 80
346. Servitudes (بندگی ها) p. 80
347. Heart Mecca (کعبهٔ دل) p. 80
348. Mecca of Presence (کعبهٔ حضور) p. 80
349. High Spirituality (رتبت ابرار) p. 80
350. Be Arrow, Not Bow (تیر باش نه کمان) p. 80
351. See For Yourself (از دیدهٔ کن روایت) p. 80
352. Fixed and Wandering Stars (ساکنان و سرگردانان) p. 81
353. Intellect's Shackle (عقیلهٔ عقل) p. 81
354. Bull-Milking (گاو نر دوشی) p. 81
355. Knowing Not Knowing (دانستن ندانستن) p. 81
356. Knowing After Death? (دانستن پس از مرگ؟) p. 81
357. Intellect Not Enough (عقل ناکافی) p. 81
358. Ant or Wolf (مور یا گرگ) p. 81
359. Whim to Breath (هوس تا نفس) p. 82
360. Non-Dualism (دو نبینی) p. 82
361. Take and Go (بردار و برو) p. 82
362. A Day Bests A Century (روز به از صد سال) p. 82
363. Fasting and Meditation (روزه و مراقبه) p. 82
364. A Mindful Breath (یک نفس) p. 82
365. Self-Mirror (خودآینه) p. 82
366. Self-Seeing (دیدن خودشمول) p. 83
367. Wave or Ocean? (موج یا دریا؟) p. 83
368. Idol's Lesson (درس بت) p. 83
369. Flimsy Branch (شاخ سست) p. 83
370. Meditate (سر کن در گریبان) p. 83
371. Open Heart's Eye (دیدهٔ دل بگشا) p. 83
372. Selfishness for How Long? (خودپرستی تا کی؟) p. 83
373. Let Go (بگذر) p. 84
374. Created or Eternal (چه محدث چه قدیم) p. 84
375. Fish and Duck (ماهی و بط) p. 84
376. Pearl of Tear (درّ اشک) p. 84
377. Drunken Awareness (مست هشیاری) p. 84
378. Mystic Wine (شراب معرفت) p. 84
379. Wine and wine (می و می) p. 84
380. Cooked or Raw? (پخته یا خام؟) p. 85
381. Wine and Raisin (انگور و میویز) p. 85
382. Drunken Wisdom (خرد مست) p. 85
383. School and Minaret (مدرسه و مناره) p. 85
384. Gnostic State (حال عارف) p. 85
385. Intellect's Chain (بند عقل) p. 85
386. Brawl, Drink, Agitate (خروش, نوش, جوش) p. 85
387. School to Tavern (مدرسه به میکده) p. 86
388. Heart's Eye (دیدهٔ دل) p. 86
389. Why Beg? (دریوزه چرا؟) p. 86
390. Ways of Hearing (راههای شنیدن) p. 86
391. Better Run Away (بگریزی به) p. 86
392. Why Futile Stress? (چرا غم بیهوده؟) p. 86
393. Better Ruined (خراب اولیٰ تر) p. 86
394. Thought's Obsession (وسوسهٔ فکر) p. 87
395. Brim-to-Brim (مالامال) p. 87
396. Wined Elderly (پیر مست) p. 87
397. Retire to A Corner (کناره گیر) p. 87
398. We Are Marbles (رخامیم همه) p. 87

399. Go Drink This Wine (رو این باده خور) p. 87
400. His Pure Wine (می طهور او) p. 87
401. Talk Until When? (تا چند حدیث؟) p. 88
402. Allowed Wine (می حلال) p. 88
403. Fall Madly in Love (مجنون شو) p. 88
404. Transcending Twoness (عبور از دوئی) p. 88
405. O God, Intoxicate Me (یا رب، مستم کن) p. 88
406. Neither That, Nor This (نه آن، نه این) p. 88
407. State of Drunkenness (مرتبهٔ مستی) p. 88

XI. Willfulness (اراده) p. 89

408. Symbol's Truth (حقیقت مجاز) p. 89
409. Won't Build A Shop (کارگاهی ننهد) p. 89
410. Futile Worrying (غم خوردن بیهوده) p. 89
411. Why Cry? (چرا فریاد؟) p. 89
412. Wax in Hand (موم در دست) p. 89
413. Life's Backgammon (تختهٔ نرد زندگی) p. 89
414. Chance's Arrow (تیر قضا) p. 90
415. Not All Due to You (نه همه چیز از توست) p. 90
416. See 'Now' (حال بین) p. 90
417. Planted and Reaped (کِشت و دَرَو) p. 90
418. Lips on Lips (لب بر لب) p. 90
419. Wine-Hair Compass (پرگار می و زلف) p. 90
420. Dome's Circling Cup (جام سپهر به گردش) p. 90
421. Never Will (هرگز نشود) p. 91
422. Breeze, Dust, Heat, and Mist (نسیم، گرد، شرار، و نم) p. 91
423. Even the Wheel Knows Not (چرخ هم بیخبر است) p. 91
424. It's Been Like This (آنچه بود بود) p. 91
425. Whole in You (کل در تو) p. 91
426. Is What Is (هست آنچه هست) p. 91
427. Prince to Garlic (میر تا سیر) p. 91
428. Sphere's Secret Confession (گفت فلک پنهانی) p. 92
429. Field of Causes (صحرای علل) p. 92
430. Poorer Wheel (چرخ بیچاره تر) p. 92
431. Don't Give In, Don't Beg (گردن منه، منّت مکش) p. 92

XII. Foes and Friends (دوست و دشمن) p. 93

432. Foe Wrongly Said (دشمن به غلط گفت) p. 93
433. My Faith (ایمان من) p. 93
434. Be Fair (انصاف بده) p. 93
435. Woman's Question (سؤال زن) p. 93
436. Hundred Bites (صد لقمه) p. 93
437. Foe's Mirror (آینهٔ دشمن) p. 93
438. My Mirror (آینهٔ من) p. 94
439. Real Hell (دوزخ به یقین) p. 94
440. They Hate Their Souls (از جان خود بیزارند) p. 94

441. Defamers (بدنام کنندگان) p. 94
442. Uncooked (خامان) p. 94
443. Stone, Wax, Bow, Arrow (سنگ، موم، کمان، تیر) p. 94
444. Famed for Talking Nonsense (به کرخی معروفان) p. 94
445. Buy-Nothing Crowd (نخران) p. 95
446. Reply to Takfiris (پاسخ به تکفیریان) p. 95
447. Bulls and Asses (گاوان و خران) p. 95
448. Who's Blood-Thirstier? (کدام خونخوارتر؟) p. 95
449. Aren't You Ashamed? (شرمت نایَد؟) p. 95
450. Blame for How Long? (تا چند ملامت؟) p. 95
451. Who Are You To Teach God? (حق را تو کجا آموختنی؟) p. 95
452. Go Fix Your Eyes (رو چارهٔ دیده کن) p. 96
453. Zoo (باغ وحش) p. 96
454. Fire and Water (آتش و تر) p. 96
455. Where Were They? (کجا بودند؟) p. 96
456. Pupil's Disrespect (بی احترامی شاگرد) p. 96
457. Jug-Breaker (صراحی شکن) p. 96
458. Wasted Sheriff (محتسب دایم مست) p. 96
459. Hello-Bye (سلام و کلام) p. 97
460. Friend or Foe (دوست یا دشمن) p. 97
461. Changing Affection (لطف پویا) p. 97
462. Enough Already (بس است) p. 97
463. Sufi Prayer (دعای صوفیانه) p. 97
464. Friendship or Ill-Intention (خویش یا بداندیش) p. 97
465. Sweet Poison, Poisonous Sweet (زهر نوش، نوش زهر) p. 97
466. Humble Rogue (رند پشت دست) p. 98
467. Don't Drip (مچکان) p. 98
468. Life's Wine-Drinking Bench (مصطبهٔ عمر) p. 98
469. Bravo Grief! (آفرین بر غم) p. 98
470. Sea's Overflow? (سر رفتن دریا؟) p. 98
471. Worse Than Death (از مرگ بدتر) p. 98
472. Ill-Wisher's Self-Abuse (خودآزاری بدخواه) p. 98
473. O Scarecrow! (ای گُه نَه) p. 99
474. O Darvish (ای درویش) p. 99
475. Hairsplitting Knower (دانا مو به مو) p. 99
476. Deed Knowing (فعل شناسی) p. 99
477. Not My Fault (من نکردم از خود) p. 99
478. How Ignorant! (عجب نادانی) p. 99
479. Suffer, Don't Cause Suffering (میرنج و مرنجان) p. 99
480. Friend to Foe, Foe to Friend (دوست به دشمن، دشمن به دوست) p. 100
481. Be Good (خوب باش) p. 100
482. Eye's Pupil (مردمک چشم) p. 100
483. Anonymous Living (زندگی گمنام) p. 100
484. From Intellect to Wine (از خرد تا می) p. 100
485. Bowl and Dices (طاس و کعبتین) p. 100

486. Time Robbery (زمان دزدی) p. 100
487. Denude From Abuse (جفا از تن در کش) p. 101
488. Cup's Show (نمایش پیاله) p. 101
489. Don't Play Their Game (تو مگرای) p. 101
490. Be Simorgh, not Owl (سیمرغ باش، نه بوف) p. 101

XIII. Wealth (ثروت) p. 102

491. Violet and Rose (بنفشه و گل) p. 102
492. Free Wealth's Danger (خطر ثروت رایگان) p. 102
493. Less is More (کمتر بیشتر) p. 102
494. Content With a Bone (قانع به استخوان) p. 102
495. Don't Be a Fly (مگس مباش) p. 102
496. Here I Am! (آید که منم) p. 102
497. Fame to Slavery (شهرت تا غلامی) p. 103
498. Greedy Poppy (سگ بچۀ مایل) p. 103
499. Brittle Hair (زلف شکننده) p. 103
500. Abusive World (دنیای مردم آزار) p. 103
501. Lancet and Scale (نیشتر و میزان) p. 103
502. Loaned Breath (نفس عاریتی) p. 103
503. Left for the Foe (به دشمن ماند) p. 103
504. Before It Gets Cold (زان پیش که گردد سرد) p. 104
505. Take A Load Off (بردار باری) p. 104
506. Don't Scatter (پراکنده مشو) p. 104
507. Wish Unfulfilled (به مراد نابوده) p. 104
508. King Between Nothings (شاه میان دو هیچ) p. 104
509. Both Worth the Same (هر دو یک نرخ) p. 104
510. None Escape (هیچکس جان نبرد) p. 104
511. It's Been Around (بودست) p. 105
512. World's Kitchen (مطبخ دنیا) p. 105
513. Be Content and Free (آسوده باش و آزاده) p. 105
514. Suppose and Go Free (گیر و آزاد شو) p. 105
515. From Skill and Parentage to Gold (از هنر و نسبت به زر) p. 105
516. Terkan's Fair Eyes (چشم خوش ترکان) p. 105
517. Goodness and Nothingness (نیکی و هیچی) p. 105
518. One Night or Two (یکی دو شب) p. 106
519. Tomorrow's Wish (هوس فردا) p. 106
520. We're All Beggars (گدائیم همه) p. 106
521. Royalty in Poverty (شاهی در فقر) p. 106
522. Endowment Bite (لقمۀ وقف) p. 106
523. Dust of Attachment (گرد تعلق) p. 106
524. Being Human (انسان بودن) p. 106
525. Keeping Promises (عهد وفا) p. 107
526. Unending Greed (حرص ناتمام) p. 107
527. Rich or Poor Both Pass (سیر و فقیر هم گذرند) p. 107
528. King and Servant Both Die (کشته هم محمود هم ایاز) p. 107

529. Kārun's Wealth (گنج قارون) p. 107
530. Not a Grain Follows (جوی با خود نبری) p. 107
531. Times' Good or Bad (نیک و بد زمانه) p. 107
532. Share What You Swallow (لقمه ات باز مدار) p. 108
533. Wish He Did It Now (اکنون کندی) p. 108
534. Freedom From Dependence (آزادی از منّت) p. 108
535. Ocean, Diver, and Pearl (دریا، غواص، گوهر) p. 108
536. I'm Happy (خوشیم) p. 108
537. Darvishhood Wealth (توانگری درویشی) p. 108
538. King's Envy (نه حدّ هر سلطانی) p. 108
539. Bravo, Live in Joy! (گو شاد بزی) p. 109

XIV. Today (امروز) p. 110

540. What's Left (چه مانده است) p. 110
541. What Good Is It? (چه جای طرب است؟) p. 110
542. What's My Fault? (تقصیر من چیست؟) p. 110
543. Water and Wind (آب و باد) p. 110
544. Wine's Shield Boat (سپر کشتی شراب) p. 110
545. Consulted You? (تدبیر با تو؟) p. 110
546. You're Not Useless (بیهوده نه ای) p. 111
547. Exhale or Not (بر آرم یا نه) p. 111
548. Last Act (آخر کار) p. 111
549. Who Can Tell? (کس چه داند؟) p. 111
550. Sorrow's Medicine (دوای غم) p. 111
551. Don't Waste This Breath (ضایع مکن این دم) p. 111
552. Death and Sleep (مرگ و خواب) p. 111
553. Times' Ignoring (کم روزگار) p. 112
554. Wise Are Ruined (فرزانه درو خراب) p. 112
555. Water in Waist (آب در کمر) p. 112
556. Don't Sadly Seek (غمخوار مپوی) p. 112
557. This Circle (این دایره) p. 112
558. Seeking Excess (بیش طلبی) p. 112
559. Wise Attitude (عاقل چو درنگرد) p. 112
560. Saw With Own Eyes (دیدیم به چشم) p. 113
561. Suppose Achieved (ساخته گیر) p. 113
562. Snowflake in Desert (برف در صحرا) p. 113
563. Donkey-Rider's Legend (افسانۀ محمر سوار) p. 113
564. Not a Moment (نه یک ساعت) p. 113
565. Let Ignorance Go (بنه تو جهل) p. 113
566. Lustful Self (نفس شهوانی) p. 113
567. Lust and Base Passions (شهوت و هوا) p. 114
568. Detach From Possessing (ترک تعلق) p. 114
569. Detachment Skill (مایۀ تجرید) p. 114
570. Bird and Wild Horse (مرغ و توسن) p. 114
571. Next Breath (آن دم) p. 114

572. Don't Fear (مترس) p. 114
573. Enjoy Now (حالی خوش باش) p. 114
574. Life's Chance (فرصت عمر) p. 115
575. Straw and Mountain (کاه و کوه) p. 115
576. Your Turn (نوبت تو) p. 115
577. Don't Let Go of Wine (می باده مباش) p. 115
578. Since You Know (چون واقفی) p. 115
579. Time's Sickle (دهرهٔ دهر) p. 115
580. Untanglings (بندگشایی ها) p. 115
581. Seek Wine Quickly (هین باده) p. 116
582. Breath's Taking (غنیمت دم) p. 116
583. World's Prime Wealth (سرمایهٔ جهان) p. 116
584. Freethinker's Way (راه قلندر) p. 116
585. Path of Blame (کوی ملامت) p. 116
586. Less or More Chance (قضا کم و بیش) p. 116
587. Not Depending on Others (ز دگر نمی باید خواست) p. 116
588. My Youth's Turn (نوبت جوانی من) p. 117
589. Drum and Falcon (طبل و باز) p. 117
590. Don't Deny the Sea (منکر بحر مشو) p. 117
591. Be Civil (آباد زی) p. 117
592. Doesn't Just Threaten (نکند گرای آزار) p. 117
593. We're All Guests (همه مهمانیم) p. 117
594. Wine That is This Word (می که همین ست سخن) p. 117
595. Freed From a Thousand Tasks (رستی ز هزار پیشه) p. 118
596. Five-Fingers (پنجه) p. 118
597. Not Quit Kissing (لب بر نگرفت) p. 118
598. Life-Giving Dawn (صبح جان بخش) p. 118
599. Two Types of People (دو نوع مردم) p. 118
600. Self-Cultivators (مجردان) p. 118
601. Not A Drop (نه یک قطره) p. 118
602. Sweet and Sour (شیرین و شور) p. 119
603. Beloved's Loving (دوست داشتن دوست) p. 119
604. Know Yourself (در خود نگر) p. 119
605. If You Lost Your Way (اگر جدا افتادی) p. 119
606. Door Opening (در گشودن) p. 119
607. No Name and Sign (نی نام و نشان) p. 119
608. Stolen Slowly (خوش خوش ببرد) p. 119
609. Advice for the Youthful (پند برای تازه جوان) p. 120
610. Sixty or More (بیش از شصت) p. 120

XV. Pottery (کوزه گری) p. 121

611. My Own Cup of Gold (جام زرینم بود) p. 121
612. Hand and Head (دسته و سر) p. 121
613. Jug's Cry (خروش کوزه) p. 121
614. Glazed Pitcher (سبوی کاشی) p. 121

615. Go Easy Please (نیکو دار) p. 121
616. Stop! (ساکن) p. 121
617. Don't You Know? (چه می پنداری؟) p. 122
618. Forefathers' Clay (خاک پدران) p. 122
619. Father in Palm (پدر در کف) p. 122
620. Be Patient Now! (دمی با من ساز) p. 122
621. Lips on Lips (لب بر لب) p. 122
622. Poor Lover (عاشق زار) p. 122
623. Don't Step On (قدم نهی) p. 122
624. Harmless Wine (می بی ضرر) p. 123
625. Jug and Pitcher (کوزه و سبو) p. 123
626. Spirit's Song (نعرهٔ روح) p. 123
627. Chatter's Slavery (اسیر عقل) p. 123

XVI. Cemetery (گورستان) p. 124

628. Eye Pupil (مردمک چشم) p. 124
629. Human Horizons (آفاق انسان) p. 124
630. Grave's Tile (خشت گور) p. 124
631. Selfless Dusts (غبارهای بی خود) p. 124
632. Heart's Howls (نعره های دل) p. 124
633. Flowing Down Water (آب فرو رو) p. 124
634. Tulip's Secret (راز لاله) p. 125
635. When You're Gone, You're Gone (چو رفتی رفتی) p. 125
636. Don't Leave Something (چیزی نگذاری) p. 125
637. One Way Street (راه بی بازگشت) p. 125
638. Grave's End (آخر گور) p. 125
639. Seen A Hundred Thousand (دیده صد هزار) p. 125
640. No News Came (خبر نیامد) p. 125
641. Seven-Thousand-Year Olds (هفت هزار سالگان) p. 126
642. Grave Tiles (خشتهای گور) p. 126
643. Drink Wine, Not Sorrow (باده خور، غم مخور) p. 126
644. Drink or Not (خوری یا نخوری) p. 126
645. No One Came Back (یکی باز نامد) p. 126

XVII. Paradise and Hell (بهشت و جهنم) p. 127

646. O Baffled One (ای حیران شده) p. 127
647. Rumors (آوازه) p. 127
648. Dog's Better Bark (سگ بهتر) p. 127
649. Things Will Be Like This (چنین عاقبت کار) p. 127
650. Cash Better Than Credit (نقد خوشتر از نسیه) p. 127
651. Drumbeat from Afar (آواز دهل از دور) p. 127
652. Sufi's Illusion (پنداشت صوفی) p. 128
653. Paradise Like Empty Hand (بهشت چون کف دست) p. 128
654. Sustaining the Situation (باشد که چنان انگیزند) p. 128
655. Worth Both Worlds (دو عالم ارزد) p. 128
656. Had They Been Doomed to Hell (گر دوزخی خواهد بود) p. 128

657. Written From the Start (از ازل نوشته) p. 128
658. What's My Fault? (تقصیر من چیست؟) p. 128
659. Sit in This Heaven (بنشین به بهشت) p. 129
660. Anyone With More Guts? (که را بود زهرۀ این) p. 129
661. Lucky He Is (به اقبال نشست) p. 129
662. Run Away from It (از آنجا بگریز) p. 129
663. Be Free of That Hell and Paradise (فارغ از آن دوزخ و بهشت) p. 129
664. Perhaps They'll Forget (شاید فراموش کنند) p. 129
665. Go Wherever You (هر کجا خواهی رو) p. 129
666. Don't Listen to Times' Rulers (مشنو سخن زمانه ساز آمدگان) p. 130
667. God Does Not Need (خدا مستغنی است) p. 130
668. They'll Regret It (پشیمان گردند) p. 130
669. They Both Sigh (هر دو در حسرتند) p. 130
670. Our Garden Temple (مزرعۀ کشت ما) p. 130
671. No Heaven But This (جز این نیست بهشت) p. 130
672. Who Said There's A Hell (که گفت دوزخ خواهد بود) p. 130
673. Whoever Knows the Secrets (آن کس که اسرار دانست) p. 131
674. One Sip Bests Both Worlds (یک جرعه به است از دو جهان) p. 131
675. Here is There (اینجاست آنجا) p. 131
676. Wine, the Teacher (رهبری می) p. 131
677. Don't Rough and Tumble (درشتی نکنی) p. 131
678. Why Am I Not There (چونست که ره نیست مرا) p. 131
679. Paradise's Address (نشان بهشت) p. 131
680. Repenting from Repentance (توبه از توبه) p. 132
681. Drunken and Loving Author (نگارنده در مستی و عشق) p. 132
682. Paradise Now (بهشت اکنون) p. 132
683. Next's Uncertain Goal (ای دانم آن جهانم باشد) p. 132
684. Longing for Rose and Wine (میل به گل و می) p. 132
685. I'm Taking the Three in Cash (این هر سه مرا نقد) p. 132

The Robaiyat of Omar Khayyam: Part 3 of 3: Songs of Joy Addressing the Question "Why Can Happiness Exist?" p. 133

XVIII. Garden (باغ) p. 135

686. Garden Time (فصل گل) p. 135
687. Neither Hot, Nor Cold (نه گرم است و نه سرد) p. 135
688. Why Did He Paint Me? (بهر چه آراست مرا؟) p. 135
689. Rose's Tale (حکایت گل) p. 135
690. Perfumer's Oppression (ستم گلابگر) p. 135
691. Torn Dress of Rose (دامن گل چاک شدست) p. 135
692. Next Week (هفتۀ دگر) p. 136
693. Drunken Nightingale's Message (پیام بلبل مست) p. 136
694. Cloud's Crying (گریۀ ابر) p. 136
695. Blood Rain (خون باران) p. 136
696. Watched Green (سبزۀ تماشاگه) p. 136
697. Nowrooz's Tulip (لالۀ نوروز) p. 136
698. When Today Nicely Goes (امروز خوش است) p. 136
699. Blood and Bounties (خون و مال) p. 137
700. Narcissus Rain (ریزش نسترن) p. 137
701. Worth the Wait (انتظاری ارزد) p. 137
702. So and So's Cup (پیالۀ فلانی) p. 137
703. Tulip and Violet (لاله و بنفشه) p. 137
704. Green Makeup (خط سبزه) p. 137
705. Who's Awakened? (هشیار کیست؟) p. 137
706. Bud's Own Robe (دامن غنچه) p. 138
707. Cypress and Lily (سرو و سوسن) p. 138
708. Garden's Joseph (یوسف چمن) p. 138
709. Riverbank Green (سبزۀ کنار جوی) p. 138
710. May Suddenly Depart (ناگه بروم) p. 138
711. Shirts and Petals (پیراهن و گلبرگ) p. 138
712. Sphere's Intention (قصد فلک) p. 138
713. Happiness Farming (برزگری شادی) p. 139
714. Where's Someone (کو آنکس) p. 139
715. You're Not a Leek (تره نه ای) p. 139
716. Grab a Cup (برگیر پیاله) p. 139
717. Don't Brag, Sir! (خواجه، مناز) p. 139
718. Don't Let (مگذار) p. 139
719. You're the Cure (به تو گشت درست) p. 139
720. Will Become For Long (بسی خواهد شد) p. 140
721. Pregnant (آبستن) p. 140
722. Before I Disappear (زان پیش که ناپدید گردم) p. 140
723. Rose's Secret (سرّ گل) p. 140
724. Oud Twins (دو عود) p. 140
725. Don't Sleep (خواب مرو) p. 140
726. Bubble's Joy (خرّمی حباب) p. 140
727. Balanced Candle (شمع طراز) p. 141
728. Divining Choice (اختیاری بکنم) p. 141
729. Repenting Now? (اکنون توبه؟) p. 141
730. World-Play (ایهام) p. 141
731. Repenting of Repentance (توبه ز توبه) p. 141

XIX. Wine (شراب) p. 142

732. Molten Ruby (لعل مذاب) p. 142
733. Wine Ink (جوهر شراب) p. 142
734. Don't Dilute (آبش مرسان) p. 142
735. Moon Veiling Sun (مهتاب حجاب آفتاب) p. 142
736. Three Conditions (سه شرط) p. 142
737. Don't Listen (مشنو) p. 142
738. Sweet Bitterness (تلخی شیرین) p. 143
739. Rogue's Sigh (آه رند) p. 143

740. Morning Sigh (آه سحری) p. 143
741. Grand-Tent Idols' Wine (می بتان خرگاهی) p. 143
742. One Sip of Old Wine (یک جرعه می کهنه) p. 143
743. Higher Ruin (خراب اولیٰتر) p. 143
744. Arrogance Remover (تکبّرزدا) p. 143
745. Why Repent? (چرا توبه؟) p. 144
746. Bring Wine (باده بیار) p. 144
747. I Can't Endure (نتوانم) p. 144
748. My Excuse (عذرم) p. 144
749. Even He Drank (میمره گفت) p. 144
750. Gourd-Maker (کدوساز) p. 144
751. Evolving Grape (تکامل انگور) p. 144
752. Enemy's Blood (خون عدو) p. 145
753. Inner Companion (دوست اندرون) p. 145
754. Best Confidant (بهترین همدم) p. 145
755. Drink or Not (خوریم یا نه) p. 145
756. Wine Scent Bests Vanity (بوی می به ز غرور) p. 145
757. Special Month (ماه خاص) p. 145
758. Drunken Until the Feast (مست تا عید) p. 145
759. Bags of Wine (خیکهای می) p. 146
760. Revelation Night Too (شب قدر هم) p. 146
761. Sorrow's Antidote (تریاک غم) p. 146
762. Stay Away! (دور از بر) p. 146
763. Wine Mantra (ورد می) p. 146
764. Grief's Snake (افعی غم) p. 146
765. World Is Wind (عالم باد است) p. 146
766. Torn Tent (پردۀ دریده) p. 147
767. Why In-"toxic"-ating? (چرا شراب؟) p. 147
768. If not now, when? (اکنون نه، کِی؟) p. 147
769. Noah's Ark (کشتی نوح) p. 147
770. Wine's Miracles (معجزات شراب) p. 147
771. I'm Not Hopeless (نومید نیم) p. 147
772. Freethinkers' Feast (بزم قلندران) p. 147
773. Mind Writing in Heart (نگاشت عقل در دل) p. 148
774. In-Between State (حال میان) p. 148
775. My Wine Drinking (می خوردن من) p. 148
776. Why I Drink Wine (علّت می خوری) p. 148
777. Four Silk Strings (چار ابریشم) p. 148
778. Throat Bleeding (خونریزی گردن) p. 148
779. Why I Don't Repent (چراست توبه ناکردن من) p. 148
780. Freeing Myself from Myself (خودرهایی) p. 149
781. Second Spirit (روح ثانی) p. 149
782. Splashing Wine (مشتی می زنم) p. 149
783. Restless Mercury (سیماب گریزپا) p. 149
784. How to Drink (طریق می خوری) p. 149

785. Avoid the Lowbred (مخور با سفله) p. 149
786. When to Drink (کِی خور) p. 149
787. Friday and Saturday (آدینه و شنبه) p. 150
788. Drink Twice on Friday (آدینه دو خور) p. 150
789. Bubbling Wine (قلقل می) p. 150
790. Simple Event (واقعۀ سهل) p. 150
791. What I Sell (چه فروشیم) p. 150
792. I'm the Ring-Leader (سرحلقه منم) p. 150
793. We're the Rogue (همه رندیم) p. 150
794. Wine Mix (ترکیب می) p. 151
795. Permissible Wine (می حلال) p. 151
796. Wine's Residue (خاک می) p. 151
797. Where Are You From? (از کجا می آیی؟) p. 151
798. Lips Rag (کهنۀ لب) p. 151
799. Meaning of Humankind (مقصود ز آدمی) p. 151
800. Feast Wine (می عید) p. 151
801. What a Pity! (حیف است) p. 152
802. Wine Thrill (ذوق باده) p. 152
803. Problem-Solver Wine (می مشکل گشا) p. 152
804. Drink While There's A Bowl (نوش چو کاسه است بجا) p. 152
805. An Hour (یک ساعت) p. 152
806. Peasant's Wine (می دهقان) p. 152
807. Wine to Wine (می به می) p. 152
808. Disgrace Until When (تا کی ننگ) p. 153
809. Wine's Knot (بند می) p. 153
810. Repent! Not! (توبه؟ نی) p. 153
811. Drink for Fulfillment (می برای کام) p. 153
812. Drunken Particle (ذرّۀ مست) p. 153
813. Purest Pearl (درّ خوشاب) p. 153
814. Emerald in Box (زمرّد در حقّه) p. 153
815. What Will Be, Will Be (هر چه بادا باد) p. 154
816. Be Ruined (خراب باش) p. 154
817. Coffin in Noah's Ark (تابوت در کشتی نوح) p. 154
818. Ways of Seeing (منگر، آن بین) p. 154
819. All Left for Wine (هر آنچه هست برای می) p. 154
820. When to Drink (وقت نوشیدن) p. 154
821. Boiling Pot (دیگ اندر جوش) p. 154
822. Shedding Which Blood? (ریختن کدام خون؟) p. 155
823. Dust on Whose Head? (خاک بسر که؟) p. 155
824. Eternally Embraced (در ابد هم آغوشان) p. 155
825. Wine-Drop Cure (دوای قطرۀ می) p. 155
826. Wine for the King, Wise, and Rogue (می شاه و حکیم و رند) p. 155
827. Hurry Up, Tend the Cup! (بشتاب، بر نه قدح) p. 155
828. What Wine Does (باده چه کند) p. 155
829. Beloved's Lips (لب یار) p. 156

830. Noah-Old Advice (قصۀ نوح) p. 156
831. Confession (اعتراف) p. 156
832. Nothing But Wine (نیست بجز باده) p. 156

XX. Love (عشق) p. 157

833. Pearl-Pouring Pen (کلک گهربار) p. 157
834. Intuitive Knowing (علم لدنی) p. 157
835. Beloved Was With Us (معشوقه با ما بود) p. 157
836. First Lesson (درس اوّل) p. 157
837. Free From Being and Non-Being (رستن از بود و نبود) p. 157
838. Heart Without Fire (دل بی سوز) p. 157
839. Love Today (عشق امروز) p. 158
840. Freedom from Duality (آزادی از دویی) p. 158
841. I Know He Knows (من دانم او داند) p. 158
842. Three Happinesses (سه چیز باید خوش) p. 158
843. The Origin of Heart (منشا دل) p. 158
844. Threshold of Creation (درگاه الست) p. 158
845. Sorrow to Love and Drunkenness (غم به عشق و مستی) p. 158
846. Light of Kindness (نور محبّت) p. 159
847. Freed From the Times' Suffering (از محنت ایّام برستیم) p. 159
848. Disobey the Wheel (مپندر چرخ را) p. 159
849. Tavern of Love (میکدۀ عشق) p. 159
850. All Is the Friend (همگی دوست) p. 159
851. What's Heart For? (به چه کار آید دل؟) p. 159
852. Head and Love (سر و عشق) p. 159
853. Go to Its End (قدم زنی محکم زن) p. 160
854. Happy in Sadness (خوشی در محنت) p. 160
855. Compass of Head and Soul (پرگار سر و جان) p. 160
856. God's Favor (عنایت الهی) p. 160
857. What to Ask For (چه طلب) p. 160
858. Moth Knows (پروانه داند) p. 160
859. Dying in Joy (مرگ خندان) p. 160
860. Immortal Sun (خورشید لایزال) p. 161
861. Lovers' Door (در عاشقان) p. 161

XXI. Night (شب) p. 162

862. Your Presence (تو در کنار) p. 162
863. Venus and the Moon (زهره و ماه) p. 162
864. Angel's Thunder and Lightning (رعد و برق آسمان) p. 162
865. Appeal to Wine-Tender (غنا از ساقی) p. 162
866. Waste Not A Drop (یک قطره رها مکن) p. 162
867. Night-Day Scissors (تراش شب و روز) p. 162
868. This is the Blessing (کرم از خداست) p. 163
869. Tight-Lipped Mouth (دهان تنگ) p. 163
870. Shine But Not Find (بتابد و نیابد) p. 163
871. Book Divination (فال دفتر) p. 163

872. Dew's Meditation (نشست شبنم) p. 163
873. Moonlight's Routine (مهتاب بی خواهد تافت) p. 163
874. Balkh or Baghdad (چه بغداد چه بلخ) p. 163
875. Nightly Raid (شبیخون) p. 164

XXII. Death and Survival (مرگ و بقا) p. 165

876. Oh, I Wish! (ای کاش) p. 165
877. Death's Knot (بند اجل) p. 165
878. Secrets of Death (اسرار اجل) p. 165
879. Home in Another Substance (مسکن در جنس دگر) p. 165
880. Time of Death (وقت هلاک) p. 165
881. Surrendering Day (وقت تسلیم) p. 165
882. My Fear (ترس من) p. 166
883. Body and Pure Soul (تن و روان پاک) p. 166
884. What You Plant Can Still Grow (ز فنا شاخ بقا خواهد رست) p. 166
885. Pity the Earth (بیچاره زمین) p. 166
886. Suppose You're In Dust (انگار در خاکی) p. 166
887. Branch of Hope (شاخ امید) p. 166
888. Rooster's Saw (ارّۀ خروس) p. 166
889. Wine-Tender Love (مهر ساقی) p. 167
890. Death Angel in Stone (اجل در سنگ) p. 167
891. Intimate Friends (یاران موافق) p. 167
892. My Wine Mindfulness (هوشم ز شراب) p. 167
893. Jug Made of My Dust (کوزه از خاک من) p. 167
894. Tavern Wall Gaps (رخنۀ دیوار خرابات) p. 167
895. Defeathered Bird (مرغ پر کنده) p. 167
896. Plain Weave (نخ ساده) p. 168
897. Wine's Fragrance (بوی شراب) p. 168
898. Wine! Push the Capstone (باده! سر بردار) p. 168
899. Pure Wine Prayer (تلقین ز شراب ناب) p. 168
900. Lose My Dusts (خاک مرا کم سازید) p. 168
901. Leaves Falling (برگ ریزان) p. 168
902. Tree of Life (نهال عمر) p. 168
903. Vine Coffin (تابوت رز) p. 169
904. When You Tryst (چو میعاد کنید) p. 169
905. Flip the Cup (نگونسار کنید) p. 169

XXIII. Liberation (رهایی) p. 170

906. Swiftly Fasten Belt (میان بند چست) p. 170
907. Grieve No More (دیگر غم نخوریم) p. 170
908. War Now (جنگ اینک) p. 170
909. Triple Divorce (سه طلاق) p. 170
910. Khezr's Wine (می خضر) p. 170
911. Wine's My Lot (می قسم من است) p. 170
912. I Don't Repent (من توبه نکنم) p. 171
913. My Pledge (قول من) p. 171

914. I Am Who I Am (چنان که هستم هستم) p. 171
915. Fiery Water (آب آتش افروز) p. 171
916. It's All About Happiness (حاصل همه عشرت است) p. 171
917. The Right Point of View (رای درست) p. 171
918. If I Had a Hand (گر دست بدی) p. 171
919. Heaven's Brink (به چرخ افراشتمی) p. 172
920. Depends On You (با تست) p. 172
921. Don't Be Lost (گم نکنی) p. 172
922. Is Is Not, Is Not Is (هست نیست، نیست هست) p. 172
923. Your job, Soul's Wine Brewing (کار تو می جان پروردن) p. 172
924. Will Pass As You Pass It (هر گونه که گذرانی گذرد) p. 172
925. Hands Together, Dance In Joy (دست انفاق، پای نشاط) p. 172
926. Sixties' Joy (ذوق شصتی) p. 173
927. Passing World (دنیای گذران) p. 173
928. True Dawn's Shell (صدف صبح صادق) p. 173
929. Last Wine (بادۀ قیام) p. 173
930. Stop Old Tales (چه جای حدیث) p. 173
931. Dying to Exist (پستی تا هستی) p. 173
932. Drink Slowly (نرمک نرمک خور) p. 173
933. O Still-Young (ای طرفه پسر) p. 174
934. It's Morning (صبح است) p. 174
935. O Unfailing Idol (ای صنم فرّخ پی) p. 174
936. Wake Up to Drink (برخیز تا بخوریم) p. 174
937. Teaching Drunkards Music (طرب آموزی مستان) p. 174
938. Depression Drug (دوای دلتنگی) p. 174
939. Morning Mourning? (غمناکی صبح) p. 174
940. Nightingale's Thousand Tunes (دستان هزاردستان) p. 175
941. Wine Cup As Prayer Rug (سجّادۀ پیاله) p. 175
942. Moses Hands, Jesus Breaths (موسی دستان و عیسی نفسان) p. 175
943. Muhammad's Wine, Ali's Pool (شراب احمد، حوض مرتضی) p. 175
944. Where Is It? (کو؟) p. 175
945. Faith Wine (بادۀ دین) p. 175
946. Your Emanation (چشمۀ فیض تو) p. 175
947. Friends' Hearts (دل دوستان) p. 176
948. Secret to Joy (راز خوشدلی) p. 176
949. Medicine Will Come (دوایی بیای) p. 176
950. Futile Threat (بیهده تهدیدستی) p. 176
951. Few Gut-Wrenched (جگرسوزی چند) p. 176
952. Wet Fire (آتش تر) p. 176
953. Tomorrow Disobeys (فردا عاقی) p. 176
954. Break Up World's Grief (غم جهان در شکنم) p. 177
955. Many Lives to Sleep Across (عمرهات میباید خفت) p. 177
956. Sweeping Tavern's Door (در میخانه رفته) p. 177
957. Cooked Soulmate, Raw Wine (همدم پخته، می خام) p. 177
958. Dress Will Tear (جامه چاک شود) p. 177
959. Here It Is (این است) p. 177
960. That's Its Elegance (نغز آن است) p. 177
961. My Way (آیین من) p. 178
962. Twisted Eye, Twisted Building (دیدۀ کج، نمای بد) p. 178
963. O Gist of the World (ای خلاصۀ جهان) p. 178
964. One Soul At A Time (یک خاطر، یک بنده) p. 178
965. I Give You An Advice (پندی دهمت) p. 178
966. Gain Stock Here (سرمایه بدست آر اینجا) p. 178
967. Die Before Death (بمیر پیش از مرگ) p. 178
968. Rebirth of Attributes (حشر صفات) p. 179
969. Your Seat Is By the Divine (عرش است نشیمن تو) p. 179
970. Your Mustache, My Beard (سبلت تو، ریش من) p. 179
971. Hot-Tempered Dear (عزیز تندخو) p. 179
972. No One Has Seen (کس ندیدست) p. 179
973. Hell and Heaven Now (دوزخ و بهشت اکنون) p. 179
974. Caravan of Life (قافلۀ عمر) p. 179
975. Wine and Divan (می و دیوان) p. 180
976. Here I Am, Free (ماییم آزاد) p. 180
977. Elixir of Life (آب زندگانی) p. 180
978. Wine, Life's Delight (می، لذت عمر) p. 180
979. Moon's Suffering (رنج ماه) p. 180
980. One More Week (یک هفتۀ دیگر) p. 180
981. Be Happy at Heart (خوشدل باش) p. 180
982. Suppose You're Not, to Be (انگار نیستی تا باشی) p. 181
983. Wine Better Than "Two Worlds" (می خوشتر از دو جهان) p. 181

XXIV. Return (بازگشت) p. 182

984. You'd Be Blind If (کوری اگر) p. 182
985. Each Particle a Universal Cup (هر ذرّه جامی جهان نما) p. 182
986. Your Building Blocks (مایۀ تو) p. 182
987. Eternal Love (عشق بی زوال) p. 182
988. Who Saw? (که دید؟) p. 182
989. Nothingness In You Is Better (نیستی در هستی تو خوشتر) p. 182
990. Your Fragrance (بوی تو) p. 183
991. Invitation to Garden Feast (دعوت به بزم باغ) p. 183
992. O Everything (ای همه) p. 183
993. You and My Impermanence (تو و زوال من) p. 183
994. Not Ashamed of Blame (از ملامتم ننگی نیست) p. 183
995. You and I (تو و من) p. 183
996. Faith is Love (مقصود عشق) p. 183
997. I Will Find Rebirth (برخیزم من) p. 184
998. News of an Event (خبر واقعه) p. 184
999. A Hundred I Became (صد ساله شدم) p. 184
1000. Mid-Gemini Dot (نقطۀ میان جوزا) p. 184

www.ingramcontent.com/pod-product-compliance
Lightning Source LLC
Chambersburg PA
CBHW072232240426
43670CB00040B/2504